ADVANCE PRAISE FOR

THE UNEXPECTED GUEST

"*The Unexpected Guest* is a deft meditation on the ordinary magic that happens when you open your heart and home, one small step at a time. Poignant, timely, compulsively readable. Konik's story of family lingers long after the last page."

> —JACK MCCALLUM, *New York Times* best-selling author of
> *Dream Team: How Michael, Magic, Larry, Charles, and*
> *the Greatest Team of All Time Conquered the*
> *World and Changed the Game of Basketball Forever*

"Just as Fisher King Mike embedded himself in Michael Konik's home, this story quickly establishes an enduring residence in a reader's mind. *The Unexpected Guest* illuminates an urgent topic with an easy conviviality."

> —JOHN TEMPLE, author of
> *American Pain: How a Young Felon and His Ring*
> *of Doctors Unleashed America's Deadliest Drug Epidemic*

The
Unexpected
Guest

Also by Michael Konik

—

Becoming Bobby

Ella in Europe

How the Revolution Started

In Search of Burningbush

Making It

The Man with the $100,000 Breasts

Nice Shot, Mr. Nicklaus

Reefer Gladness

Report from the Street

The Smart Money

Telling Lies and Getting Paid

The Termite Squad

Year 14

The Unexpected Guest

HOW A HOMELESS MAN
FROM THE STREETS OF L.A.
REDEFINED OUR HOME

MICHAEL KONIK

DIVERSION
BOOKS

For more information, email info@diversionbooks.com

Diversion Books
A division of Diversion Publishing Corp.
443 Park Avenue South, suite 1004
New York, NY 10016
www.diversionbooks.com

First Diversion Books edition, May 2020
Paperback ISBN: 9781635767292
eBook ISBN: 9781635766981

Printed in The United States of America

1 3 5 7 9 10 8 6 4 2

Library of Congress cataloging-in-publication data is available on file.

For Charmaine, creator of possibilities.

Contents

ONE

A Knock at the Front Door

"**G**ood morning," he grunts. "Hey, look, sorry to bother you, I need to ask . . . Do you think I could borrow a pair of pants? I had an accident."

It's a little after 7 a.m. on a sleepy Sunday morning in 2016. Fisher King Mike is standing at our front door, having let himself in the closed (but unlocked) sidewalk gate. And judging by the smell wafting over the porch, this time he's telling the truth.

"Pants? Yeah. Sure," I stammer, still startled and bleary from unexpected early-morning knocking. "Let me find you something."

He fingers one of the five leather crucifixes necklaced on his chest. "No, no it's not that. I didn't mean to bother you, sir. It's just—The Center isn't open yet, and I can't walk around like this, can't do my work. And, you know, all my stuff is in Calabasas, in the Valley, and I can't get there like this."

"I understand," I say, not sure if I actually do, but too frazzled to make further inquiries. "No problem. Yeah. OK. Let's see, we're about the same size. I mean, I have a bigger waist, but, sure, it shouldn't be a problem." I smile reassuringly as he looks down and mumbles, the rotten odor intensifying. "I'll be right back, Mike."

Trudging upstairs in my bathrobe, I have a moment to consider what I'm getting into. Fisher King Mike has previously asked for

1

little things: a leftover sandwich, a pair of socks. Now he wants to "borrow" pants. In the few seconds it takes to reach the closet in our upstairs bedroom, I conclude that whatever dungarees I loan will never be returned—and that'll be just fine. I can live without them.

Eventually he'll ask for something else, probably money, and boundaries will have to be considered and all that, but right now the man needs a clean pair of pants and a change of underwear. I feel simultaneously grateful and mildly ashamed; grateful that I can help and mildly ashamed at how grateful I am that it's not me in Mike's position.

"What's going on?" my wife Charmaine groans from bed, slightly alarmed.

"It's Fisher King Mike," I whisper. "Are you awake?"

"I am now. What's wrong?"

"He soiled himself so I'm giving him some pants."

Charmaine shoots me a look that communicates her complicated feelings on the matter. Then she says, "OK," sighing lightly and nodding. She smiles. "That's very nice of you."

I kiss her face, and I tell her, "We all do what we can. Some of us discover we can do more than nothing." Charmaine chuckles softly at our familiar mantra—the one she's gradually teaching me to believe in. Now I'm telling myself *you can do more than nothing* as a gentle encouragement to pick up litter in my neighborhood and dog poo at the park. I also started telling myself I possessed some kind of secret superpower, because I seemed able to do something (grab detritus off the ground) most people streaming past on the sidewalks and trails seemingly couldn't.

It worked. Now I feel *responsible* for picking up any litter I see—because I'm one of the "gifted" few, the able.

I can do more than nothing.

We own a spacious house in a historic district of Hollywood

and never go to sleep hungry. We have closets full of unworn clothes and racks of untrod shoes. And a car and bicycles and computers and dishes and glassware and furniture and stereo equipment and a grand piano and a million other possessions. And electric power and hot water on demand.

An objective observer would determine we have all we need and possibly far more.

Fisher King Mike doesn't.

I find an old pair of brown denim jeans and a sweatshirt, too. Maybe a collared shirt? Would he want that? Would that be useful? It's springtime; the weather's mild. Still, nighttime temperatures—maybe a sweater is what he needs.

As I rummage through the markers of my big American success story—eight pieces of wheeled luggage? Twelve tailored suits?—the urge to be generous grows, and as it grows, and the more I find to give away, the finer I feel. Why don't I do this more often? Why isn't this my default mode, constantly giving stuff away? Thumbing a long-ignored jacket, it occurs to me: If being generous makes *everyone* involved feel good, the giver as much as (or more than) the receiver, maybe this could be a new paradigm. I could make a habit of being generous every chance I get, blissing out on kindness.

"DON'T GO ANYWHERE," I tell Charmaine, who mumbles sleepily and curls into a tempting croissant. Plucking one more shirt from a seldom-used pile, I return downstairs, where Mike is slouching, hands in pockets, eyes downcast, radiating defeat and resignation.

I don't have any comforting nostrums to make the truth go away. No matter what fantastic stories he tells about himself, at this moment he needs help. Here he is, a man almost sixty I would suppose, a Vietnam vet, homeless and incontinent. There's nothing

I can say to ease the pain and humiliation—except, maybe, a different truth. "Here you go, Mike," I say, handing him my hand-me-downs. "I want to thank you for giving me the opportunity to do the right thing. I really appreciate it. Thank you."

"Well, no, no, see. It's not that. I didn't want to bother you and your wife. It's just—The Center isn't open yet, and I can't walk around like this, can't do my work. And, you know, all my stuff is in Calabasas, in the Valley, and I can't get there like this," he repeats, verbatim.

I nod but don't answer. He's wearing mirrored sunglasses. I can see myself in him.

The man wearing the glasses looks morose, defeated by life. The man staring back at me in the mirrors, with the stubble and the bathrobe, looks very happy, and also, somehow, very sad, as though all the bounty and fullness of his life has left him inexplicably empty.

Mike shakes his head, like a dog emerging from a bath. "Hey, listen. No, it's not that. I'm sorry for bothering you and your wife."

"Not a bother," I say, uselessly.

"Well, no, no, it's not that. It's—see, what people don't understand is, and I tell them this—it's like they see people walking around in Hollywood—they see movie stars and they walk around and it's like, hey, this is what I do. You know? And people don't get that. Because, see, I can't do my work like this. Ordained Minister of God, military chaplain. And, and, so, no, no, I'm just saying."

Ushering him out, I say, "Be well, Mike," and I'm wondering how that's going to be possible.

TWO

The Legend of Fisher King Mike

———

M ike tells me he owns a private jet.

    Mike tells me he lives on an estate, next door to Kanye West.

Mike tells me he performs "special ops" for the Department of Defense.

Mike tells me he's not permitted to discuss his military history.

Mike tells me he's married to Selena Gomez.

Mike tells me he's married to Selena Gomez, and they have two children.

Mike tells me he's married to Selena Gomez, and they have two children, and it's very hard to be away from his family, to be separated, but she's got her work and he's got his, and he's sure I know what he means, a man does what he's gotta do, even when he knows family comes first, and nothing is more important than family, and, sure, he misses them, because, you know, there's nothing more important than family, but he's a pastor, a street pastor, and he has to do his work, has to minister, because there are a lot of people out on the streets, people who need help, and even though he's married to Selena Gomez and has two beautiful children, a boy and a girl, what people don't understand, they think it's all movie premieres and paparazzi, and he tries to tell them, what people don't understand is there are people who need him, people he has to minister to, because he's a military chaplain, and also Special Forces.

When Fisher King Mike rhapsodizes out loud, the stories sound magnificently glamorous and exciting, and, of course, utterly incredible. He's not a habitual liar, not in the conventional, desperate politician sense. He seems to believe his tales are real, and he assumes you believe them, too. I find myself wishing that somehow, as in a Marquez novel or the subtext of a poem, Mike's magical claims—*surprise!*—will turn out to be totally authentic, not the ravings of a deluded fabulist. All along, while our hero sputtered and fumed and no one believed him, he was telling the truth!

I wish it were so, that there was some chance, even the remotest chance. But Mike's rants typically occur at the bus stop on the corner of Sunset Boulevard and Gardner Street, or at the bus stop on the corner of Hollywood Boulevard and Fuller Street. Where he sits for hours. I once made the mistake of engaging him in pleasant repartee while waiting to cross the street. Three cycles of "Walk" signs passed before I could extricate myself from Mike's flamboyant oratory.

His possessions crammed into a backpack and a canvas tote-bag, Fisher King Mike meanders around our Hollywood neighborhood, known as "Sunset Square," an idyllic pocket of century-old bungalows and tree-lined sidewalks tucked inside the teeming, angry city. He and his fellow transients usually stick to the main avenues, the business districts, where they're more likely to scrounge food and cigarettes. But each year we see more homeless people settling closer to our residential streets.

It's not that the problem is being ignored or explained away.

The voters of Los Angeles *want* to help. In 2016, the overwhelming majority of us voted for Measure HHH, which increased our taxes in order to pay for $1.2 billion in bonds earmarked to build housing for the homeless. Three years later, the City of Los Angeles has built precisely zero units with that money.

Although our mayor, Eric Garcetti, has publicly pledged to "end homelessness" in Los Angeles—indeed, it was one of his campaign planks in 2013, when he was still an ambitious City Councilmember—the number of people without housing, in fact, *rises* every year. The latest figures, released in 2019, showed a sixteen percent increase, despite more than $600 million spent to procure the opposite result. Like the failed "War on Drugs," we're badly losing our war on homelessness—and almost all the small battles, too. Contemporaneously, members of the Garcetti administration, the City Council, and the Board of Public Works are being investigated by the FBI for a long list of crimes, including, naturally, bribery and extortion. The main source of these solicited "donations"? Real estate developers.

While squalid encampments populated with nylon tents and cardboard boxes are springing up all around Los Angeles in catastrophic numbers, the wise elders of our city keep approving one luxury skyscraper-and-condo-project after another, displacing long-time residents and depleting the stock of rent-controlled apartments. Almost every Angeleno, in every neighborhood that's not Bel-Air or Beverly Hills, sees and understands that we have a growing humanitarian crisis on our hands. Yet the City behaves as though we're facing a luxury Airbnb shortage, not an affordable housing shortage. Like San Francisco, Los Angeles is in many ways becoming a place where only the wealthy can pay the going rental rates. More people than ever live in their cars, dodging tow trucks and parking officers. One impound or theft, and their temporary housing is gone.

Soon, if we don't collectively do something to ameliorate this slow-motion disaster, what always appears to be "someone else's problem" will be outside our front windows.

Or on our front porch.

A FEW MONTHS before Mike shows up looking for clean pants, I'm in the front garden one morning, weeding and pruning. A low hedge of rosemary and roses separates the soil from the sidewalk, the private from the public. I'm bent over, pulling interloper bamboo shoots from the kale patch. When I look up, Fisher King Mike is standing on the other side of the low fence. He's wearing a baseball cap that says "Hollywood" on it, and his necklace of crosses, and mirrored sunglasses, and two jackets. He's painfully thin, all elbows and knees, but his hair and mustache are trimmed neatly, and he smells freshly bathed.

"Hey, Mr. Punky, Mr. MK Punky," he says, using my poetry-comedy-spoken word handle. "Good morning, sir. Hey, look, I was just passing by—gotta get to the Valley to take care of some business. My wife. You get it. Because, and I don't have to tell you this, what people don't understand is, yeah, OK, look, he might not always dress flashy because he wants to blend in with the regular people, but, you know, you're a performer, you're MK Punky, you're famous, you understand, you know, you get it, we're just normal people like everyone else, me and you, and, yeah, you can *talk* to us, and I try to tell them, I'm like, *Look, Punky and me, yeah we're used to the photographers and everything but we're just normal if you get to know us, like when we hang out at the Meltdown with the other comics, it's like, like, like—*"

He throws up his hands. Speechless. For a moment.

"Good morning, Mike," I say. "Would you like to try a tomato?" I'm thinking: *Be generous. Be kind. Treat him like you would any other neighbor who stops by to chat.* But I'm also thinking: *Now he knows where we live.*

I hand Fisher King Mike a just-picked cherry tomato. He puts it inside one of his coats without comment. "Thanks. But no, no it's not that. It's—look, you're here in your garden, right? I tell people, what they don't understand, I tell them," he changes his voice slightly, to the tone of an impatient pedant, "*Look, MK Punky has been on TV and, and, of course he's got books, a lot of people know he's a best-selling author and, and everybody knows that*, but what people don't understand is, and I tell them, you do stand-up comedy, you do poetry, and, and when you walk by *he's in his garden growing vegetables. For the community.* They don't get that."

Although it's true that we put extra veggies from the garden on an old wooden table fronting the house, I'm not sure who "they" are; I'm quite sure that no one has ever asked Fisher King Mike if I'm down-to-earth. Just as I'm quite sure he's not really married to a pop starlet thirty years his junior who's linked to Justin Bieber.

In the four or five months I've known him, a total of maybe twenty encounters on the streets and at several nearby open-mics, where Mike often puts his name on the list to perform, I've learned not to cross-examine his assertions. Mike doesn't entertain impertinent questions. He does, however, use any inquiry, no matter how innocuous or innocent, as a launching point for a rambling, tenuously connected monologue that might be fleetingly entertaining as a piece of performance art, part of an experimental, off-off-Broadway, one-man show.

On the streets of Hollywood, after a few iterations, Mike's soliloquies tend to grow less amusing and more confusing. Eventually—and what people don't understand—you learn to avoid inspiring them, or risk becoming a passively captive audience, a sold-out symphony hall of one, a friend who may as well not be there.

"It's a beautiful day to be outside in the dirt," I say, innocuously, trying to keep Mike's focus on the here and now.

"Well, no, no, it's not that," he replies. "See, what people don't understand is, you can do the poetry and the comedy, and when you're onstage it's like, OK, yeah, this is what I do, but what people don't understand is you're growing vegetables for the neighborhood."

"Trying," I say, fussing with some new radish sprouts.

"Well, no, no, it's not that. No, see, that's the thing."

I nod cordially and return to weeding, wondering if our encounter this morning is truly a random coincidence of "just passing by and look who I ran into!" or if Fisher King Mike has been staking out our house, shadowing my perambulations around the neighborhood.

He's never struck me as dangerous, or aggressive. Unpredictable and inscrutable? Oh, yes. But for all his weirdness and conversational volatility, in the whole time I've known him Mike hasn't uttered a single threatening or mean-spirited word about anyone. Indeed, he usually finds ways to praise people. Physically unimposing—he must weigh 120 lbs., at most—and unarmed (as far as I know), Mike is essentially a gentle man. Not a "gentleman," in the social sense, but as harmless as a butterfly with injured wings.

The first time I met him was at Elderberries, a new age vegan café located around the corner on Sunset Boulevard dedicated to the somewhat obscure philosophies of Waldorf School founder Rudolf Steiner. The proprietors live together communally, in a five-bedroom bungalow with a giant garden out front, called "Have Seeds House," which hosts travelers from around the world and serves as the Los Angeles headquarters for a beautiful cult of kindness. In 2015, Elderberries was hosting a potluck Thanksgiving for their regulars and anyone in the neighborhood who might randomly show up. Mike showed up—along with another transient he seemed to know vaguely. They walked in after seeing a welcoming sign on the door. No one knew where they had come from, or how they had discovered our community dinner. Neither man wanted to talk much, but both were hungry. Ferociously hungry.

They offered their gratitude throughout the evening, and we reciprocated. "Thank you for joining us, for the opportunity to share." It was all deeply satisfying, a profound illumination of the concept and meaning of Thanksgiving liberated from offensive fake histories and rampant over-consumption. But near the end of the meal, the homeless man sitting beside Mike arose from his chair, glared across the table at the nice Quaker man seated next to me, the film festival curator who'd brought a savory green bean dish, and accused him of killing children.

And of being the devil and a host of other sins. He pointed a menacing finger. "You! You hate homeless people!" he shouted.

The Nerdist Showroom, one of the best "alt-comedy" rooms in Los Angeles, is also around the corner, a few doors from Elderberries; I often hang out there with a gaggle of genius comedians, smoking weed in the parking lot. For a second, I thought I was witnessing one of my buddies pulling off an astonishing satire.

Then I realized it wasn't funny.

The homeless guy was genuinely incensed, and he seemed dangerous. Threatening.

The Nice Quaker Man was dumbstruck, obviously frightened. Mike, I noticed, turned away, shaking his head, disavowing the loud lunatic—who promptly grabbed a handful of mashed potatoes, shoved them in his pocket, and stormed out into the Hollywood night. Mike never said another word about him, a volatile ghost who came (and feasted) and went, never to return.

Mike stayed. Indeed, over the next few weeks, whenever I popped into Elderberries, he was there, sometimes enjoying a courtesy meal, "a blessing," he called them. Sometimes he was sitting alone at the end of the counter, poring over his bible, bags tucked neatly beneath a stool. Sometimes he was deep in (mostly one-way) conversation with Chris, another homeless man who often slept in the alley behind Elderberries, next to a bustling car repair shop. Other times he was behind the counter, doing dishes. In the brief time it takes to transform a stranger into a friend, Mike was granted membership in the Elderberries Community, becoming one of its irregular regulars, a Knight of the 21st Century in search of his lance.

No one seems to recall who started calling him The Fisher King, or Fisher King Mike. It could have been Dottie, the visionary founder of Elderberries, whose brand of "craziness" is based on self-less service. It could have been Daniel, the Swedish Viking, tall and red and pale, who showed up one day at the front door of our home, saying, "I saw the little library and the vegetable table out front, and I thought I should meet whoever lives here." It could have been Caleb, the Itinerant Canadian in his early twenties whose inner calm and loving demeanor suggest that of a much older person. Or maybe it was Frank the Artist, stepson of a famous jazz musician, a multi-instrumentalist and painter and woodworker, whose strange yet oddly pleasing ambient music issues forth from the small Elderberries stage. Or it might have been someone else.

Whoever dubbed him Fisher King Mike was probably referring to *The Fisher King*, the 1991 Terry Gilliam film starring Jeff Bridges and Robin Williams, who plays a homeless man convinced he knows the Manhattan location of the Holy Grail. The film is based on an ancient Celtic myth that's been retold through the eons with minor variations. The story, in all its forms, is a fable about sinful pride. The movie roughly follows this version, per Wikipedia:

The Fisher King was charged by God with guarding the Holy Grail, but incurred an incapacitating wound for his sin of pride. A Fool asks the King why he suffers, and when the King says he is thirsty, the Fool gives him a cup of water to drink. The King realizes the cup is the Grail and asks, "How did you find what my brightest and bravest could not?" The Fool says, "I don't know. I only knew that you were thirsty."

If Mike disliked or took offense to being called Fisher King Mike, he never said so. Aside from all the metaphorical possibilities held in the name, practically speaking, he was a man on a quest for the holy, and he'd tell you so every chance he got. "I'm a street pastor, ordained minister, military chaplain," he'd say. He also considered himself a kind of modern royalty: someone in the entertainment industry, married to a famous starlet. The wounded part he didn't talk about.

I often wondered what sequence of events led him to Hollywood, California. How did he end up on the streets? Like this?

When did he break so badly he couldn't put himself back together?

Fisher King Mike began attending each bi-weekly edition of "Revolutionary Words," a social-justice open-mic I hosted at Elderberries, drawing slam poets, comic improvisers, and prophetic provocateurs. He was always one of the first to arrive, to put his name on the sign-up sheet ("Michael James"), and the last to leave. He shared handwritten poetry and highly improvised sermons, and was known to sometimes exceed the 5-minute limit. But Mike was always a keen listener and a weirdly engaging performer. A man of letters.

A gentle man. A poet at heart.

So why, on this serene springtime morning, am I wary of having him loiter in front of our home?

Maybe because I know what's coming: The Ask.

Eventually, after the philosophizing and explicating, the subtle flattery and misdirection, Fisher King Mike is going to want something from me. He always does.

Why does this trouble me? What's so bad about being needed?

My dread, I realize, comes from being of two minds on charity, a dialectical tension between the desire to do well and the realization that I'm possibly doing the opposite. None of us wishes unwittingly to encourage anyone to remain homeless or paralyzed by hopelessness. We want to *help*. Yet when we give cash to a career beggar with obvious substance abuse issues, we're positively reinforcing his choices, ensuring, on some level, more of the same, leading to nothing good—especially when the panhandler is parked outside a liquor store.

Is giving food and clothing different? While you still might be affirming a negative behavior—begging for a living—you're also having an immediate salutary effect. You're feeding a hungry woman. You're clothing a shivering runaway teenager.

Perhaps it's patronizing and condescending to imagine I have any moral claim over a homeless person, or an addict, or someone with mental illness, simply because I give them money. They are, after all, independent, if disadvantaged, adults. All I know is I want to do the right thing, even if I'm not sure what that is. I want to be righteous, compassionate, philosophically Christian.

If ever I am cold and hungry and unable to feed or fend for myself, I pray someone will be kind to me. I pray they won't succumb to the cruelty of apathy. I pray they won't be in thrall to stirring philosophies of self-reliance. I pray they will simply help, understanding that, in cases like these, the Golden Rule is the only one that matters.

I decide to not wait for The Ask. "Hey, Mike, can you wait here a minute?"

"No, no, it's not that. I was on my way to the Valley, to take care of some business, and what people don't understand—"

"I'll be right back!" I shout dashing up the porch steps and into the house.

Inside the kitchen I find a buffet of semi-eaten, semi-neglected, completely edible leftovers. A chicken drumstick. Half a pear. Noodles. We have a tiny, antique GE refrigerator from 1948 that, at least a few times a year, threatens the sanctity of our marriage. Charmaine hates the old beast and actively campaigns for it to be replaced by something from this century. She thinks the GE is inconvenient and inefficient, and she's mostly right. (She also thinks it's stylish and classic, and she's right about that, too.) I think the refrigerator is all those things and something maybe more important: an omnipresent reminder to consume less.

Our small fridge forces us to shop lightly and to keep our provisions in view, neatly arranged and ready for inspection. There's not a lot of room to hide in there. Because of this (and a bunch of other reasons), Charmaine and I throw out drastically less food than the average American household. The statistics are astonishing and immoral: in the United States, according to the FDA, something like 40% of all edible food gets wasted, at a cost of $165 billion a year.

Like almost every chronic problem vexing humanity, hunger is not caused by scarcity; it's caused by poor distribution. There's enough food to feed every single person in the world, it's just distributed badly. So badly that while millions starve, those of us who have access to more calories than we'll ever need must buy memberships to "health clubs"—we're blessed with six high-end exercise and training facilities, including a pole dancing academy, on a two-block stretch of Sunset alone—to burn off the results of our gluttony. Yet we collectively still manage to toss nearly half of our food into the trash.

As I snatch an almost-finished yogurt tub from our controversial icebox, peering into the tundra I realize Fisher King Mike has helped me understand a simple idea.

There's no shortage of anything in this world, except compassion.

Nothing. We suffer only from a shortage of compassion. *I* suffer from a shortage of compassion.

But maybe compassion, like everything else, is distributed poorly, concentrated disproportionately in our saints. We tell ourselves not everyone can dedicate her life to serving the poor, that it takes an unimaginably special person to work with the hyper-needy, the diseased, the damaged. We convince ourselves we can give funds and support good works remotely, and "in spirit," but the actual work of tending to the least among us is best left to others.

Bundling the makeshift meal in a paper carryout bag from a "gourmet," gluten-free cupcake shop—hello, Ridiculous Abundance—I return to the front garden, where I find Fisher King Mike fiddling with an earbud attached to a device. I want to ask him, *Is that an iPhone? And how did you acquire such a fine gadget?* I'm reluctant to get him started, so I announce matter-of-factly, "This is for you, brother. A little something for the road."

He takes the bag, peeks into it for a nanosecond, and says gruffly, "Thanks. No, no, it's not that. I didn't want to bother you while you're working in your garden." He leans in conspiratorially, accelerating, "I was just on my way to the Valley to see my wife, Selena Gomez. The singer? One of the hottest women on the planet? My wife, mother of my children—say no more. *Puh-shweep!*" He makes a wiping motion.

"Right," I say. "A snack for the trip."

After several false starts and reiterations of his calling, his lifelong mission, to minister to "people who need help," Fisher King Mike finally departs, shuffling up the street, skinny legs bowing outward and narrow shoulders dipping side-to-side, like two sides of an old-fashioned scale.

I won't be surprised if I never see Mike again. Hundreds like him have come and gone in the twenty-five years I've lived in the neighborhood, shooting stars that vanish into the ether.

I wish him well on his journey. And I wish I felt better about being so thoroughly relieved to see him go.

THREE

The Better Angels

In 2015, Charmaine and I organized a ten-day, free-to-all, completely volunteer-staffed experiment in kindness called The Better Angels Festival. It sprang from a recording Charmaine had made with the jazz pianist and arranger Laurence Hobgood, eleven songs of hope that they called *The Better Angels*. (On the album, Charmaine recites a portion of Abraham Lincoln's 1861 inaugural address containing the phrase "the better angels of our nature," while Hobgood and the band play the American folk song "Oh, Shenandoah.") After releasing four albums in the traditional fashion, including three straight records that reached the *JazzWeek* World Music Radio Chart Top 20, Charmaine had grown disillusioned with the music business, of making music meant to last forever that, nonetheless, had to be sold in the here and now. She wanted to do something bigger, more lasting, than a mere album release.

"I want to start a movement," she told me one night over dinner. "A community."

And so that's what she did. Charmaine is like that.

When she decides she can do something—that she *must* do something—she does it. This has been going on since she immigrated to America with her Filipino parents before her junior year

19

of high school, speaking English as a second language to her native Tagalog. Two years after arriving in a new, intimidating country, Charmaine graduated as the valedictorian of her private Catholic School class (which is both a testament to her brilliance and a mild indictment of native English speakers). She went on to earn a Master's Degree in Physical Therapy, from Cal-State University Northridge, and, after CSUN, worked for fifteen years in hospitals and clinics around Los Angeles, building her therapy chops.

All that time, Charmaine was picking up extra money—and having a great time—gigging as a back-up singer for Filipino pop stars on tour in Los Angeles. She also worked on the weekends as a "KJ," a karaoke host, at a Filipino fried-chicken restaurant, Max's of Manila.

Charmaine has always been a singer. Her mom reports that Baby Mae sang before she spoke, in her crib, at six months, mimicking a popular pro-Marcos tune that played on the radio constantly. At the age of three, she was serenading passengers on the bus traveling between Manila and her provincial town in Subic Bay, near the U.S. Naval Base. At school and church, she sang the solos.

Her parents worked for the Americans as office administrators, and in return for their service they were granted a visa to immigrate to the Land of Opportunity. It was a tough move for a teenager, and the living circumstances upon arrival weren't pleasant—the whole family in one room of a cousin's house. Eventually, both parents found jobs with the State of California, administering the State Fund for Worker's Compensation. Having achieved one version of the American Dream, Mom and Dad Clamor hoped their little Charmaine would have stability and security, a regular salary, a pension. That their gifted daughter perhaps might sort of maybe have been *meant* to be a singer did not occur to them.

And so it didn't really occur to Charmaine, either. Singing was a hobby, something everyone did (she claims it's not a proper Filipino household without some form of karaoke machine on hand). She had long since stopped practicing the piano, an instrument she excelled on during childhood, and she certainly didn't "practice" vocalizing. She went out with friends and *saaaang*.

On one of those nights, in the mid-nineties, the founder and music director of a vocal harmony group named Crescendo was in the audience while Charmaine performed her version of Whitney Houston's "I Will Always Love You," a karaoke classic. The music director, a Filipino immigrant named Bobbie Garcia, asked Charmaine if she sang jazz—yes, she had grown up listening to Ella Fitzgerald and Frank Sinatra—and if she would like to audition for the alto position in Crescendo.

She became the group's newest member.

Seven years later, after more gigs than she could count, and more sopranos coming and going than backstage at the Los Angeles Opera, the group's long-time tenor departed to take a position with the L.A. Master Chorale. Crescendo posted audition notices in *Backstage* and other industry rags (back when they still existed), seeking a singer with a strong background in the "classic" jazz repertory—Ellington, Basie, Shearing—and a love for harmony.

I applied.

After passing the initial audition, and not without some nervous flubs, I was invited for a call-back with the other singers, a kind of blending test. That's how I met Charmaine. She was the alto who I stood near and vibrated with, making beautiful harmony. Of course, I fell in love with her.

In 2005, with the blessing and support of the four other members of Crescendo, Charmaine released her first solo album of jazz standards, arranged and played by some great local musicians. That's when the storybook stuff started happening.

Charmaine Clamor—pronounced like *amour*—was instantly recognized by critics and taste-makers as "one of the most important new voices of the decade," as Don Heckman, the long-time *Los Angeles Times* jazz critic wrote. The *New York Times* anointed her as "a gifted vocalist." She does indeed have a remarkable, one-of-a-kind voice, and a singular biographical path; when Charmaine stormed onto the World Jazz scene, she really had no competition; she represented her own category.

That "genre" was a newly developed hybrid called *jazzipino*, a mix of Filipino music, languages, and indigenous instruments, with American jazz. Charmaine scatted in *Taglish*, a blend of her two languages, and melded church spirituals with Filipino folk songs. She blazed a new path. Her own.

We were married in 2007, at Catalina Bar & Grill Jazz Club, where I hosted a long-running weekly series called "Tasty Tuesdays," and where Charmaine headlined a couple of times a year. (Our epic wedding band included blues legend Linda Hopkins and perennial Grammy nominee in vocal jazz Tierney Sutton.) That year, Charmaine's album "Flippin' Out" made history: after a guest appearance on NPR's "Weekend Edition," the recording reached the Top 5 in both the *JazzWeek* World and Jazz radio charts, a first for a Filipino recording artist. Soon thereafter, Charmaine started touring the world, performing in concert halls and festival stages from Mexico to Malaysia, Finland to South Africa.

Now known as the "Queen of Jazzipino," Charmaine curtailed her physical therapy work to one or two days a week (when in town), supervising a clinic. Even as being a performing artist became a full-time job, she never stopped practicing her healing arts.

In between her solo albums and concerts, Charmaine collaborated with David Byrne and Fatboy Slim on "Here Lies Love," a disco song cycle about Imelda Marcos that became a smash off-Broadway musical. She served as Chairperson of JazzPhil-USA, a nonprofit that for ten years produced the first Filipino-American JazzFest, featuring the very best Filipino talent Charmaine could find, including the Thelonious Monk Competition champion Jon Irabagon and the ukulele master Abe Lagrimas. And she gave a command performance for the president of the Philippines, Benigno Aquino, Jr, at the Malacanang Palace in Manila. Charmaine's mom and dad were there in the front row, and they got to take pictures and chat with the president afterward. For one night, at least, no parents could have been prouder that their daughter was a singer, one of the best in the world.

As the jazz guys say, Charmaine's a heavy cat. She's got some gravity about her, a calm that people find welcoming and comforting. No doubt, singing in front of thousands of people has trained her to be relaxed and tension-free when "the pressure" is on. But Charmaine is also one of those rare people who understands that *pressure* and *stress* are largely mental constructs that we can deconstruct in an instant if we choose to. Except during certain times of hormonal imbalance—and don't we all go through that occasionally?—Charmaine exudes what's commonly known as "inner peace," which might be another way of saying "wisdom." She's a beautiful person who magically makes everyone around her a bit more beautiful.

So, when Charmaine declared in 2015 that we were going to launch The Better Angels Festival, I said, yes, sure, of course—having no idea whatsoever how one did such a thing. I just knew that when Charmaine Clamor decides she can do something, something more than nothing, something gets done.

Flowing from the music on *The Better Angels*, all of it concerned with connecting to a higher vibe, The Better Angels Festival featured free healing services by day, including nearly a dozen volunteer physical therapists, and free cultural programming at night, created and performed by volunteer artists. Free meals for all participants were prepared on site by volunteer chefs using donated ingredients. The space, Search to Involve Pilipino Americans (SIPA), a cultural center in the heart of Historic Filipino Town, was donated. Nothing was for sale. There was no "merch." Every transaction at The Better Angels Festival was a form of sharing, sharing the best of ourselves—the better angels of our nature. For me, the whole experience was revolutionary, improbable, and utterly beautiful, the finest coming-together I've known, a congregation built on twin pillars of compassion and kindness. For ten days, we were at our best, all of us.

It was in the lead-up to The Better Angels Festival that I started talking regularly with our homeless brothers and sisters. Some of them attended the event, and one man, Kevin, volunteered to do security. He escorted me on a visit to where he lived: a tent encampment beneath a freeway underpass, two blocks from SIPA.

As part of my contribution to the Festival, I performed a one-hour spoken word piece called "MK Punky's Better Angels," which included a monologue inspired by a Hollywood transient who called himself Homey Prophet.

Before he disappeared, I used to see Homey Prophet around Sunset Boulevard, near the Meltdown store, home of the Nerdist Showroom. Everything about the man's appearance and demeanor would earn him the "crazy" label, but then nearly everything he proclaimed in his street-corner soliloquies seemed pretty close to my version of The Truth: We're all one family; there really is no Us and Them, only We; the power of love will overcome the love of power. Homey Prophet, as far as I could tell, had grooming issues and an outlandish predilection for ill-fitting wigs, but there was nothing amiss in his thinking. He was just tuned into a different frequency than most of us are, able to dial-in broadcasts few homeowners are able to receive.

Having made one of those "sounds good, but not as easy as it sounds" resolutions for the New Year—namely, to try to do something every day slightly out of my comfort zone—I started talking regularly with homeless people.

When confronted by human misery and squalor, my instinct, like most folks, is to turn the other way, or stare straight ahead, voluntarily blinding myself to avoid seeing the painful truth. Around the time of The Better Angels Festival, I decided to stop behaving like an ostrich with his head stuck in the ground and, instead, tried to be present and open with everyone I encountered, even our society's "untouchables." Nothing too intense; just the amiable banter we share with strangers passing on the sidewalk: A simple, "Hello. Good morning. How are you doing today?" Sometimes, I'd ask a person on the street his name. Sometimes, I'd shake a dirty hand, or pat an unwashed back. And sometimes, when it was obvious that the man on the street wanted a hug, I hugged him as if he were an old friend. Like the Generosity Effect, these moments of human communion, of what felt like genuine fraternity, left me, the one who didn't really want to talk-touch-hug a homeless person, probably feeling better than the unfortunate guy craving warm physical contact did.

I made early-morning donation runs to Skid Row, in downtown Los Angeles—the "other Los Angeles"—bereft of trees, adequate toilet facilities, and celebrities. The scandalous conditions are worsened by local businesses, many of which (illegally) dump their trash onto the streets, knowing the poor and disenfranchised can't stop them. Conditions here are literally *inhumane*. Few properly housed visitors can't spend more than a few minutes in this sad district without feeling there's something profoundly wrong—with L.A., with America, with us.

At Skid Row, and in Hollywood, and Koreatown, and Little Ethiopia, and every other neighborhood of L.A. I found myself in, I talked with hundreds of people. But I mostly listened, willing myself to be an intake receptor for the ones no one wants to hear. When you're invisible, you're also mute. The cardboard sign you carry screams into a vacuum, its message as irrelevant to achievers in their cars as the person holding it. Almost nobody's interested in your story, which always involves some kind of abuse, or injustice, or bad break. And for sure nobody is interested in what you have to offer our gleaming society, because, even though few are so cruel as to say it to your face, you're pretty much worthless to many devout devotees of capitalism. A net negative. Someone who contributes nothing to America's bottom line—except providing ballast at the bottom.

The invisible. The mute. There are legions of them on the streets of Los Angeles, constantly reminding me of my hypocrisies. I willed myself to do the "difficult" thing and connect with them, and one day I realized it was actually ridiculously easy. *I* was the difficult part.

For about a year I engaged in what I thought of as a Listening Project. Just listen. Don't try to solve everyone's problems—don't try to solve *anyone's* problems. Just listen. Let someone know, if only for a few minutes, that she's not alone.

The culmination of the Listening Project was an eight-piece suite of prose-poem monologues I wrote called *Report from the Street: Voices of the Homeless.** Several of the soliloquies were inspired by Fisher King Mike, who could be a brilliant (albeit unorthodox) social critic, someone with ample time to observe the bustling world hustling by him, and ample time to compose sage commentary on what he saw. The radical psychoanalyst Wilhelm Reich, after three decades of studying schizophrenic minds, determined in his book, *Character Analysis*, that "they look through our

---

* See Appendix.

hypocrisy, our cruelty and stupidity, our fake culture, our evasiveness, and our fear of the truth." The broken and insignificant have the capacity for profound insight; they call into question our standard definition of "mentally ill."

I wanted to share the finished *Report from the Street* with Mike, to tell him how much he inspired me. But no one had seen him for months. After I stopped doing "Revolutionary Words" at Elderberries, and after he was banned from the Nerdmelt—given a probationary time-out, according to the management—Mike drifted away.

In my fantasy, he and his imaginary family hop on his imaginary jet and take a much-needed vacation to someplace with warm blankets, foamy mattresses, and an open buffet.

In reality, Fisher King Mike was probably living at a homeless shelter somewhere nearby (or accessible by public transportation), deftly skirting the violence and disharmony commonly found in such places, talking off the ear of another unlucky vagabond waiting for his private plane to depart.

These days, months later, I don't miss Fisher King Mike. But I don't forget him, either. In fact, I think about him often, especially when I'm trying to access the better angels of my nature. I wonder how he survives. (I always assume he's alive. He's resilient and resourceful. He *must* be alive.) I wonder where he sleeps. And what he eats.

Everything I take for granted on a daily basis—all the while declaring my alleged gratitude for having so much—people like Fisher King Mike have to worry about constantly. Next meal, next place to defecate, next shelter from the storm. I wonder where he's going. And where he really comes from.

And I wonder if something Fisher King Mike told me one night, in the lot behind Nerdmelt, is the most heartbreaking part of our national failure to provide dignity to so many of our fellow citizens. He said, "No, no, see, what people don't understand is what you call the homeless problem, so many people on the streets, it's, it's not that. It's that we have a system, a society, and the way that system is set up, OK, there's *gonna* be people on the streets. It's *inevitable*. The system makes it that way, so people don't care about each other. Christians. Christian nation. We don't care about each other. So, OK, see? The homeless problem, all these people on the streets, it's *inevitable* and totally *preventable* at the same time."

Inevitable and preventable. That's not a system I support, yet I support such a system every day of my life, no matter how begrudgingly. I'm part of the fabric, part of the whole. I may not agree to the terms and conditions set forth to become a member in good standing of our fine society, but I'm a member nonetheless. However incrementally, I contribute to the inevitability of someone less fortunate, someone very weak in some key area of getting by, ending up living in circumstances so undignified and unrighteous you might call them *unacceptable*. Yet I accept it all.

I personally haven't made anyone homeless. I've never evicted a tenant and forced them to brave the elements, never demolished a rent-controlled apartment building to construct a glass tower. Still, the way our marvelous system is currently calibrated, I know that in order for people like me to live in luxury, many other people must live in less splendid environs. That's the curious way we've got things organized at this moment in history. I don't make the rules, but I involuntarily benefit from them.

Maybe, I tell myself, there's a way to share the bounty of my Good Life. Maybe there's a way to make another person's life altogether better without making my circumstances any less wonderful. Maybe there's truly enough for everyone.

My yoga teacher and friend, Dharma D, sets aside one night a week to feed the homeless, handing out sandwiches and warm drinks. Another friend makes weekly early-morning clothes donations. Surely, I remind myself, I can do those things.

And perhaps more. If I'm able to will my stocky middle-aged body to run marathons, and my tired middle-aged brain to write books and learn new languages and master the game of chess, and my timorous heart to face the frightening and the unknown with a modicum of courage—well, then, maybe I have what it takes to do more than nothing.

Maybe the better angels of our nature aren't as distant and inaccessible as most of us imagine. Maybe all that's required to access and embrace these angels is to decide consciously and willfully that we've got everything we'll ever need, with plenty of extra to share.

If I'm able to access the better angels of my nature, then maybe I can change the world, my tiny little inconsequential part of it, without even trying.

FOUR

The Porch Watcher

———

We're huddled behind the Nerdmelt, waiting for the Monday night open mic to commence. Someone is telling a story about a comedian who used his precious three minutes of stage time to slowly, wordlessly remove all his clothing—except one sock.

"Remember that other crazy dude that used to come here?" Kyle, the host, interjects. "With the Selena Gomez stories?"

"Mike," I say, nodding. "My man, Fisher King Mike."

"Yeah. Him. So, I'm walking down Sunset, on my way here, and I see Mike at the bus bench over there by Chipotle. And, I swear, no shit, he's wearing an *alligator costume*, like, a furry felt alligator, like, a mascot, and he's got a big smile on his face, just, like, oblivious."

"Maybe he'll come to the mic like that," I say. "Gator comedy is very alt."

Kyle laughs. "Fisher King Mike is all about the *alt*, you know what I mean?"

We nod and chuckle and add tags onto what's been said before, a subtle current of one-upmanship rippling beneath the jokes. You can detect strenuousness behind our brand of funny, the effort to find laughs. Guys like Fisher King Mike don't have to try.

31

"So when's the last time you saw him?" I ask.

"Like, literally ten minutes ago."

"Yeah? I haven't seen him in a while. When's the last time he did the mic?"

"Seems like forever," one young comedian says. "Months?"

Kyle takes a deep drag from an omnipresent cigarette. "Yeah, I wanna say, like, it's been about three months since he did a set here."

"All that time I haven't seen him once," I say. "He used to do 'Revolutionary Words' over at Elderberries. Religiously. Never missed it."

"Didn't you have to ban him here once?" another guy asks Kyle.

"It wasn't, like, an outright ban. I just had to remind him about some of the ground rules. Like, the light. You gotta respect the light."

Murmurs of solemn assent. "No doubt." "Fo sho." "You *gotta*."

I'm about to mention logorrhea, compulsive talkativeness, but I know in this crowd such a word will only lead to discussions of watery stool, so I keep it to myself.

Fisher King Mike can't stop once he starts. He seems to have the same desires and compulsions as all the talented, striving young comedians grinding their way through the dues-paying mill of Los Angeles. All of us performers crave an audience. We all want someone—or a whole bunch of someones—to listen and laugh, as though what we have to offer the world is necessary and unmissable, when, in reality, it's often of interest only to the guy on stage. Fisher King Mike, unlike Hollywood aspirants who own cars and live in apartments, has no self-editing function, no superego mode to impart shame and insecurity. *Of course*, he runs the light. And of course, he's wearing an alligator costume today. Why wouldn't he?

Mike and I once went back-to-back at one long-forgotten

show. To my initial alarm and eventual delight, he used most of his set—and some of the next person's—to offer a detailed commentary on what he'd just watched before he was called to the stage: *my* set. It wasn't a review or a critique, really, and it wasn't a reiteration, either. My set served as a kind of jumping off point for Mike's digressions, a starting line with no finish in sight. The mystery and surprise of where his disjointed rant might lead was kind of funny and sort of mesmerizing, and, in the end, utterly inscrutable. If it weren't a schizophrenic homeless man delivering the performance, people would call it boundary-breaking, genre-smashing, comedy genius.

Delivering an entire stand-up set dressed as a cartoon alligator—and never referencing the outfit—would be something I'd like to see. Alas, Mike doesn't show up for the Nerdmelt event that night. Or the following one, or the one after that.

But the next week, when I amble into the parking lot on a mild Monday night, Fisher King Mike is there, standing by himself, off to the side, looking very much as he did when I last saw him three or four months earlier strolling on the sidewalk outside our front garden.

He's wearing dark sunglasses and his Hollywood hat, which seems to have been inscribed with bible verses on most of the available fabric. Mike's outer coat is also covered with hand-written messages, some of them Jesus quotations, some of them incomprehensible. "Mr. Punky," he says as I approach.

"Mr. Mike," I reply. "Good to see you. How you been?"

"No, no, it's not that. Had some family complications. My wife. My kids. You know how it is."

I nod. But, I have no idea, actually, how it is when you're able to hear obscure messages emanating from distant corners of consensus reality.

We go inside together and put our names in the bucket, on

crinkled slips of paper. They choose twenty-five (from about 150 entries). Neither Fisher King Mike nor MK Punky gets picked.

"Good to see you again, Mike," I say, slipping out the back door. Five minutes later, I'm home.

"Did you win the lottery?" Charmaine calls to me from her upstairs office.

"No. I've probably already used up my share of luck this time around," I say, flashing Charm a look that indicates she's the big lottery prize in my life. Which is true. I'm loved and I give love, and that's the greatest luck of all. But my partnership with Charmaine isn't the exception in my life; it's closer to the rule. I've been extraordinarily, incomprehensibly *lucky* in this lifetime. Although I could surely catalog all the elements of what I consider my great good fortune, my privilege, let's merely start with the fact that I was born a white male in the United States of America. That's a pretty good break.

So I don't buy lottery tickets, and when I enter a charity raffle it's really charity, because I don't harbor a tiny feeling (or desire) that I might win. I feel like I've already won, that I've already gotten more than my fair share of good breaks and golden opportunities. I've already used up my good luck inventory; better for someone less lucky to enjoy a taste.

Just then, when I'm feeling altogether jolly about my high ideals and blah-blah-blah, I hear knocking at the front door.

"Are you expecting anyone?" Charmaine asks.

"No. Maybe it's a solicitor. I'll check."

"Please don't open the door until you know who it is," she implores.

I assure her I will. A few weeks earlier, on a mild weekday night, Charmaine was robbed at gunpoint in our driveway by two masked assailants. Her calmness served her well. They took Charm's phone and wallet, but, mercifully, they didn't hurt her physically. They never touched her. Emotionally, though, the wounds were deep. The fear lingered.

Now we take extra care with security. We do a full 360-degree scan of the street and sidewalk, like Secret Service agents, before getting in or out of Charmaine's car, and I installed motion-sensor floodlights around the property, bright enough for nighttime tennis. Still, when the sun goes down, Charm sometimes feels a little frightened, a little anxious.

I open the window shutters beside our front door and peer onto the porch, illuminated with LED bulbs. No one's there.

Then I look down the path leading toward the front gate. On one side of the gate is Fisher King Mike; on the other side are all of Fisher King Mike's bags.

"Babe, it's Fisher King Mike," I call out. "I'll go talk to him outside."

"Isn't it a little late?" Charmaine asks.

"Yeah. It is. I just saw him at the open mic. He didn't say anything, didn't say he was coming. Don't worry. I'll be back."

"All right," she says, in a tone that I understand to mean *everything is not all right*. "I'm going to lock the front door. Take your key."

Sure. Whatever makes her feel better about living in the heart of this enormous, sometimes-violent city.

I step outside. "Mike! Everything OK?"

"No, no it's not that. I didn't want to disturb you and your wife—I know how important family is, family is the most important thing there is, nothing comes before your family, and I know you know that, and so I *knocked* on your door but I thought I should wait here, down here, where, you know, I'm not intruding on your space, giving you your space, you see what I'm saying?"

"Thanks for your courtesy," I say, with as much patience as I can muster, which, I confess, is not something I manage with great success. "What's up?"

"No, no, it's not that," he says, shaking his head and making a small dismissive wave of his hand. "I just didn't want to disturb—"

"I got you, brother. And thank you for that. So what's going on?"

Mike looks down at the path, avoiding eye contact. (He's wearing dark sunglasses tonight, anyway.) "Look, I hate to ask you this, and, and if you," he holds up both hands in a *hey-it's-no-big-deal* gesture, "if you can't . . . I just was wondering if you would have a problem with me leaving my bags behind your hedge over there, where it's out of sight, won't be in nobody's way."

He's got two canvas bags, slightly larger than airplane carry-ons but smaller than a traveler's duffel. "Sure," I say nonchalantly. "How long do you want to keep them there?"

"No, no, see, it's not that. I just have to get to the Valley for a couple of days, and, see, what people don't understand is, I have to get back here to do my work, to minister, because I'm a street pastor and there are so many people here who need help, they need help, and no one wants to help them, and so I've got to help them, and, and, if I can leave these bags here for a couple of days—"

"A couple of days," I repeat. Not a question. A statement of fact.

"A couple of days," Fisher King Mike repeats. "While I'm in the Valley. Gotta take care of some business there with my family."

"Right," I say. "So we'll keep your bags here for a couple of days."

"A couple of days. *Puh-shweep.*" He gestures like he's wiping off a counter.

"OK. You got it."

"Thanks. Look, I didn't want to disturb you and your wife, but I gotta take care of some business in the Valley, and, and, you know, what people don't understand is that when you're a minister, a street pastor, you've got a lot of responsibilities."

"Well, thank you for your good works," I say amiably. "We're glad we can help you out." And before he can launch another monologue, I grab his bags and plod toward the front porch, where a six-foot-tall hedge does indeed provide full privacy from street views, and from the neighbors and their children. In my rush to make things all better, I neglect to ask my wife if she's cool with making our front porch a temporary storage facility for a loquacious homeless fellow.

Fisher King Mike follows me, carrying his backpack and a white plastic takeout bag filled with his sundries. "Here," I say, sliding the bags beneath a low square table flanked by wooden chairs. "We can stash them under here."

He nods affirmatively several times, and sighs heavily. Then he shakes his head "no" several times, and sighs heavily. "Hey, look, I just want to say . . ." his voice trails off, and his frail, bony shoulders begin to tremble.

I'm about to make a comment about how rare it is for the great orator to be at a loss for words, when Mike begins to sniffle and dab at his eyes. "Oh, man, it's OK," I tell him. "Everything's going to be OK. We'll take care of your stuff. It's no problem. You didn't disturb anything. Everything's fine, Mike."

Before he trudges off to wherever he's actually going—and maybe, in some alternate universe, it really is his estate next to Kanye West's—Fisher King Mike flashes a knowing smile at me, a comedian's smile, someone who's in on the joke, who gets the irony and absurdity of the humor. A smile that says, *Sir, you are one funny dude. 'Everything's fine. Everything's fine.' Yes, sir, you are hilarious.*

His bags stay on our porch for three days and nights, talismans of Mike, symbols of all he has and doesn't have. And every time I look at them, they seem to flash me the same myth-busting smile.

Never again am I going to tell Fisher King Mike that everything's OK, I resolve. I'm going to help him *make* everything

OK—even if that "everything" is, in the grand scheme, almost nothing.

Because something is almost always more than nothing.

IN THE INTERVAL, before Mike comes back for his possessions, Charmaine has the opportunity to school me on the importance of making bilateral decisions about the use of our household, particularly when it involves the warehousing of bags that contain *who-knows-what* and have been previously stashed *who-knows-where.*

Noted. Must consult the wife. Got it. Because, and what people don't understand is, there's nothing's more important than family.

Even when that family consists of two people.

We don't have children. We don't own a dog (or a cat or any other creature). After Ella, our white greyhound-Labrador mutt memorialized in my book *Ella in Europe: An American Dog's International Adventures* and on the Animal Planet show "Ella & Me," died at 15 ½, a couple years after we were married, the timing was bad to adopt another pet. We were grieving for a great friend, yes. But we were also traveling all over the globe for Charmaine's concerts, and to the Philippines for family visits. Taking in a puppy from a shelter—no other option works in our canine value system—"rescuing" often means dealing with abandonment issues. We didn't want to be a mom and dad who were seldom there.

These days, we're traveling less. Charmaine's parents, Baldomero, 87, and Nieves, 82, are both in declining health. Dad is on dialysis every other day. Mom has precancerous internal lesions and mobility issues. Charm doesn't like being away from them for more than a week at a time, and almost every Sunday that she's in town, she visits them at their two-bedroom condo in the valley, nowhere near Kanye's place.

I'm not welcome, having been declared *persona non grata* by

Mom Clamor as a result of losing my cool and speaking harshly (loudly) to her—and then immediately apologizing for my momentary lapse of decorum. She determined it was all unforgivable.

They used to live with us, in the retrofitted garage that today serves as Charmaine's private therapy clinic. Now they're forty minutes away and growing more distant by the day. Getting ghosted by Mom, I eventually realize, is a wonderful affirmation of how the most disparate world cultures are often surprisingly similar, that even the most devoutly Christian person can behave exactly like an Orthodox Jew. *You're dead to me! [ripped shirt thrown disdainfully to the floor].* More proof, to my mind, that We Are One. *Namaste.*

When Charmaine hangs with the 'rents, I putter in the garden, read on the back deck, write poetry in my head. On Sundays, I try to disconnect. After posting my Thought of the Week essay on my website and doing a sweep for any urgent emails, I shut down the internet. Since I don't have a smartphone and I don't text, I'm blissfully removed from the constant noise that emptiness makes.

I find that Sundays are some of my happiest days. The more I'm away from a computer screen and the more I'm in the dirt, growing things, the better I feel. The opportunity to muse, to ponder, to cogitate—it seems our modern culture allows fewer and fewer chances to simply *think.* Setting aside an entire day for reflection, a Sabbath, if you will, has made me slightly more centered than I was the month before.

Sometimes, though, after hours alone pulling weeds—alone except for the birds and worms and squirrels—what's missing is a companion, someone to chitter-chatter with. Or be silent with. Someone whose presence affirms that you're not alone in the world.

A friend.

I don't have many. Definitely a quality over quantity situation, which suits the writer's need of solitude. Still . . .

As if on cue, as though I'm able to manifest my wishes through meditation and positive imaging, an exceptionally skinny fellow wearing two coats and a "Hollywood" hat appears at the front gate. When Fisher King Mike returns for his bags three days after he left them, not quite as promised but close, I'm outside in the garden, planting onion bulbs. "Hey! Mike!" I say, genuinely glad to see him, and even gladder that he's sort of followed through on his pledge. "You're back!"

"Yeah, yeah, I know. I *told* you I was coming back in a few days," he says, astonished that anyone would doubt Mr. Reliable. "Selena is getting ready for a big tour, going away for the whole summer. Europe. And, and, you know how it is."

"I have some idea," I say, noncommittally. "You OK? You hungry?"

"No, no, I've got plenty to eat," he says, holding up a Wendy's bag. "You want some fries?" He tilts the bag toward me. It's filled with wrappers and ketchup packages and a giant soda-filled cup with a straw in it, and possibly some potatoes hiding somewhere.

"No, thank you," I say. "I'm on a celery binge at the moment."

"Yeah, yeah, I know. Hey, look, I was wondering," he says, setting down the carryout bag on our vegetable donation table stationed between the sidewalk and the curb, on what's technically known as "the parkway." Wendy, the pigtailed, freckle-faced mascot who seems super happy that you've purchased such a nutritious meal from her company, smiles magnanimously over our garden, content in the knowledge that the food grown here will never end up in her restaurant. "I was wondering if you could let me stay with the bags tonight."

"On the porch?"

"I need to get my head together. I just need a night to get my head together. See, what people don't understand is, and I tell them this, you know, you can't help all the people that need a street pastor, you can't help them if your stuff is in one place and your family is in another, and, and, I'm having some problems with, you know, holding it, and, and if I could just get my head together." He nods and chews his lips.

"So, you want to sleep on the porch?"

"I just need to get my head together, going back and forth, and, and, the bus stops running after ten, and all my stuff."

"You can leave it here," I assure him. "Your bags are safe."

"No, no, it's not that, I just need to get my head together."

I nod. "As far as I'm concerned, it's OK. You can stay on the porch tonight. But I've gotta ask the wife. I'm sure you know what I mean."

"Yeah, yeah, I know," he says, chuckling wearily. "Check with the boss."

I instruct Mike to make himself comfortable, take a seat, have a rest while I go inside and get official permission from the Executive Committee.

My moral barometer says that if we're able to let strange bags sleep on our porch, we should be able to let a human being do the same. Why wouldn't we?

Instead of philosophical arguments, when I find Charmaine upstairs in her office, singing in Tagalog, I frame the Fisher King Mike pitch as a home-security move. Sure, I tell her, it's unusual to have a homeless person sleeping on our front porch. But, given what Charmaine went through in the robbery, wouldn't having a night watchman on the premises give us an added level of comfort and confidence? Fisher King Mike could be a kind of early-warning system if anyone suspicious walks down the driveway or loiters near our gate—something his bags, fully approved and permitted for porch-sitting, can't do.

"And where exactly is he planning on sleeping?" Charmaine asks.

"I'm not really sure. I think he might have a sleeping bag, or a mat or something. I get the feeling that anything is better than the street."

"Or the shelter?"

I shrug. "From what I'm told, the shelters are notoriously dangerous, so our front porch is a big improvement."

"And the bathroom?"

I tell her, "We didn't really talk about that. I think he goes to the church, on Hollywood, when he needs a toilet. Or the supermarket, the Ralph's on Sunset."

"And it doesn't worry you that he's mentally ill?" Charmaine inquires, a bemused smile curling her lips.

I think about it for a second. "No doubt. He's definitely experiencing a different reality than we are. But he's also totally harmless. All his ravings, I mean, they're weird and strange, but he never talks about hurting anyone, nothing violent. And as far as I know, he doesn't drink. I don't get any threat vibes from him. Do you?"

Charmaine agrees. She doesn't think Mike's dangerous, just unpredictable. "It's hard to make arrangements and agreements with someone like that," she reminds me.

We decide to let him stay for one night. *One night*—boundaries clearly defined. Then Fisher King Mike, Wendy, and all the bags will have to move on, going wherever Mike's ministerial services take him.

I bound downstairs and find Mike on the porch, asleep on one of the wooden deck chairs, his spindly legs thrust outward, his sunken jaw resting on his chest. His mouth—I figure he must have done a lot of meth at some point. He's got that look: desiccated facial muscles, skin like a chicken's after boiling, missing teeth.

Plus, he chain-smokes Camels and guzzles Coke—regular, caffeinated, corn-syrup-infused Coke, no effete diet stuff. All that's got to wreak havoc on your dentistry.

I watch him doze. He smells better than the last time he was on this porch.

The sun is beginning to set. I leave Fisher King Mike to his slumber, wondering when he last slept soundly, wondering where he goes to when he disappears into "the Valley," wondering if he really does have a family who worries about him and misses him and counts on him. Not Selena Gomez. But someone.

Before Charmaine and I have (a non-Wendy's) dinner inside our warm, capacious home, I check on Mike, ready to slide him a sandwich and a cup of tea. When I peer through the dining room shutters onto the porch, he's no longer in the chair; he's moved to the concrete, sleeping in the fetal position, a knapsack his pillow. I go back inside and grab a throw pillow from the living room couch and a wool blanket slung over an armchair.

Placing them on the ground beside him, I whisper, "Good night, Mike." He doesn't stir. The city, that mean, cold place just two blocks from here, has gone silent, the sounds of traffic replaced by chirping crickets and Fisher King Mike's shallow, rapid breathing. There's a certain rhythm and harmony to their sounds, a kind of nocturnal music formed in the blending. I add a sigh to the choir and go back inside, where a bed, with a mattress and feathery pillows and a comforting snuggling partner, awaits.

IN THE MORNING, I rise early with the sun and go downstairs to check on our porch tenant. He's not there.

His bags are, but Fisher King Mike is gone, only a couple of torn and emptied sugar packets in the ashtray left behind.

Before I return upstairs, I shuffle in my bathrobe to the corner of our driveway, just yards from where Charmaine was robbed.

We have a tiny community library there, founded in 2012 and built entirely from found materials, including an old picture window frame that serves as the library's see-through door. In addition to keeping the books organized and the guestbook up-to-date, the library offers poems for the people—"Free! Take One!"—two different poems every day, on each side of one piece of paper. Most of them have been previously published on my website, as part of semi-annual MK Poetry Festivals featuring new material for a week or two, or until I can't come up with anything worth sharing. But one of my resolutions for 2016 is to submit my poetry for publication, whether in magazines and journals or anthologies and collections. (Another resolution is to try to get *Year 14*, a novel my literary agent has found to be un-sellable, published somewhere, anywhere.) I have no ambitions or expectations of the poetry world; I'm not sure I even belong there. Sharing the work, as pretentious as it sounds, is reason enough.

The Vista Street Community Library is well-stocked this morning. Someone has left eight books from a cat mystery series, a genre with which I am not familiar but which I'm certain pays better than poetry.

As I'm assessing the Free Poems inventory—I like to keep four to five in stock—I hear the crackle of jacaranda pods on the sidewalk behind me. It's Fisher King Mike, shuffling down the street with what appears to be a *grande* coffee in hand and a white earbud in one of his earholes.

"No, I was just at the church," he announces. "Little breakfast. Doughnuts."

"Was everything OK last night?"

"No, no. Fine." He walks past me to the porch. I follow him.

"So, what's the plan today?"

"Listen, do you think I could leave my bags here while I do my work?"

"You mean, today? During the day?"

"No, no, see, it's not that—"

"Yes," I interrupt him. "Yes, you can. You may." I'm relieved it's only the bags and not their owner occupying our front porch. I imagine, by nightfall, Fisher King Mike will move on to whatever comes next in his improvised adventure.

"Thanks. See—and that's what people don't understand—when you're ministering to the homeless, when you're a street pastor, and you've got a family that counts on you, I just need to get my head together."

"I'm glad we can help," I say, sincerely, silently wishing we could do more, but relieved that, for now, we don't have to do more. "Have a good day, Mike. I'll see you later."

"Yeah, yeah, I know." He checks the pockets on his outermost coat, fishing out a pack of cigarettes, purchased by mysterious means. "Don't worry. I know, I know: no smoking on the porch."

"Or the garden! Charmaine doesn't like it."

"No, no, see, that's what I'm saying." He chuckles and shakes his head. "I'm not gonna do nothing that don't respect the space." He looks at me like I'm nuts. Then he ambles away, his possessions left on the porch.

He's gone all day. Periodically, on breaks from work in my home office, I check out front. Mike's bags are undisturbed, untouched while their owner's on walkabout, doing whatever he does on a hot Los Angeles day. I figure he'll be back by sundown.

Charmaine says not to count on it. "You have to be careful about having any expectations," she warns me over lunch. "You're not dealing with a normal person. He's not really capable of keeping his word, even if he means to. His brain just doesn't work that way."

He came back for his bags, I remind her. "Just like he said he would—you know, a day later."

"Just be careful," she counsels. "I know you want to help, and that's lovely. So kind. But some people are very difficult to help."

As if to demonstrate his reliability—his *normalcy*—Mike knocks on the front door just as the sky is turning dusky. "Hey, sorry to disturb you, I don't mean to cause any problems, it's just that, I was wondering, it's going to be hard to get to the Valley right now, and, and, I was wondering if, you know, I could crash here tonight. With my bags. Stay with my bags. I won't make any noise or nothing."

"You want to sleep on the porch?"

He looks at the ground and nods, chewing his lips.

"Let me ask the boss."

Charmaine doesn't see why not. "Sure," she says when I seek her blessing. "As long as all the boundaries are clear . . ." We agree Fisher King Mike can stay one more night on our front porch, and so can his bags—and that he can have the pillow and blanket, and that we can make his slumber a bit more comfortable with an old exercise mat we'll donate.

Neither of us feels inordinately magnanimous letting a refugee from the streets spend the night on our front porch. If we were to really go above and beyond, we'd offer Fisher King Mike a night in Weed Hollow Cabin.

In the back corner of the backyard, tucked beneath a blood orange tree canopy, and with a tangerine tree outside the front door, we have a one-room redwood cabin, with a proper shingle roof, functioning electricity, and a queen-size bed. There's no plumbing. The previous owner of our house used the cabin to play video games and smoke weed; Charm and I turned it into a quaint hideaway, an adorable bed and breakfast without the breakfast. Over the years, we've hosted dozens of guests: family members, social justice travelers, friends-of-friends, musical collaborators, entitled freeloaders, parents and children, people in need. One friend, between jobs, stayed there for more than two years. Another friend, post-divorce, stayed there for six months.

And once we let a homeless man sleep there. We were trying to be generous. The cabin was unoccupied at the time. We wanted to help.

It didn't go well. Boundaries were not respected. Cleanliness was not maintained.

The wife was not happy.

We agreed that would be the last time a transient would stay in Weed Hollow Cabin—unless, of course, they were of the privileged young backpacker variety, couch-surfing for a few nights between Burning Man and their flight to Cambodia. Weed Hollow isn't meant to be a casual crash pad, not for random crashers or society's crash victims, the denizens of the street.

And nor is Charmaine's backyard clinic, Be Well Therapy. Formerly the in-law apartment, it has a full bathroom with a shower, a working kitchen, and a Murphy bed. But it's also her healing space by day and almost never available to guests. Numerous people with our financial interests at heart have encouraged us to rent Be Well and Weed Hollow on a short-term basis. We've chosen to hold the spaces rent-free, ready and available when there's a need.

It doesn't occur to me that "there's a need" for Fisher King Mike to sleep in Weed Hollow Cabin. Or Be Well, or our empty guest bedroom, which we use as a screening room, or on the couch in the living room, or the couch in my office, or on an auxiliary blow-up mattress we keep in the closet.

He's got our porch, and that's a whole lot better than the bus stop, isn't it?

Fisher King Mike performing at "Revolutionary Words"
social justice open mic.

FIVE

Mr. Fixit

———

For the next two nights, Fisher King Mike sleeps on our front porch, in all his clothes, under a wool blanket. During the day, he disappears for long stretches, eventually returning to our house, where he sits and reads. He reads voraciously: scripture, poetry, comic books, novels, self-improvement manuals. I don't know where he gets the books and magazines, which, like their reader, are tattered and worn from overuse. Sometimes he makes notes in a spiral notebook journal; sometimes he thumbs through his phone, watching Selena Gomez videos. Mostly, he reads.

I don't avoid Mike—he's on my front porch; I can't—but I avoid engaging him in "conversation." On this day, though, we need to talk.

"Michael!" I say, trying to see his eyes beneath the dark sunglasses. "I've got some important news to share."

He looks up from his King James Bible and shakes his head "no," so at least I've got his attention. "Mike, you can stay on the porch for the next two nights. In fact, we would *like* for you to stay here. We're going out of town for the weekend, and it would be great to have you doing security while we're gone."

He smirks—as you might expect from a former Navy SEAL

and CIA agent with high Department of Defense clearances who's been asked by some *civilian* to do home security. "Yeah, yeah. OK."

"And I'm going to leave you some food, and a little money in case of emergencies."

Fisher King Mike shakes his head "no" and shrugs. "Nah. Nah. OK."

"I just wanted to be clear: you're not only welcome to stay here for a couple more nights, you're *wanted*. Just to keep an eye on the place."

"No, no, OK. Look, could I please use the hose? I got something on the bottom of my shoe." He holds up one of his sneakers—it's gigantic, like NBA-player-size. Wedged in the waffle sole is a dark gloppy spot that could be any number of things.

I escort Mike through the driveway gate to the side of the house. "You should lock that thing," he grunts, gesturing at the driveway gate. He nods repeatedly. "No, no, like a chain lock. More secure."

I tell him he's right—"and here's the hose. Do your thing."

"No, I was just—hey, you know you got a leak?" He points at the faucet, where the hose connects to the water pipe. There's a little drip, which I've patched with duct tape.

"Yup. A little one. Probably needs a new washer."

"No, no, it's not that. What you got here—and, and, I'm only guessing before you take it off—I'm guessing you got an old hammer valve here connecting to a ball valve, you know, the one that's like a circle, and it just closes up, and then you got it connected to a hammer valve, with the block, and, and, you know, *that's* not going to work!"

"So it needs a new washer?"

He laughs, his lips stretched thin. "No! You need a new valve, not a washer."

"I'm not very handy," I tell him.

"Yeah, yeah, I know, it's just that you need a new valve. Probably take you longer to get one than to replace it." Mike seems highly amused at this irony.

"Maybe for you," I say. "This is not my area of expertise, Mike. Obviously."

"No, no, if we go to Home Depot and get the part, I can change this in thirty seconds."

"Really?" *Like you've got your jet parked at Van Nuys airport?*

"Dude, I can build a house from the ground up. This is, this is," he waves at the faucet dismissively, "this is . . ."

"I understand. We'll get it fixed soon."

"No, no, see, if you wait, it's only gonna get worse. And then there ain't nothing you can do once it blows. It's just gonna be water everywhere. You gotta replace this valve, sir." He looks at me gravely. "You gotta replace this valve."

"OK. But don't you have to wash your shoe?"

"Yeah, yeah, I know. But you gotta replace this valve. Do you gotta wrench?"

"An Allen wrench?"

"No!" he guffaws. "Just an adjustable wrench, a plumber's wrench."

I tell Mike I think we have such a thing, but I'm not certain. Maybe we should look in the basement, where forlorn items like tools and unsold CDs gather mold.

We descend eight concrete steps into the cellar, a space beneath our kitchen with its own door and lights. The fuse-box is here, as well as a seldom-used table saw, a neglected workbench, and an unorganized storage cabinet. "Dude!" Fisher King Mike exclaims. "You got a workshop down here!"

"Sort of. Yeah. Right now it's more of a storage space. Do you see the wrench?"

"Here," he says, plucking it from a wall mount. "All you need. And some plumber's tape. You got plumber's tape?"

We might. I invite Mike to investigate.

"You should finish this basement. Put a ceiling in, some walls, re-do the floors. Nice workshop." He holds up a small ring of blue tape. "This is all you got. Might need some more tape. You got clamps?" He riffles through a box of odds-and-ends. "I could turn this place into a workshop. Power strip over there, and, and some shelves. I can build a house from the ground up. Easy. See, what people don't understand, and I try to tell them, we used to have to build houses for training exercises, so they could get shot up, but they had to be real houses, and we had to build them cheap, no furniture, just, you know, a house, with drywall and electrical and water, and then they'd use it for training exercises, and we'd just have to build another one."

In a flashing moment of clarity, I realize having Fisher King Mike replace a water valve on the side of my house might not be the wisest idea.

"Well, now we know I've got the right wrench," I say, guiding Mike out of the cellar. "And some plumber's tape."

"Yeah, yeah, I know. You might need more."

"Man, I really appreciate your guidance on this, Mike. As you can tell, I'm not good with this stuff."

"Yeah, yeah, I know. But, see, with an old house like this?" He shakes his head and shrugs.

I nod.

"No, no, it's not that."

"Thanks, Mike."

THE NEXT MORNING, at sun-up, I brew a pot of coffee and take a cup to our porch watcher. I want to make sure I see him before we leave for San Diego, where Charmaine has a gig. We need to exchange phone numbers, and talk about plant watering and a dozen other minor details.

When I open the front door, Mike is standing with his hands in his pockets, facing the postal box, as though he's been waiting for my arrival. Before I can greet him or offer him a mug, he says solemnly, "C'mere. I gotta show you something."

He walks to the driveway gate. I set down the coffee and follow him in my bathrobe. He pushes the gate open and gestures for me to go in. I do. He leads me to the garden hose, coiled against the side of the house. The little drip is now a big drip.

"No, see, I put a bucket under there before I went to bed." The bucket has several inches of water in it.

"Not good," I whisper, unhelpfully.

"No, no, it ain't, and it's only gonna get worse. Eventually, it'll just be like you're running the hose, even when it's turned off."

Unhandy though I am, I quickly calculate that there's no bucket on the property large enough to deal with this issue. "OK," I announce. "We're going to Home Depot."

"Yeah, because if you don't replace it, what I'm saying is, you gotta replace it or else, if you don't, see, you need a new ball valve, two-and-quarter, I already measured, and, and, see, if you *don't* replace it, well—"

"We're going to Home Depot!"

"Yeah, 'cause all you need is this one piece, with the connector."

"We're going. Let's go." I'm not thinking, but I'm deciding. I'm acting very presidential.

Charmaine and I have to leave in a few hours, and I still have to pack, and the water is leaking. Attention must be paid. Worst case, Mike helps me find the correct part and I call my general contractor friend Sagi to help me change it out. I don't own a car, and I seldom drive, but I have a valid license and a home-maintenance issue on my hands: we're going. "Let's do it."

"I need to stop at the store," Fisher King Mike tells me. "Grab a Coke."

"Sure," I agree to his breakfast choice, if that's what it takes to get the job done. "Let me put on some pants and grab my wallet. We'll leave in three minutes!" This is feeling like a mission, a secret one I'm not allowed to talk about with non-coms.

Charmaine's still sleeping. I leave her a note so she knows her car was borrowed, not stolen, and slip out quietly.

We get in her twelve-year-old Volkswagen Jetta, and, immediately, I'm acutely aware of Fisher King Mike's aroma, sour and unclean, with an overtone of tobacco. I roll down the windows.

He puts on his seatbelt and rests his hands on his knees, like he's accustomed to zipping around L.A. in chauffeured automobiles. Before I've backed out of the driveway, Fisher King Mike commences a five-minute monologue on the importance of addressing water leaks *early* in the process, before they become a deluge. "See, and what people don't understand is, it ain't just something that don't work right, it's *water*. It can damage your house."

"And you don't want to waste it," I add.

"No, no, see it's not that."

"Well, it is that. That's one of the things."

"Yeah, but, see, what I'm saying is, it's *water* and, see, if you let that go, it can damage your house." He shakes his head and adds wearily, "the foundation."

Mike directs me to a convenience store on Sunset Boulevard near La Brea, where homeless folks congregate near Starbucks and Subway. I park. He gets out of the car and strolls inside, saying nothing. "I'll be right here," I announce to his back, fully expecting him to return but also knowing there's some possibility that he might not.

I savor the quasi-silence—and think. Mike's right: it would be imprudent to leave town with a growing water leak on the side of your ninety-nine-year-old house. I want to get it fixed quickly—or at least temporarily repaired—but, see, what people don't understand is, Fisher King Mike doesn't operate on the same schedule as the rest of the world, and, also, parenthetically, his biography and *curriculum vitae* are almost certainly elaborate fictions.

A wave of anxiety nausea washes through me: I've allowed a potentially serious plumbing problem to fester to the point of crisis—and instead of calling a professional, I've enlisted an aromatic homeless man for the job.

Maybe it's me who has the mental problems.

Where he gets the money, I don't know, but Fisher King Mike eventually emerges, with a two-liter Coke in one hand and a lighter in the other. Without acknowledging me, he stands next to the store entrance and sparks a cigarette dangling from his mouth. Then he swigs some soda. Then he smokes. Then he swigs. Caffeine-Nicotine-Caffeine. Then he sets the bottle on a window ledge and retrieves his phone from a coat pocket. Then, smoking, he appears, from my obscured perspective, to be scrolling through social media accounts.

I lean out the window. "Yo, Mike. You almost ready to roll?"

He holds up his free hand, like, *just wait a sec.* And continues to smoke and look at his phone.

Does he understand? Does Fisher King Mike know that, at least right now, at this peculiar moment, I need him more than he needs me? Not only do I lack the skills to replace a ball-valve—or is it a hammer-valve?—I wouldn't even know the correct connector to purchase, let alone what to do with it. I watch him smoke and scroll. Calling a real plumber, or handyman, or whomever deals with mechanical issues frail poetic types can't handle, seems like a better and better idea by the second.

Then Mike tucks the phone into a pocket, takes a long, valedictory drag on his cigarette, and tucks a nearly full bottle of Coke into another pocket. He gets in the car. "OK," he says.

"We can go?" I ask dryly.

"Yeah, yeah, that's what I'm saying." He looks at me like I'm out of my mind, and then stares straight ahead.

We cruise down Sunset Boulevard in the early-morning light. It's not yet 6:30 on a Wednesday; the city is still sleeping. As we pass tent– and box-encampments on the sidewalk, Fisher King Mike says nothing. Stopped at a light beside the CNN building, where the lobby monitors seldom display televised reports on homelessness, we see a bedraggled man with a sign asking for help; Mike says nothing. The ride takes about ten minutes, and neither of us speaks. *Inevitable and preventable.* Driving with a chronically homeless man, passing talismans of all that's wrong with Mike's life and our diseased society, allegedly powerful attributes like *eloquence* and *insight* feel useless and absurd. Because lingering behind all the sophisticated explications and rhetorical hand-wringing, the question remains, always unanswered: *What are you going to do about it?*

Pulling into Home Depot's massive, mostly empty parking lot, populated mainly by day laborers looking for a gig, Mike clears his throat and says, "Let me out here." He gestures toward the store entrance. "I gotta use the bathroom."

We agree to meet in the plumbing department after I park the car. I offer Mike my cell number, in case of complications, but he waves me off and hustles to the toilets in the back of the store. I watch him go, the sour smell drifting away with each stride. His posture suggests a semi-erect question mark; his clothes are too big for his scrawny frame; and he's wearing two coats. Other than that, he looks like any other home improvement shopper.

I avoid the Depot—and all the other big-box stores—shopping here maybe once or twice a year, mostly for garden-related merchandise. It's overwhelming: so many power drills, so many wall sconces, so many nails. For the non-handyman, it's like visiting an exotic country where you don't speak the local language. *What's in all those unfamiliar packages? How do you know which hammer is right for the job? Are there multiple uses for a stud finder?* Wandering semi-lost in the aisles, my mind drifts to questions of philosophical significance, such as how many extra ball-valves—and screwdrivers and paint thinners—must Home Depot sell to pay Tony Stewart for the privilege of painting his orange NASCAR racer with their corporate logo?

And I wonder how many people Habitat for Humanity, or a similar organization, could shelter using only the materials found in *one* Home Depot location.

With the help of a friendly "associate" wearing an orange apron, I locate the plumbing section, where a menagerie of tubes and pipes and unidentifiable commodities taunt me from the shelves. There's one guy squatting in front of some rubber rings, and one other pawing through what I strongly suspect are washers. Fisher King Mike is M.I.A.

I start at one end of the plumbing aisle and search-party it to the end. No Mike.

I find the bathrooms in the way-back corner of the store, near the employee break-room. No Mike.

I go back to plumbing. No. I check the bathrooms again, calling out Mike's name. No. I pull out my flip-phone and realize I don't have his number—if he actually has a working number.

Trying to determine whether or not I should go home without him, I make one last stop in plumbing, clinging to the preposterous fantasy that I'm suddenly going to be endowed with magic powers of pattern recognition that will give me the ability to recognize the exact part I need for my leaky water pipe, distinguishing it from the million impostors begging me to take them home.

There's Mike. Blithely window shopping the merchandise.

"Mike!" I shout, partly relieved, partly annoyed. "Where you been? I've been looking all over for you."

He removes the earbud. "Yeah, yeah, I know. I had to use the bathroom."

"Right. But we were supposed to . . ." I take a deep, calming breath. "All right. Anyway. Here we are. So. Let's get the part and get out of here before the morning traffic."

"Yeah, yeah, I know, I already got it," Fisher King Mike says, slightly exasperated.

"The valve?"

He holds up a metal thing that looks almost exactly like the thing that's attached to my house. "Told you it would take longer to buy it than for me to install it," he says, letting the profundity of his pronouncement sink in.

"That's cool. Because it's taken, like, twenty minutes already," I note, attempting a subtle shade of irony.

"No, no, see, it's not that."

I laugh. "It *is* that!"

"No, no, it's not that, I was waiting for you so I got the part, already measured it, and, and now we can install it, *that's* all I'm saying."

Well, that would be marvelous, I'm thinking. *A crisis averted.* "All right, then. Let's go install it."

We're walking toward the checkout. "I'm going to use the bathroom one last time," Mike says.

I stop myself from saying *you just went*, realizing there in Home Depot that Fisher King Mike is wearing adult diapers. They peek out over the waistband of his sagging trousers. "OK," I say. "But let's have a plan. We're going to meet right outside the checkout, at the exit. I pay; you go to the bathroom; we meet at the exit. Yes?"

"Yeah, yeah, that's fine," he grumbles.

I fulfill my part of the plan in about five minutes. After fifteen minutes, Mike is still off the radar. Now we're definitely going to hit traffic. After twenty minutes, I power-walk to the bathrooms, which are as far away from the checkout as possible, about an eighth of a mile. Mike's not there—unless he can't hear me over the Selena track blasting in his earbud.

I can't leave without him, but I also can't spend all morning waiting for Mike's continence to return. I make a mental note: *this will be the last time you collaborate with the Fisher King—on anything.*

I trudge toward the front of the store, where I have the idea to page our missing Mr. Fixit over the intercom, as if that would do any good. No need. There he is, with a heavy chain in his hands.

"What are you doing, man?" I ask, trying poorly to be amused.

"You need these," he says, holding up the chain and a lock. "For security. And if you get me the right fixture, I can change out that area light you got on the corner of the house, the one that ain't working."

What I'm thinking is *although this all sounds nice, unfortunately you have no credibility whatsoever, and I'm slightly ashamed that I played along with your delusions.* What I say is, "Thank you for caring, Mike."

"No, it's not that. It's you gotta protect your family, that's number one, and, and after what Miss Char went through, you know what they say, the more lights the better—no, no, I'm serious, you gotta fix that light." He nods affirmatively.

"Let's just deal with the water leak. We can do the light another time. That's a big job, with electricity involved. And also I'm sort of in a hurry now."

"Yeah, yeah, I know. But we're here. I can do it for you, no problem. You don't have to pay me. No expectations. Whatever you want to bless me with." Fisher King Mike might be a world-class salesman or I might be a world-class sucker, but the way he's talking I'm starting to believe he's skilled enough to do what he claims. Maybe the *just believe in yourself* mantra we're given from sports and televised singing competitions is really true. Maybe he's convinced me because he's convinced himself.

I figure there's only one way to find out. "OK. Fine. Let's get the light."

The Fisher King immediately sets off toward the back of the store, where our quarry lurks. "Yeah, because you understand, you get the importance, you know: *nothing is more important than family*. And the more light you got around your property at night?" He throws up his hands and marches on.

Mike locates what we're looking for, up-sells me to a solar version, and suggests maybe he should make another bathroom visit—which I oppose, knowing that unless I accompany him as far as the stall he's using, there's a strong chance that he'll wander off on another hard-to-explain detour. Desperate, I blurt, "You can use the bathroom at my house. Let's just get home."

We're back at the checkout. We've been at Home Depot for fifty-two minutes. I'm beyond ready to go. I'm fantasizing about being beamed back to Vista Street. Then: "Hey, MK, I was wondering," Mike says, lowering his voice conspiratorially. "Can we get some breakfast before this job?"

I think a thousand things, none of them encouraging, but say nothing. He doesn't have a kitchen and a refrigerator full of leftovers. He's hungry. I just nod my head and smile.

He directs me to a Burger King across the boulevard from the Depot. Fast food restaurants, like big-box stores, aren't my deal, as Tony Stewart and his NASCAR cohorts might say. Set aside every legitimate criticism one might have of their foodstuffs and business practices and you still won't find me in a place like Burger King more than maybe once every year or two—on a blazing hot day, for a frozen cherry slushee. I don't eat meat or dairy, so, nothing personal, the King and I probably aren't meant for each other.

But with the help of an unwitting accomplice—enter Fisher King Mike—we're brought together, forced into a partnership, and, to no one's surprise but our own, find ourselves (eventually; just wait) very much in love. At this point, early in the First Act, we *hate* each other, cannot stand being around each other. We sing mocking, disdainful songs that somehow telegraph a nascent interest, an awakening of desire. Still, at first meet, we're not enthralled.

I'm ready to leave. "What do you want, Mike? A breakfast sandwich?"

"Yeah, yeah, that's fine," he says. "I'm gonna use the bathroom."

"Two Croissanwiches for four bucks," I report to the air as he leaves. Then I repeat the phrase to the nice lady behind the counter, adding an order of tater tots for the driver. Mike's decided, I infer, that using the bathroom isn't necessary at the moment; he's outside, smoking, looking at his phone.

In California, certain restaurants are required by law to post easy-to-see nutrition information for their customers, who, by and large—and more large than by—don't waste time counting calories. But there it is, right next to styled and enhanced pictures of sausages and bacon strips looking fabulous and not remotely carcinogenic. I'm pondering the calorie content of the King's breakfast menu when, *bing*, just like that, order's up. *Fast* it is, indeed.

I intercept Mike on the sidewalk. We walk to the car. Mike doesn't get in. He's finishing his cigarette. I'm trying to control my breathing, trying to be yogic in the face of opportunities disguised as challenges.

A last drag. A last phone check. And now he's back. "No, I was just saying that once we bought the right part, we can install it, that was all I was saying."

"Yeah. I got it," I say, handing him the breakfast bag, the deep-fried smell of which briefly overpowers the stench of smoke and body odor that swirls around Fisher King Mike like a cartoon cloud.

"Thanks," he says, putting the bag between his feet. "No, but what I'm saying is, like I was telling you, it's just a matter of if you got the right tools and, and you got the right part, it's, you know . . ." He throws up his hands and shrugs. "Piece of cake."

"I appreciate your confidence, Mike."

"Dude! We did it, I'm telling you." He's grinning now.

I attempt reasonableness. "Well, actually, Mike, we've done part of the job, the getting the valve part, and, by the way, thank you for that, but we still have to do the changeover, the fix."

"Dude, I told you," he says, incredulous at my ignorance. "You got the right tools and the right part, *puh-shweep*. Done. Don't worry. It'll take me thirty seconds." Mike's starting to use the same semi-smug tone he employs when bragging about his celebrity friends and neighbors.

"Great. I'll time you."

"No, no, I'm just saying."

On the way back, on a stretch of Sunset Boulevard that's home to a Catholic Church, a famous recording studio, and a strip mall abutting a U.S. Postal Service office, Mike gestures vaguely out the passenger window. "That's The Center."

"Where? Which one?" I'd heard of a Homeless Center in the neighborhood, but I always thought it was inside the church.

"Behind the church," Mike grunts.

The Center at Blessed Sacrament, a non-profit that works in conjunction with Los Angeles County, has a noble mission: End isolation, end chronic homelessness—one cup of coffee at a time. I've never been there, but the neighborhood street denizens speak highly of the place, notwithstanding The Center's inability—or anyone's—to fulfill its lofty goal. As homelessness gets worse in Hollywood, service providers like The Center are often a beacon of hope for those who have none; but even hope has its limitations when you're looking for a place to lie down at night.

"Do they have beds there?" I ask Mike, figuring a gentle way to ask where he sleeps when he's not on my front porch.

"No. Daytime only," he replies tersely. He's sitting very still, concentrating on something in the distance, like a sea-sick land-lubber staring at the horizon.

I realize then Fisher King Mike is "holding it," and the sooner we get him to a toilet, the better. What actually happens at The Center on a daily basis remains a mystery to me, but I sense that whatever it is, something good is going on there. Mike's said as much, and this story I believe.

When we pull into the driveway, before I can outline a plan for our ambitious valve repair, he utters one word: "Bathroom."

I hadn't thought this one through fully. Now what? Charmaine isn't going to appreciate someone in Fisher King Mike's pungent state traipsing inside the house—and I sense that a quick pee in the back garden isn't going to satisfactorily answer this particular call from Nature. "Follow me," I say, leading Mike quickly through the unlocked driveway gate and into the back yard.

There's a very nice bathroom in the Casita, inside Charmaine's physical therapy clinic. In a moment of marriage-saving foresight, I realize that inviting Fisher King Mike into the harmonious space Charmaine created for her patients would be akin to pouring a shot of espresso over a glass of fine Bordeaux. The only other choice is the downstairs bathroom, off the kitchen, next to the laundry room. Inside the house.

"Please take off your shoes," I request, opening the back door. "It's straight back. Sliding door. And, Mike," I say, as if it will make a difference, "Miss Charmaine is still sleeping, so—"

"Got it," he says, hustling past me.

I keep telling myself, *this was an emergency*. I think that's how I'm going to explain it to Charmaine. *It was either find him the nearest bathroom or do unspeakable damage to your car.* Of course, knowing Charmaine, she's probably going to ask me what Fisher King Mike was doing in her car in the first place, and why I thought it was a good idea to avoid calling a professional plumbing service and, instead, entrust our house, our home, our most valuable asset, to a bipolar schizophrenic known to tell the very tallest of tales.

It's a good question. While I wait for Fisher King Mike to emerge from the bathroom, I think to myself, *There's definitely something wrong with you.* This kind of questionable decision-making goes beyond frugality; this is one of those situations where my willingness to give people chances, to be optimistic and to write optimistic stories in my head, clouds good judgment. I wish I could blame it on pot, but it's too early for me. (I'm not a wake-and-baker; more of a late-afternoon break-taker.) Fisher King Mike, according to reasonable people, confuses his fantasies with reality. If I'm being reasonable, I have to acknowledge much of my life has been about trying to make my fantasies into reality.

Sometimes it happens.

I can hear Fisher King Mike using the sink, which I take as a good sign on many levels. There's a shower in there, too . . .

I suddenly feel strongly that he should use it, for the good of everyone.

I don't know how I'm going to explain this to Charmaine, because I can't really explain it to myself, but no good reason comes to mind why—other than he's *filthy*—why I shouldn't offer a man who desperately needs to bathe the use of my (hot and steamy) shower, copious amounts of soap included with compliments of the management.

Before I can insist, Fisher King Mike bounds out looking

somewhat refreshed but not completely cleaned, his face a polished apple with wax residue. "No, I just washed up a bit. Cleaned up after myself." (That claim I'll confirm in the near future, and I'm not looking forward to it.) Behind his sunglasses, Mike seems to be smiling.

I ask him if we've got everything we need to get the party started. "Let's do this!" I say, encouragingly.

"Hold on," Mike says, his voice now taking on the tone of an Air Force Colonel. "Gotta have a cigarette and gotta check my sugar."

I feel a surge of adrenaline rushing through my monkey brain, which is telling my body it's time to bare teeth and throw feces. Then I remind myself that I'm "working on" being less exasperated and impatient. "OK. But please take it away from the doorway."

He waves me off. "Yeah, yeah, I know. I'll go across the street."

"You don't have to, Mike," I reassure him, my patience stretched so thin you could pluck it like a guitar string.

"No, no, it's fine."

"Mike, you can smoke back here, just keep it away from the doorway." If I let him go across the street to smoke and "check his sugar"—*check his sugar?*—this fiasco will be extended by at least another fifteen minutes, and maybe forever, because something urgent might come up at the Pentagon.

He grunts and shakes his head "no." Then he walks toward the back of the garden, near the cabin, shaking his head the whole way and mumbling unintelligibly. I watch him light up and scroll through his phone, earbud implanted; then I retreat to the cellar, where I attempt in vain to help with the repair.

I survey the space: it's confusing and unwelcoming, screaming *you don't belong here.* When I return to ground level, Fisher King Mike is still smoking, still doing something on his phone. The sun has fully risen, and the sound of cars begins to join the chirping of birds and squirrels cavorting in the ficus tree canopy. It's still early, but almost late enough that I can call a repairman's office and make an appointment. Which I'm about to do.

"You got termites back here," Mike announces, way too loudly for the hour.

I shush him and pantomime "keep it down."

"Yeah, sorry," he stage whispers, walking toward me, extinguished butt in hand. "I was just saying, you got termites in the roof beams over there. Nice little house. Redwood. Termites love their redwood, yes, sir, they do. No, but that's another job."

"Right."

"No, I didn't want to"—he indicates the filter of his just-smoked cigarette—"I wouldn't just throw it. See, what people don't understand is, when you're a guest at someone else's place, you got to treat that place like it's, you know, you don't just throw stuff anywhere, pardon my French."

"Your courtesy is much appreciated. Now let's see if we can fix that frickin' leak, pardon my French."

He shakes his head emphatically. Apparently, I just don't get it. "Dude, I told you."

"Yes, you did," I agree. "You've told me a lot of things." Statement of fact. That's all I'm saying.

"Gotta turn the water off. You don't want . . ." he's cracking himself up now. "You know where the main is?"

A maintenance question I can answer! We go and shut 'er down, Mike trying to convince me I don't have to tell Charmaine that the water's off, because the job will be finished so quickly.

No sale. "Wait here!"

I dash upstairs, where Charmaine is still in bed and nowhere close to using the facilities. I dash downstairs, where I find Mike lingering near a potted avocado tree, mumbling. "All right! Good to go."

He ignores me and heads to the leaky pipe. It's dripping steadily now, like it's crying. Muttering to himself, Mike retrieves supplies from a coat pocket and stares down the situation. I sense another unscheduled intermission is about to commence.

"Here. Hold this right here. Like this." He grips a wrench, or maybe it's a kind of pliers, on the neck of the pipe, as though he's trying to throttle it. "Pull it towards you, like this." He demonstrates. "OK. Now just hold that there."

We switch places. Mike puts another wrench on the nose of the pipe and pulls it in the opposite direction of me. Nothing happens. He pulls more, audibly exerting himself, his face scrunched and determined.

It's stuck. Frozen. Or maybe he's pulling it the wrong way?

"That thing's really . . ." he shakes his head vigorously. "Wow. Hoo boy . . . Hey, you wanna try? Maybe you're stronger."

"Are you sure we got the right tools?"

"Yeah, yeah, I'm *sure*," he keens. "It's probably just rust."

"And the pipe won't break if I pull too hard?"

"*Noooooo*," Mike wails in a three-second glissando of impatient despair.

"All right," I say, shrugging. "Here we go."

We switch places again. This time he holds the clamp and I tug on the wrench, like it's the handle on a giant slot machine. With a pleasant little pop, the pipe starts to turn. "Yeah, see, that's what I was saying," Mike declares.

"Hey! It's working." I feel like I do when the wife needs me to open a bottle top. I'm *useful*.

I'm also expendable. "Yeah, I know. OK, I'll take it from here," Mike says, sending me off with a royal wave.

I pull palm tree seedlings out of the garden while Fisher King Mike *hecks* and *shmecks*. I hear metal on metal, and squeaky gaskets—I think gaskets are involved—and then: nothing. It's eerily silent. I look up. Fisher King Mike is standing in front of the pipe, hands on narrow hips, assessing.

I walk over and stand beside him.

The pipe appears to be fixed.

"Go turn the water back on," Mike orders. I bop over to the main and come right back. "Now turn the faucet on."

The nozzle goes on, the nozzle goes off. Pretty smoothly, I note. And it doesn't leak.

"Done," he says dramatically. If he had a mic, I feel like he would drop it.

"Yes! Thank you!"

"No, no, I told you it would take longer to get the part than for me to put it in."

"That's true," I affirm. "It's been more than two hours since we left. You were right about that, because once we got down to business . . ."

"No, that's what I'm saying. Simple job. You give me the right tools, see, I can do it in thirty seconds. I'm fast, I get stuff done fast, *puh-shweep!*" He makes that wiping motion and raises his eyebrows. "*Fast.*"

I laugh. What else can I do? No amount of patient explaining is going to make Fisher King Mike understand that nothing he does is *fast*, except talking. *That* he does with great alacrity. But putting aside our differing interpretations of Mike's labor velocity, or lack thereof, the fact remains: the worrisome leaky pipe is no longer leaking. And I've got a cute new nozzle that goes on and off easily, employing the latest ball-valve technology.

"Man, I really appreciate the work. Wow. Great job. It's fixed!"

"That's what I'm saying," Mike replies, in a tone that sounds like *Why does nobody get it?*

I shake his bony hand. "Mike, thank you. This is a big relief. Now, hang out here for a moment. I'll be right back." Before he can get another verbal juggernaut launched, I run inside to get some money and some food.

The food part is easy; we have nutritious leftovers and ripe fruit. But I'm not quite sure how to think about the money. What's right? Should I give Mike what I'd give a pro? An hourly wage? Something else based on something else?

Money is a necessity, a fact of life, a tool, a cudgel, whatever metaphor you prefer—but that doesn't necessarily make it an interesting subject. These days I almost never talk about money and seldom think about it, other than the compulsory moments when I must. Money doesn't occupy my daydreams or fantasies. The less attention I give it, the better I feel.

For several decades I gave money plenty of attention, hoping one day I'd be able to put my focus on more fulfilling reasons for being alive. I was much heavier then, and not unhappy, exactly. More like "never quite content," never quite satisfied with everything I had (and didn't have). Although I published hundreds of magazine articles and essays, and a dozen books, a significant portion of my income was supplied by gambling, beating casinos at their own game(s), particularly sports betting.* It was a tremendously profitable endeavor that, in the final analysis, does nothing good for society, satisfies no spiritual imperative, and devalues human connection and cooperation, encouraging the strong to prey on the weak in the best tradition of "survival of the fittest." Dealing with bookies and bankers, NBA touts and NFL teasers, left me feeling affluent yet unfulfilled.

Some people feel they always need more; they'll never have enough. The luckiest moment of my gambling career came at the end, when I realized success didn't obligate me to continue betting. I wasn't infected with More Syndrome. I had enough.

---

*The details, sordid and otherwise, are recounted in my 2005 memoir *The Smart Money: How the World's Best Sports Bettors Beat the Bookies Out of Millions.*

I quit—fled?—that world, where nothing matters but winning, and redirected my energy toward less mercenary pursuits, where everything matters except winning. Nowadays, when faced with money valuation decisions, I don't know the "correct price," and I tend to resist a *laissez-faire* "whatever the market will bear" strategy and try to figure out an arrangement that feels fair and satisfying to all parties involved.

In this case, it's tricky. Understanding that whatever I give Fisher King Mike will probably be converted to corn syrup and Camels, I tell myself that he's a grown man, an adult, my elder, and I've got to let him make his own choices, no matter how much I disagree with them.

He doesn't buy booze. He doesn't buy crack. He doesn't buy switchblades. He buys their legal equivalents, Coke and cigarettes and candy—and highly drugged "energy" drinks. If Mike were a dragster, they'd say his fuel mixture is ultra-rich, but somehow, he keeps making it across the finish line of another day. Somehow, he keeps surviving on the streets.

I settle on $60 and a satchel of snacks. When I return, Mike is examining the newly pristine pipe on the side of the house. "Making sure the seal is holding," he reports.

"Thank you, Mike. I really appreciate your assistance." I hand him three crisp Twenties and the bag of food.

He barely acknowledges the transaction. Pocketing the money and holding the bag, he says, "Thanks, look, the light is going to take a lot longer, I'm just warning you, and, and you're gonna have to turn off the juice, 'cause I sure as heck don't wanna get fried up there." Now he's cracking himself up. "Don't wanna mess with high voltage, that's for sure!"

"Let's talk about the light when Charmaine and I get back from San Diego. I gotta get going. Still haven't packed."

"No, I was just saying this job was a piece of cake but the light is going to take longer, because, you know, you don't wanna mess around." He's giggling again.

"OK. So, look, Mike, here's the plan: You can hang out on the front porch until we leave. But Charmaine and I are going to have a talk with you before we go, so don't wander off too far."

"No, no, I'm just going to the store."

I remind him there's plenty of food in the bag. He reminds me that he's got a serious diabetes problem and he's got to keep his sugar right, and he's got a system (unknown to me or the medical community) for doing so that involves Milky Ways and Coke.

Then he resumes talking about his glamorous wife and their wonderful children.

I compose several appropriate-sounding responses in my head, but, ultimately, realizing that whatever I say isn't going to matter or compute, I say nothing—except, "Mike I really appreciate your help. Thank you again. You've been an angel."

He waves me off and continues rhapsodizing about Selena Gomez.

MY WIFE, I confirm upon returning upstairs, definitely exists. I'm not imagining her. "Hey, I *do* have a wife!"

Charmaine is making the bed. "So I *do* have a husband! Where were you?"

"Fixing the leaky pipe." I tell her what happened, kind of leaving out the part about Mike using our downstairs bathroom— which, *oops*, I still have to check/police/fumigate. I help her fold the comforter. "It's all done. It's fixed. We're good."

"Fisher King Mike helped you?" The idea seems ludicrous and faintly amusing. "Really?"

"Actually, it was more like I helped him."

"Really?"

I know how Charmaine feels. But, yes, really.

She smiles and nods and furrows her brow. "All right, then. Good. So you're confident the house isn't going to explode or something?"

"I'm pretty sure everything is going to work out," I say. Then I start packing.

Before we leave, shortly after noon, I send emails to my neighbors, letting them know we'll be gone and that someone will be watching the front of the house. No worries, but please call if anything seems out of the ordinary—like, say, a small pond forming in our driveway.

I also compose a kind of "safe passage" letter for Fisher King Mike, in case anyone wonders what a guy with writing on his clothing is doing hanging around our front door.

June 29, 2016
To Whom it May Concern,

Michael James is a friend of mine from the Elderberries Café Community. I have given him permission to be on my property at 1█████ N. Vista Street.

From Wednesday (6/29) through Saturday (7/2), Charmaine and I will be out of town. In our absence, Michael has permission to do handyman work in my backyard. He also has permission to be on my front porch at night to keep watch over the property.

If you have any questions or concerns, please call me: 323/ █████████.

Your Neighbor,
Michael Konik

Before we depart, I find Fisher King Mike on the porch, with his shoes and socks off. "Got a blister," he announces. His feet look clean and reasonably healthy. But I make a mental note to get him some new socks.

"Take it easy," I tell him. "Rest your legs."

"Yeah, yeah, I know, a lot of walking lately, like, the other day I walked almost twenty miles. It's a long way from the Valley and the bus stops running earlier now."

Fighting off volleys of non-sequiturs, I attempt to deliver a "While We're Away" briefing, with phone number exchanges and plant-watering instructions and what-to-do-in-case-of-emergencies, as one does when one entrusts one's domicile to a house-sitter.

Mike seems to be listening, on some level. He nods a lot, impatiently.

I stress that should anything out of the ordinary occur—*anything*—he should contact either Josh and Kristen, the neighbors to the left, or Chris and Rolin, the neighbors to the right. *And* call me or Charmaine.

I stress that the doors to the house will be locked, and he'll have to use the bathroom facilities at the church or The Center.

And I stress that there are to be no visitors whatsoever, no invitations extended to friendly vagabonds.

"Yeah, yeah, I know," Mike says gruffly.

"And before we leave, I wanted you to have this for while we're away. Something to read." I hand him a signed copy of one of my books, a novel called *Becoming Bobby*. It's about a middle-aged man who wills himself to become the man he always wanted to be, a Vegas bigshot. (It's a satire.)

Mike takes it in both his hands, riffling the pages, examining the front and back. Then, not speaking, not acknowledging the gift, he starts to read the book. "Somehow I thought you might like this one," I say, knowing it doesn't matter what I say.

"Yeah, I'm gonna read this," he replies, barely looking up.

When Charmaine and I load our luggage fifteen minutes later,

Mike's where I left him, reading my book. His legs are splayed straight out, resting on his heels. When he realizes there's a lady present, Fisher King Mike sits up straight and tucks his feet underneath his chair.

Too late. Charmaine has already seen his blisters.

"Mike, we need to treat your feet," Charmaine tells him. "We don't want them to get infected."

He shakes his downcast head, unable to look at her.

Charmaine turns to me. "We need to treat this."

"Now?" As always, we're running a bit late, and the later we are the worse the traffic . . .

"If we wait four days—it could get serious. Let me just treat him quickly and we'll get out of here." Charmaine instructs me to fetch antibiotic gel from the medicine cabinet, and a big plastic bucket we use for soaking dirty vegetables. She fills it with hot water and bath salts, and she brings it to Mike on the porch, me following with the tube of antiseptic.

Talking in her Medical Professional voice, Charmaine addresses the patient. "Mike, we need to clean those blisters first. OK?" It's sort of a question, but not really.

"Yes, ma'am," Mike replies, and I can almost detect a faint Southern accent in his gentility.

"Good," Charmaine says, and gets down to business, kneeling before Mike's feet, dabbing softly at the blisters with a cotton swab drenched in germ-killer. (I notice she's put on rubber examining gloves.) Mike winces slightly at each contact, but says nothing. I feel certain that Jesus Christ and Pope Francis and other famous foot-washers are not on Charmaine's mind at the moment. This isn't about symbolism. She's in healer mode, treating Mike the way she treats her paying clientele: as best she can.

Satisfied he has no infections, only hot-spots, Charmaine slides the tub underneath his chair, rolls up Mike's pants to his knees, and guides his feet by the ankles into the bath, foamy as a cappuccino. "Hoo boy!" Mike exclaims.

"Too hot?" Charmaine asks.

"No, no, it's OK, it's OK," Mike says. "Nah, I'm fine. I'm fine."

"Great," Charmaine says flatly. "So you're going to keep your feet in here for about five minutes. Got it?"

"Yes, ma'am."

She sends me back to the medicine cabinet for some bandages, and to the laundry room for a disposable washcloth. While Mike soaks, we finish loading the car, carefully stepping over and past the podiatric patient. The Fisher King is on his throne, his feet weary from the quest. And, even though he's wearing sunglasses, you can tell he's falling asleep.

We leave the contact list, a copy of Mike's safe-passage letter, and a box of adhesive bandages and cotton puffs on the porch table. Quietly as we can, we slip out of the house and into the Jetta, only an hour behind schedule.

As I back the car out of the driveway and onto the street, Charmaine waves. "Goodbye, house. I hope you're here when we get back."

I laugh nervously. "It will be. It will be."

Charmaine smiles and raises her eyebrows. "Babe, Fisher King Mike is on our porch. Just sayin'."

She has a point. When the Fisher King is introduced into a previously stable situation, heretofore unimaginable variables complicate your usual prediction model. But no matter what Mike does or doesn't do in our absence, short of setting the place on fire—and he's not supposed to smoke on the porch—our ninety-nine-year-old home will live to see her 100th birthday. I'm certain of it.

Well, certain enough to drive away.

"Goodbye, house!" I cry. "Please be here when we get back!" And I'm pretty sure I'm only joking.

SIX

While You Were Away

———

Traveling south down Interstate 5 through Los Angeles County and into Orange County is exactly like scenic Highway One meandering through Big Sur—minus the grandeur of nature and fresh air. Instead, the scenery includes strip malls, RV dealerships, and smokestacks. We've been on the road for more than ninety minutes, and for approximately eighty-nine of them Charmaine and I have been discussing the Fisher King, allowing him to occupy our thoughts (as well as our front porch) like some kind of mythic hero.

But we don't call. We don't hover. We're not helicopter home-owners.

Another strip mall. Another railyard.

Factories. Warehouses.

I crack first. "Maybe we should check in with Mike. What do you think?"

"Definitely. Let's call him," Charmaine says.

"We'll just check in. See how he's doing. Get an update," I propose. What we won't ask are some of the questions we've been considering in the car: *What's his real story? What brought him to Hollywood? Where's his former home?*

When he's not on our porch, where does Mike live?

Where does he sleep? How does he get money? How does he get food? How does he bathe?

Where's his family?

What happened to him? What made him this way?

Before I can dial, my phone rings. It's Scotty, a friend who lives up the street a few blocks, near Runyon Canyon Park. "Yo, MK. I'm in my car, driving past your place, and there's a weird looking dude in your driveway, near the library."

I thank Scotty for keeping an eye out and tell him not to worry. "That's Mike. We know him. He's sort of watching the house while we're away. Very strange looking, for sure. But he's harmless." I can hear myself trying to be reassuring—to myself.

Scotty agrees to stop by tomorrow to check up on our security guard.

I tell Charmaine that everything seems to be all right. "According to an eyewitness at the scene, our house is still there."

"Let's still call anyway," she says.

I hand her a slip of notepaper. "He wrote it down. This is allegedly his number."

Charmaine doesn't like participating in what used to be known as a "wild goose chase" back in the days when chasing geese in the wild was still tenable. "You don't know if this works?"

"I think it does. That's a real area code, like around San Francisco, I think."

"I don't want to talk with him. I'm too tired," Charmaine announces, handing me her phone, faintly buzzing as it dials Mike's number.

"Even if he has fabulous stories about hanging out with all your favorite celebrities?"

"Well, in that case . . ."

On the fourth ring, the call goes to an automated voicemail, with a robot voice. I leave a message, a digital letter in a bottle, unlikely to be retrieved, maybe never to be heard.

"Mike has *voicemail?*" Charmaine asks.

Charmaine's phone rings. I hand it back to her. She looks at the screen and hands it back to me. "It's Mike."

"Hey, Mike!" I say, answering.

"Yeah. You called?"

"Yes, I just left a message on your voicemail. Just checking in, making sure everything's OK."

"Everything's OK."

"Good! Well, you know, if you need to reach us, you got the number."

Mike sighs audibly. "Mmm-hmm."

"OK, thanks, Mike."

"Mmm-hmm."

"Ask him about his feet!" Charmaine says.

"Oh, yeah. Mike, how are your feet?"

"They're OK."

I'm starting to feel like I'm bothering Mike, that my inquiries are keeping him from a previously scheduled nap. "Great. I'm glad everything's working out."

"Yep."

"Cool. Thanks, Mike. Talk to you soon."

"Yep."

"Bye, Mike."

"Yep."

After disconnecting, I return the phone to its owner. "Everything seems to be OK."

"He didn't seem to have much to say," Charmaine notes.

"I think he might have had to go to the bathroom. He gets real terse."

"Or maybe it's just part of his personality disorder?"

"Or that."

FOR THREE DAYS and nights, I call Mike's phone. From our San Diego hotel, during a beach walk, while I'm waiting for Charmaine to finish with her business; mornings, afternoons, nights—he doesn't answer. The first couple of times, I leave a cheerful voicemail; eventually the futility of shouting into the wind dawns on me and I stop.

The first day, Thursday, I don't panic. Friday, I don't panic, but I do enlist Scotty to do some reconnaissance. He calls me in the late afternoon. "The porch light is on, and you got some bags here out front," he reports. "But no Mike."

On Saturday, I semi-panic, calling our neighbor Chris, who has a key to the house. I'm hoping he can do a quick walk-through to make sure Mike hasn't smashed in a window and ransacked the place. But he and his husband and their daughter are in Palm Springs. I call a couple other friends and ask them to have a look.

An hour later, my comedian friend Ryan calls. "Hey, so, I don't see anyone here, but I looked through the windows inside and it all seems normal. A couple of lights on. No dead bodies." He also says that the driveway gate is locked with a heavy chain.

We *did* purchase one of those, as well as the outdoor floodlight. Nice to know the chain is being used. Even nicer would be if I had a key to the lock. Because now, short of clipping it with the Jaws of Life, the only other person who has the ability to open my driveway gate seems to have evaporated.

I'm too embarrassed to tell Charmaine. This is an example of that Reliability Issue she was talking about, how it's hard to make arrangements and agreements with a person like the Fisher King. She's always reminding me: I give people too much credit. I create fantastic expectations in my head; inevitably, I'm disappointed. Not a good cycle.

We'll be home in the early evening on Sunday. Until then, there's nothing to be done except avoid obsessing over how we're going to open a lock for which I have no key.

In search of tranquility and happy memories, I visit "Dog Beach," a nearly two-mile strip of oceanfront dunes adjacent to the wonderfully hippie village of Ocean Beach, in northwest San Diego. Dogs are welcome off-leash (something that can be said of only two public beaches along the entire Los Angeles County coastline). Before Ella died, Charmaine and I made a valedictory trip with her here, so she could move her arthritic hips in the water and revisit one of her favorite places in the world, where every step leads a happy hound toward another olfactory adventure, and where a digger can four-paw a hole in the moist sand without getting in trouble. Ella had gone to Dog Beach a few times in her life, including when she did a *paw-tographing* session at a bookstore in La Jolla, and she always had great fun, running and splashing and sniffing. But it's possible her owner had more.

So many dogs. So many happy dogs. Dogs being dogs.

Dog Beach is like our local Hollywood treasure Runyon Canyon Park, but with tides and driftwood. And just like at Runyon, I'm the guy—and he's at every dog park—who doesn't have his own dog at the moment, and, therefore, accosts every mutt he encounters with slightly too much enthusiasm. "Who is *this*? Hello! Hello, [insert apposite adjective here, *e.g.* "fluffy"]. Hello, gorgeous boy! May I pet him?" I stroll on hard-packed sand, still moist from receding waves, guessing at breed mixes, grinning at canine acrobatics. One day, I daydream, I'll come back here with a new friend. Not now, but sometime, some day in the indistinct future, when all the circumstances are right.

Feeling sated with dog love and slightly sun-and-wind-burned,

I stop for a last look at a clutch of noisy pelicans and turn back, retracing my steps. When I get to the parking lot, to what we call civilization, no ironic quotation marks necessary, I try calling Fisher King Mike one more time.

No answer.

By now, I don't really expect him to pick up, but I'm also starting to question my memory. This *is* his number, right? Didn't I talk with him in the car, shortly after we departed?

Boundaries. I can't let another man's madness become mine. Yes, this *is* his number. He's just not answering it, for any number of reasons. I start to run through hypotheticals in my head. *Dead battery.* No, I've already seen him use the outlet on the porch to charge up. *He lost his phone.* How, I can't say, but it seems eminently possible. *He wandered off and left all his possessions on your porch.* Yep, probably.

Then I stop worrying. Whatever has or hasn't happened to Fisher King Mike and his magnificent device is a mystery that will or won't be solved. So long as the house is more or less as we left it—and all advance scouts report as much—I'll figure out how to cut the chain or pick the lock or whatever one does to gain access to one's own driveway. It will be another relatively inexpensive life lesson.

But, please, Lord, let the house be more or less as we left it.

WE'RE IN THE carpool lane going eighty, thanks to Charmaine. If she wasn't around to supervise, I'd surely be going closer to ninety. Driving too quickly to get somewhere you think you want to be is like attempting to fast-forward your life, as though it were a video you can scroll through. But what if that place you wanted so desperately to get to is, in fact, not at all how you imagined it? Then you might feel like you've been racing through life only to arrive at death a few minutes earlier.

I'm thinking of telling Charmaine all this, but watching the mile markers unfurl in slow-motion, I'm doing all I can to remain calm and unworried. No matter my determination to "stay in the moment," I want to find out what happened to our house and the man who was supposed to be watching it.

Breathe in, breathe out. We're a little closer. Breathe in, breathe out. We're a little closer—but, also, and I don't want to harsh anyone's mellow, we're still in a car on the 5 Freeway while a man, a nice man, a nice homeless man, has gone missing.

"He probably just walked away," I conclude out loud. "Got an idea and went with it."

"Honey, I just don't think you can count on Fisher King Mike for anything. He's not a bad guy, but you can't trust him. You're just going to be disappointed."

"I just hope he's OK . . ."

"You said it yourself. He probably just—you know how he gets! He could be anywhere." Charmaine looks at me tenderly. "I know you want to help. You've been really nice to him, but, sweetheart, really, Fisher King Mike is one of those people, no matter how much you try, you can't really help them because they can't help themselves."

I've heard legions of A.A. friends talk this way after attending meetings: The addict can ask for help—and get it—but he's got to really want to help himself if he ever wants to get better. How, I wonder, can a guy like Fisher King Mike want to help himself if he's not even sure who "he" is?

"Mental illness," I say, letting the phrase hang there, like persistent air-freshener.

"It's a tough one," Charmaine says.

How many former friends and colleagues have I carefully excised from my life, avoiding regular contact and interaction with, because their mental disturbances became too much to bear? The chronically angry, the chronically depressed. The narcissists. The drunks. Shielding myself—and our tranquil home—from a bipolar, paranoid schizophrenic (or whatever Mike is) shouldn't be difficult.

And yet . . .

When we finally exit the freeway, turn off Hollywood Boulevard onto our residential street, and pull into our driveway, a little ahead of schedule, Charmaine exclaims cheerfully, "Our house is still standing! That's a good sign."

It's dusky, and the light is low. But everything looks normal from the outside. I get out of the car and bound onto the porch.

"Welcome home."

"Mike! You're here!" He's dressed exactly as he was when we left. And it looks as though he might have bathed.

"Yeah, yeah, I can get going if you need me to leave."

"No, you're fine. I'm just—I've been calling you all weekend." I turn back to the car. "Charm! Mike's here!"

Charmaine approaches the porch warily. "Hi, Mike."

"Hello, ma'am."

"Mike, we've been calling you all weekend," I say, foolishly expecting a cogent explanation.

"Yeah, yeah, well, I had a lot of stuff to get done. How was your trip?"

"Fine. But, you know, we were sort of worried when you didn't answer all weekend." I smile and shrug. "You know?"

"Yeah, I know. But, look, like I was telling you, the new pipe is good, I checked, and, and you don't have to worry about that. But—and I don't want to lay this all on you all at once—but you got," he clears his throat theatrically, "you got *critters.*"

Charmaine excuses herself. "Mikey, can you . . ." we both turn to her. "No, the *other* Mike. Mike Number One. Mr. Konik, please bring in the luggage when you're done with your meeting." She closes the door, leaving me and the *other* Mike on the porch, where it's transitioning from dusk to dark.

"No, see," he starts in, "you got rats, and, and you got termites."

"Yeah, I know," I say glumly.

"No! I'm serious," Mike declares.

I nod, already feeling overwhelmed by all the attention our old house requires, knowing I'm unsuited to the task. Thankfully there are fellows one can call, gigolos of certain talents, who lavish themselves on needy dowagers like mine.

Fisher King Mike stands with his hands on his hips, looking toward the sky, like he's searching for a constellation—maybe the one he and his pop starlet wife wished upon at the end of their first date. He begins to nod. "Yup. Yup. Should be *just* about dark enough."

He motions at the driveway, beside the front porch. "C'mere. C'mon. I want you to see something."

"Yeah, I saw you put the chain on the gate. And a lock—which, by the way, I need the key."

He waves me off, "No, no, see, it's not that. I want you to look at something."

We're standing beside the locked driveway gate. I can see through the rusted wrought iron bars into the gloom of my backyard. "Man, this is going to have to wait until the morning," I say. "I just can't do it now, Mike."

He looks at me disapprovingly. "Yeah, yeah, I know, but it can't wait until the morning, because in the morning there won't be nothing to see."

And just then, a click and a soundless explosion. Of light.

The entire area behind the driveway gate, beyond the back corner of the house, is lit up like Dodger Stadium.

Mike folds his arms over his chest. "Yeah, yeah, it's pretty bright. You might want to show your wife, and, by the way, I hope you don't mind, I had to borrow your ladder, but I put it back already so like you wouldn't even know I used it, but I had to, because, you know . . ."

He looks in the direction of the beaming fixture, and he's smiling. "While you were away, you and Miss Char, I went ahead and installed that security light."

SEVEN

Lots of Stuff to Do

———

During my childhood, I not only read all the *Encyclopedia Brown* solve-it-yourself mysteries, I strongly identified with the boy detective. I may have even "opened" my own Encyclopedia Konik bureau of investigation. (OK, I did, and it had to close almost immediately because of an absence of clients.) Figuring stuff out, solving puzzles and problems—this was my youthful passion, and it turned into a kind of career when I became old enough to play games for money, in casinos and card rooms.

Throughout a family road-trip from Milwaukee to Aspen, Colorado—this was more than forty years ago, before Aspen was Beverly Hills-with-a-chairlift—I hunkered down in the backseat of our VW Bug (two adults, two children, one space the size of a loveseat) for thirty hours or so, attempting to complete a book of geometry puzzles based on Pythagorean concepts. When I couldn't figure out two or three of the 200 shapes, I wrote to the manufacturer for a clarification in a fit of nine-year-old precociousness: were they truly solvable or were they possibly misprints?

Now, I'm still a boy detective, albeit with salt-and-pepper

hair, and I'm on the case. *The Case of the Disappearing House Sitter.*

I do what every good boy detective does at the start of his investigation: interview the chief witness, primarily to develop an expository outline of what happened, a general narrative to be authenticated—or exposed as a fraud!

That proves fruitless, as the chief witness in this case is also the chief suspect in his own disappearance. Said witness, this detective notes, does not seem factually reliable (or particularly cooperative) when questioned.

So now I'm looking for clues, for physical evidence—tangible proof immune to Fisher King Mike's oratory.

Everyone's gone at the moment; Charmaine at an appointment, Mike somewhere in the state of California, I presume. (He said he was coming back at the end of the day. Breath is not being held.) I'm canvassing the property, making sure everything that was here before we left hasn't vanished. So far so good.

The most novice detective could tell Fisher King Mike has been in the basement; the light is still on, and the fuse-box, which he must have visited to turn off the power before installing the security light, is slightly ajar. *So he's been downstairs . . .*

I conduct a half-hearted inventory of the flotsam stashed in our cellar. If only Mike had absconded with most of it—I should be so lucky. But, no, everything seems to be more or less where it was left, although I do notice a few tools hung up on the neglected tool rack, like they belong there. *Suspect appears to have committed no larceny, but engaged in un-requested organizing.*

Ah-ha! What about the wine? The *wine.* Of course, *the wine.* Did it not occur to you, sir? That would explain why no one saw him all weekend. *He was on a basement bender.* We have a small wooden rack, with maybe ten bottles on it, of which we drink one or two a year. It's back by the crawlspace, conveniently near the rats, and why would gnawing vermin stop anyone in search of a drink?

I investigate.

The wine appears untouched. *Fingerprint check conducted on film of dust encasing bottles. Negatory.* I remain clueless.

Next, I check the Be Well casita. Despite my encyclopedic knowledge of investigatory techniques—the name should have given it away—I'm unable to detect any sign that the suspect has been inside this building. *Process of elimination: There's only one place left.*

I step into Weed Hollow Cabin. I pull the light cord. I make a determination. *Fisher King Mike has not only been inside Weed Hollow, he's slept here!*

How did Encyclopedia Konik know, you ask? *Everything was completely undisturbed and untouched. But the quilt on the queen bed had a faint indentation in the shape of a skinny question mark.*

Also, there was a ripped and empty sugar packet on the floor.

I close the door behind me—it's a symbol for closing the case. *This one's solved.*

No wonder no one ever saw him: he was hiding out in the back corner of the yard—when he wasn't up on the ladder installing a spotlight? The clues tell different stories. The chief witness/suspect tells different stories. But [cliffhanger alert!] Encyclopedia Konik finds one more clue that explains everything.

"HERE," FISHER KING Mike grunts, handing me a folded sheet of copy paper. "I spent the weekend making a list. Lots of stuff to do. Lots of stuff to do. I'm gonna go smoke across the street, check my sugar." Then he walks away.

I'm standing on the front porch, watching him retreat to the curb diagonal to our front door. I unfold the paper. In 24-point handwritten block letters, it says:

PROJECTS TO DO

FIX AND PATCH AND PAINT SIDING   REPLACE BAD PIPE

    MORE SECURITY LIGHTS

    REDO OLD WIRING IN BASEMENT

ORGANIZE WORKSHOP   FIX PORCH GATE [BROKEN LATCH]

    TERMITE SPRAY   FIX IRRIGATION SPRINKLERS

REPAIR AND RESTAIN DECK   TRIM BOOGANVILLA BACK

    TAKE CARE OF RATS

FIX WINDOWS

    PAINT HOUSE

That night, we give Mike dinner on the porch while Charmaine and I eat in the breakfast nook, the sun room—with a splendid view through French windows of the garden below . . . and Weed Hollow cabin looming in the corner. Knowing Charm isn't going to be pleased to learn the "facts" of Mike's behavior during our time away over the weekend, I lead my presentation with physical evidence.

"Mike gave me this," I say, handing her his project list. "I think he compiled it while he wasn't answering his phone."

Charmaine quickly reads it. Chuckling slightly, she says, "He's a very good speller. Is that what makes you think he can really do all these things?"

"Well, I've seen him do two things so far. Maybe he really is one of those guys who can build a house from the ground up."

Charmaine shakes her head. "Babe, even if he had those skills, he's not in any shape to do anything with them. Someone like that shouldn't use power tools. Seriously. He could hurt himself, and possibly others."

"I don't think painting requires power tools," I point out. But I get it. There's a reason certain highly skilled, supremely talented people can't hold jobs, and why a certain percentage of them end up sleeping on bus benches. I don't know if Fisher King Mike is one of those people—he's certainly not able to hold a job, but, then, neither am I.

Charmaine looks again at the list. "Yeah. I don't know."

"Are you insinuating that Mike would claim something about himself that's untrue? What gave you that idea?"

We both laugh, and conversation drifts to other topics of greater importance: our careers, our social lives, *us*. And all the time, with every bite of our sumptuous supper, insistent reminders of a larger reality sit on our porch and in our yard, and we don't speak of them.

When our meal is finished, and the dishes done, as we're about to retire to the upstairs, Charmaine peers in the refrigerator, surveying the Tetris field of containers. "I'm going to give this to Mike," she says, extracting a grilled chicken thigh. "Will you come with me?"

We find him sitting in a chair on the porch, earbud implanted, baseball cap cocked, spindly legs outstretched. When Mike notices Charmaine, he sits up and assumes a quasi-military bearing, ten-*shun*.

"Hi, Mike," Charmaine says. "I've got some chicken for you." She hands him the leg.

"Oh, thanks," he blurts, his eyes downcast.

"You OK out here?" she asks.

"Yes, ma'am."

"Do you need a blanket or anything? Another pillow?"

"No, no, no. I'm fine, I'm fine. I just got to get my head together, just got to, you know, for a couple of days. I'm sorry to bother you. See, but my wife needs me, and, and the people I minister to need me, and I don't want to let them down."

Charmaine assures Fisher King Mike he's not a bother. She reminds him that she's happy to have another person on the premises, someone else looking out for her, keeping an eye on things. She doesn't explore out loud what would happen if Mike were actually to encounter an intruder. (Mesmerize him with stories from his Navy SEAL days? Offer him Selena tickets?) Instead, she reminds him, "You're totally welcome here on the porch, Mike."

"I know, I know. It's not that, see, I can't help people, can't do my work, if I don't get my head together."

We both tell Mike we understand, and then we bid him good-night and retreat into the gilded sanctuary on the other side of the door.

Before we've fully climbed the stairs to our queen size, organic cotton, equivalent-to-a-luxury-hotel Achiever Mattress, the weirdness of our current living situation sets in. The imbalance. Something's not right with this picture. And we both know it.

Charmaine's the first to speak. "Babe, maybe we should let Fisher King Mike sleep in the cabin, in Weed Hollow."

I want to be reasonable about this, and careful, and fair to everyone. I want to be coolly rational, like a chess master; I want to be Encyclopedia Konik, the guy you can count on when you need a problem solved. But all I can think to say is, "You're my hero."

MIKE SAID HE was OK. Said the porch was fine. Pretended he didn't already know how soft and comforting the bed inside Weed Hollow Cabin is. But eventually, with gentle cajoling and encouragement, he trudged down the driveway and off to sleep with a roof over his head, a shingled roof, covered with an impenetrable ten-foot-thick bramble of purple bougainvillea and raccoon warrens.

Now, at daybreak, when I go to check on him—and, incidentally, the state of our rustic cabin—Fisher King Mike is gone.

The driveway gate normally squeaks and rumbles loudly whenever it's moved. I didn't hear him leave in the night.

The cabin looks untouched; the bed's made and all the quaint knickknacks and Victorian books and tea wafers are undisturbed. You'd swear Mike was never here.

I check the casita. Spotless.

I look in the basement, just in case. Nothing.

He's vanished. Again.

But his bags, the repository of his possessions, or at least the things he's willing to carry wherever he roams, remain stashed on our front porch, underneath a low table flanked by two wood chairs. I wonder if Mike's bags are completely secure here; over the years, bikes and boots and UPS packages have been stolen from this location. Mike's duffel and knapsack? Thief bait they're not. They look unappealing, vaguely greasy. But they're all he has.

Without getting formal approval from the Executive Committee, I transfer Mike's bags to the backyard storage shed. Behind the driveway gate. The gate with the chain and lock. The lock only Mike and I—now the possessor of a key granted by the gatekeeper—can open.

My "thinking through the situation" takes less time than it does to type these words. It goes like this: *We have extra, unused space; someone else has no space; we're happy to share.*

And happy to move toward balance and harmony, inching toward some kind of vague equilibrium. It's July 2016. The major party primary elections, that ghastly freak-show of mendacity, are over, and my country is more divided and mistrustful than ever before. For now, it seems as though the majority of my fellow Americans have rejected our household's preferred candidate, Bernie Sanders, a man whose political ideas essentially boil down to "take care of each other."

Take care of each other. These days, it's a revolutionary act.

WHEN I EMERGE from a post-hike shower and look out the upstairs bathroom window, which overlooks the back yard, I see Fisher King Mike moving a large wooden bench positioned in front of Be Well Therapy. It's faded from the sun, but it's solid, and quite heavy. Mike's moving one side, then the other, a few feet at a time.

I bound down the back deck stairs. "What's going on, Mike?" I ask, careful to not sound accusatory. "You need some help?"

"Yeah, sure. No, I was just, when you were away at yoga, at Runyon, I was talking to Miss Charmaine and she said she wanted her bench painted, and, and, so, I showed her what you got to choose from in the basement, and, and she gave me permission, no, no, don't you worry, she gave me permission to use this paintbrush I found down there, and like I've been saying, she wanted her bench painted, and I told her I could do it, and you don't have to pay me or nothing, 'cause you two have been so nice to me."

He nods three times. And then he turns away and starts dusting off the bench with a wet rag.

"Mike."

"Yeah."

"Miss Charmaine told you she wanted you to paint this bench?"

"Yeah."

"She said she wanted her wooden bench—this one, not a different one, not, like, that one over there—she said she wanted *this* one painted?"

"Yeah, that's what I've been saying."

I tell him I'm going to go inside and have a chat with Charmaine; I'll be back soon, before he can drip our driveway into an unintentional tribute to Jackson Pollock.

Charm's not home. She left while I was showering, kissed me goodbye. And now she's not answering her phone; she's in a rehearsal.

On the way back downstairs to my office, I compose a diplomatic speech that I hope won't hurt Fisher King Mike's feelings and probably relies too heavily on a good-cop/bad-cop formulation. *If it were completely up to me . . .*

I know it's my duty to protect my wife's property, but I also know that Mike means no harm; he just doesn't fully grasp what's going on. I need to let him down easy.

Too late.

When I look out the window I see Mike slathering Charmaine's wooden bench with white primer. On the driveway. (The walkway clients take to reach Be Well Therapy.) Without a drop-cloth.

Fisher King Mike is on our driveway painting my wife's wooden bench without a drop-cloth.

I survey the scene: not one speckle has besmirched the concrete. The open can of primer sits on newspaper King Mike must have fished out of the recycling. He dips into the white syrup with a forceful jab, slaps it against the inside of the can a few times, and applies the loaded paintbrush to the bench. Moving confidently, purposefully, he crouches and kneels and stands—and, *puh-shweep,* one side of the bench is completed. Totally white. No drips.

"You appear to have done this before," I say, walking up the path.

He's muttering to himself, ignoring me. Then I realize he has his earbud implanted, blaring what sounds like seventies rock. He doesn't look up.

I watch him from a safe distance, like I'm on safari. When Mike finishes the other side of the bench, he stands up and admires his handiwork.

"Great job, Mike," I say, genuinely impressed by his painting skill.

He pulls out his earbud. "No, no, that's just the primer. It ain't done yet. Wait when it's done."

"And I notice you're not using a drop-cloth."

He snorts derisively. "Drop-cloths are for amateurs."

I laugh. He's right: *I* would use a drop-cloth. But then again so would a great many professionals.

"No, no, see, what people don't understand is, you only load the brush with what you're gonna use, and, and that way you don't get no drips. That's how a pro does it."

Apparently this issue is settled, at least as far as Mike is concerned. "Now I'm gonna let this dry, and I'm gonna smoke a cigarette—*I know*: 'not on the property,' I know, I know—and, get my blood sugar straight, and, and then I'll put on the paint."

Other than being the homeowner, I don't feel qualified to contradict The Pro.

I return to my office, where I spend the next hour trying to write, with little success. I'm having a hard time averting my gaze from the driveway, where Fisher King Mike is rapidly painting Charmaine's faded old bench fire engine red.

At this point, I'm assuming this color choice was also discussed with the Lady of the House. Surely this is what Charmaine wanted. *Surely*. No one would unilaterally paint someone's wooden bench fire engine red without getting clearance. Not even Fisher King Mike.

Well, maybe Fisher King Mike.

He's slouching in a canvas deck chair, chugging a liter bottle of Coke. It's the same chair my late father, Eugene, liked to sit in during his last weeks, dying of congestive heart failure, when all he wanted from the day was to feel sunshine on his face and bird-song in his ears. My dad was a Marine; the Marine Corps Hymn was the first song I ever learned. He introduced me to Ayn Rand; he did not question the legitimacy of capitalism. I wonder what my dad would make of Fisher King Mike. And what he'd make of his firstborn, the other Mike.

"Gotta dry," the Fisher King announces.

"It looks amazing, Mike," I say, genuinely amazed at the transformation.

"Yeah, but see, that's not it. When it dries, *puh-shweep*."

At the risk of offending cliché-mongers the world over, watching paint dry actually *can* be exciting, so long as you're doing it with an amiable companion keen on telling fairy tales. While we wait for Charmaine to come home, Fisher King Mike regales me with war stories that sound like a mash-up of every Hollywood blockbuster ever made about Special Ops. His tales have the plausibility of a movie aiming at quasi-verisimilitude, but, eventually, the logic-chain falls apart and you're left wondering why you spent two hours in the dark with Jason Statham.

He claims to have seen atrocities no one should have to witness. But he won't tell me where those atrocities occurred, or when, or the precise nature of the atrocities. "You don't want to know," Mike tells me, sounding very much like a world-weary Bruce Willis.

No, see, that's not it. I *do* want to know. I want to hear details and facts that will allow me to determine what's real and what's imaginary. I want to know which part is Story and which part is Life. And at that moment I realize, in a way, Fisher King Mike's madness, allegedly the least communicable of diseases, might be starting to seep into my brain. I catch myself giving some measure of credence to Mike's delusions, knowing rationally that they don't warrant being taken seriously. The man is mentally ill. *But still, however, if only, maybe . . .*

Then, as if to relieve me of my troubling illusions, Mike's military monologue morphs into a reverie about his famous wife—who he hasn't been able to see in a while, because of the important stuff he's gotta do in Hollywood. She's world famous, he reminds me.

I'm about to excuse myself when *my* sort-of-famous-in-certain-circles wife pulls into the driveway. Charmaine parks and rapidly exits her car, which she's made a habit of since the robbery. I jog up the driveway and meet her at the gate, administering a hug and kiss before blurting out, "Mike painted your bench. I'm assuming—please tell me you authorized—"

"I did. He asked me if I wanted anything painted, and, actually, he was the one who suggested it might be cool to paint the bench red." Charmaine looks at me quizzically. "He did that?"

"Right this way, please," I say, *maître d'* style. We walk down the driveway a few steps and curve left, when the Be Well Therapy casita comes into view. And sitting on the patio, flanked by tired white wicker furniture, Charmaine's old wooden bench gleams like a tomato in the sunlight.

She doesn't hesitate. "I *love* it! Mike! It's like a new bench."

Mike springs from his chair. "Yeah, I know, like I was telling MK, he was asking me if you wanted it painted, and I say 'yeah,' and, and see?" He shrugs, putting his hand in the innermost of his pockets.

Charmaine walks around it, like a judge at a dog show. "Wow. Mike, it looks great. I'm so impressed."

"Yeah, I know, but, see, it's all cleaned up for you already. Like I was telling MK, a professional doesn't use a drop-cloth because a pro don't drip, right?" He chortles and points at me. "Right?"

"Pro-level work, for sure," I say, nodding, the dopamine of relief bathing my body. (Another) fiasco avoided!

"Mike, you're a really good painter," Charmaine says. "You must have other skills we don't know about."

Fisher King Mike, redolent of adult diapers and cigarette smoke, says, "Yeah, I know, but you should see me clean. I'm a white glove cleaner. You can eat off the floor when I'm done with it. Hands and knees. Scrubbing. Little Murphy's oil? *Pu-shweep!*"

Maybe it's true, maybe it's not. Me and Charm? We're suckers for unwarranted optimism, for hope. *Let it be true. Let some of it be true.*

Charmaine catches my eye. She's grinning, and I can tell I'm not the only one who's been infected.

EIGHT

A Trio of Visitors,
One of Them Sane

———

For reasons nobody can explain or understand, Mom and Dad Clamor get a dog.

A puppy.

A three-month-old, exuberantly playful, white-and-gray mop of purebred adorableness. A tiny *Shih Tzu.* They name her Chareze.

Approximately forty-eight hours after acquiring their furry impulse buy, Mom and Dad, both in their eighties, begin to have buyer's remorse. It hasn't occurred to them that the little pup, all four or five pounds of her, won't immediately grasp the concept of house-training, and that their two-bedroom condo will soon become a two-bedroom latrine—especially because neither one of them is ambulatory enough to take the pooch out for regular walks.

Chareze spends all day confined to a corner of the apartment, tearing up anything she can get her teeth on. The dog needs attention and training; the Clamors aren't able to give it. Help!

I know all this because it's what Charmaine tells me over dinner, right before she wonders out loud if maybe *I* could help train their puppy. "We could keep her for the week, give her some guidance. Be a good influence," she says, shrugging.

Then she shows me a few photos on her phone. The dog is definitely cute.

"And when we return her to Mom and Dad?" I can see where this is heading: sooner or later, and probably very soon, we're going to inherit this dog. They can't handle the responsibility of caring for a pet, and Charmaine and I will become the new Mom and Dad for a family member we really didn't choose.

Plus, I'm prejudiced. I'm a canine bigot. *Hey, man, it's just the way I was raised.* I grew up with German shepherds and Collies and Irish Wolfhound-Rottweilers, not gerbils on a leash. Small dogs are cute, but are they really dogs? When a breed is categorized as a "toy," hasn't any claim to full membership in the canine republic already been abdicated?

I harrumph and grumble, but eventually I say, "Sure. The puppy can stay here and we'll do our best." Now we'll have *two* incontinent guests on our property.

The plan is for Charmaine to make her usual Sunday afternoon visit with the parents and to bring Chareze back to Hollywood in a travel case. She'll undergo *Shih Tzu* boot-camp for a week and return a week later to Canoga Park an impeccably behaved princess.

In the meantime, we have another visitor arriving, from New York. The Editor is a great old friend of mine. He gave me one of my big breaks at a young age, and we've traveled together on assignment to many magical places, sharing our joys and heartbreaks. He's a delightfully peculiar, one-of-a-kind chap, this Editor, and I love him like a brother.

And I worry about him. He's often miserable. Distant. Unreachable. After a calamitous divorce and serial episodes of depression, he succumbed to alcoholism, had a breakdown, and finally checked into rehab. Now, the Editor is almost thirty days sober, and Charmaine and I are excited to see his renaissance in person for the first time. We've asked Mike to vacate the cabin for the two nights the Editor is staying in Los Angeles. The porch, we remind him, is still available.

Mike mumbles and nods and waves us off. "No, no," he says, which I take to mean, "OK."

When the Editor pulls his rental car into our driveway, I greet him before he bumps into Fisher King Mike. I haven't told the Editor about Mike. (I haven't told anyone Mike's staying here, including the neighbors, since I suspect he'll be gone before long.) I don't want my New York friend to be startled to find a "vagrant" behind the shrubbery.

When the Editor emerges from his car, it's I who's startled. My friend looks hollowed out, skeletal. His eyes are puffy and purple from sleeplessness, his scalp dry and exuding dandruff. He must weigh 120 lbs., at most.

"Mikey!" he exclaims. "This is me, version two-point-oh. I'm back!"

We hug. I can feel his ribs. "How you doing, my friend?"

"Mikey, I tell you—it's like I was saying to my lover—her name is Rachael, a beautiful Jewess—we met—she's also in recovery—so, we were talking, and I was saying, you know, Mikey, when one is in Eden one must have the good sense to recognize that one is in Eden."

I nod. "All right then. Welcome to Eden." If I had to guess, I'd say the Editor has had a few too many espressos.

"And very glad to be here, indeed, sir," he replies, appending a delayed smile to his declaration. "A return to Weed Hollow Cabin! Here, sir, is a little something to wet your whistle." He hands me a four-pack of artisanal ginger ale, in fat brown bottles. "Wine is off the list, as you know, for yours truly. However—and I should like to make this easy on everyone—you and Miss Charm are welcome to imbibe whatever you wish. So let's have a *faux-jolais*! A toast to sobriety, as it were. And then—and I won't hear a word of opposition on this matter—I shall take you and your lovely wife out for supper wherever you choose, on me, wherever you'd like to go, my treat."

"You're our guest," I complain. "We'll take care of—"

"No, no! I won't hear of it. I shall take you and Charmaine out for a fine supper—although, I confess, I don't think I have a necktie!" He laughs uproariously. "Ah! And who is this?"

Fisher King Mike ambles up the driveway. "No, I was just—the cabin is all ready for you."

"Mike, this is my good friend the Editor I was telling you about. And this is Mike, he's a friend from the Elderberries community."

"And a fine community it is. Hello, sir!" The Editor extends his hand. Mike grasps it limply.

I gesture around the garden. "Mike has helped me with a couple of projects."

"Ah, I see! Outstanding. Well, it's a pleasure to meet you, sir, and I thank you for your contributions to Eden."

"Well, no, it's not that, I just fixed the pipe back there. It was leaking."

"Mike's very handy," I say, going for the Editor's bags. "Here. I'll take these to the back for you."

"That's very kind of you, sir," he says. "I'll just fetch a few things from the car and meet you there." He looks around the front garden for a second, bird-like in his appraisal. "Splendid! Out-standing!"

"And I'm going up the street," Mike says, indicating the church around the corner.

After a round of *pleased to-meet-you*s, we go our separate ways. I walk down the stone path and deposit the bags inside Weed Hollow cabin, which looks pristine. When I return to the driveway a few minutes later, looking for the Editor, he's still standing beside his car, deep in conversation with the Fisher King.

I watch from the porch. Mike seems to be briefing the Editor on his military exploits, and the Editor, trained journalist that he is, seems to be asking some good expository questions. Where was this? When did this happen? Who did you say you were married to?

They seem to have reached a level of familiarity usually reserved for college roommates.

I'm concerned. Viewing their silhouettes side-by-side, I'm concerned. From the back, you can't tell who's the Harvard-educated publishing titan and who's the Fisher King. Listening to them deliver incredible monologues to each other, with an intensity and conviction worthy of the better evangelists, you'd be hard pressed to determine which one's "crazy."

Eventually, when Mike excuses himself to use the toilet, Charmaine, the Editor, and I trundle off to dinner at a nearby Indian restaurant—"My treat! I insist," the Editor announces (again).

On the walk there, and after we order our meals, I try to give him a little background on Mike, ensuring that future interactions aren't too confusing, but he doesn't seem to grasp that the Fisher King is delusional. "Well, you know, Mikey," the Editor begins, "what constitutes a healthy mind is a fascinating subject, and I shall very much like to explore it in the near future, during one of our Weed Hollow hang-outs, as it were. But for now, dear ones, I'd like to share with you my Next Big Idea. Ready?"

We nod, warily munching on *papadum*.

Charmaine attempts a few polite interjections, but for the next ninety minutes, in lieu of a polished magazine pitch, the Editor delivers a tangential, stream-of-consciousness internal monologue about his children and ex-wife and ex-girlfriend, all of whom, he assures us, have helped him with a newfound understanding of himself.

He doesn't eat. He doesn't drink. He doesn't really pause, except to sporadically rub his forehead and scalp with tremendous force. Interrupted only by curry-bearing waiters and water-refreshing busboys, his performance rivals Fisher King Mike for endurance and obliviousness.

"There's something wrong with the Editor," Charmaine tells me later, when, mercifully, he excuses himself after dinner to attend to some pressing emails and phone messages. "Like he had forty cups of coffee. He might be sober, but, I'm sorry, he was much easier to take before, when he was still drinking."

I nod, sadly. My friend the Editor seems to have lost the ability to edit.

THAT FRIDAY AND Saturday expire in a blaze of self-absorbed filibusters punctuated by sporadic bouts of inappropriate comments directed at much younger women. By the time the Editor departs Sunday morning, Charmaine and I are deeply worried about our New York friend and almost too exhausted by his mania to do anything about it.

Eventually, I write a letter to his children, describing the Editor's visit and outlining my concerns. They respond with full agreement and commiseration, and, eventually, several months later, they'll be compelled to have him admitted involuntarily to Bellevue Hospital's psychiatric ward.

For now, I'm relieved to have fifty percent fewer bipolar men on the property. Charmaine's off in Canoga Park, visiting her parents and, according to a plan finalized five minutes before she left, she's going to bring back the puppy, Chareze, to begin boot camp. I'm in the garden, doing some of my best puttering, when Fisher King Mike walks up beside me.

"No, I was just saying, you know you could paint them railings." He points at the low fence posts bordering the back deck. Technically, they're "white," but years of being outside have earned them a patina of grime stylishly accented by stains and splotches of indeterminate origin.

"I used to have a giant bucket of that white, but I think it went bad. Do we still have some?" I wonder out loud.

"No, see, that's not it. You got some paints down there, I went through them, and, and, OK, you got several colors, various amounts, and, and you got a salmon down there, a little less than a gallon, plenty for the railings." He nods repeatedly and chews his lower lip. "Like a reddish pink. Salmon is what it is. Here—I'll show you."

He trudges off to the cellar. I set aside a spray bottle of neem oil, a non-toxic pest deterrent made from bitter nuts, and follow the paint man. In the wake of the Editor's startling visit, I'm slightly more tolerant of the Fisher King's lunacy.

"See?" he says, popping open the lid, revealing a creamy orangey-pink pigment. "And you got the rollers and brushes, and, and you got a pan. And you don't have to give me nothing, I just accept whatever blessings, you know?"

I can't tell if Fisher King Mike really thinks "salmon" is the right color for our tired white railings, or if he's out of cigarettes and really wants the job. Either way, I figure almost anything would be an improvement on the current iteration of tired posts and pickets. Even salmon.

Worst case: Charmaine hates it, we can always paint over it with fresh white primer—which, come to think of it, isn't that the best idea anyway? "Mike, shouldn't we just be covering these with a coat of primer anyway? Like, isn't that standard procedure?"

"Look, when you're painting over white, as long as it's a dark enough color, and, and this salmon is definitely dark enough, *you don't need to use a primer*. OK? It ain't necessary, not unless you just want to waste your money. And come on," he shakes his head in amusement, "we both know you can't waste money when your wife wants to take the private jet everywhere, even when she's not on tour. Right?"

Perhaps schizophrenia is contagious. I'm hearing competing voices in my head. One is saying, "*This man believes he's married to Selena Gomez, and you trust him to paint a prominent architectural feature of your house?*" The other voice is saying, "*Salmon might be interesting.*"

Although he doesn't wear a watch, Fisher King Mike looks at his wrist, like he's checking the time, and says, "Look, if you let me get started now, I can have it all done before Miss Char gets home. Surprise her." I'd swear he winks behind his mirrored sunglasses.

I look at Mike. I see myself in his glasses. I look at the railings. I see the neglect, all the care I haven't given them.

"OK," I say. "Let's paint the railings salmon."

WHEN CHARMAINE COMES home, around five in the afternoon, she *beep-beep*s in the driveway. I go out to greet her at the porch gate. "There's somebody who wants to meet you!" she cries, reaching into the passenger seat. "Cha-REEZ! Cha-REEZ! We're here! We're here!"

She hands me a small bundle of hair, soft as silk, deliciously aromatic with *eau du puppy*. "Isn't she adorable?"

"Hello!" I say, cradling the guinea pig-sized squirmer against my chest. She appraises me with black nickel eyes, and licks me on the nose. "Oh! Yes, adorable. And *soft*."

"And, Mikey, this dog is so smart. She already knows her name at three months!"

"Chareze!" I say, and she cocks her head. *Adorable.* "Chareze!" She cocks it the other way, staring intently in my eyes. *Way too adorable.* With her slight under-bite, floppy ears, and square-ish head, the pup resembles a dancing dragon at a Chinese parade—only way, way more adorable.

"I think she likes you!" Charmaine says, her normally contralto voice jumping into a coloratura soprano register.

"Oh, my god, this doggie is *so* cute!" I exclaim, momentarily channeling a thirteen-year-old girl on Instagram. Was there ever a time when I disdained small dogs? Have I ever not loved tiny toy dogs like they were Golden Retrievers? "Cha-REEZ! You are *so* cute, I can't stand it!"

Charmaine looks on approvingly. "I knew you'd like her. How can you not?"

The puppy licks me on my forehead, and all resistance melts. I'm a teenager again. I hear Donny Osmond crooning on the record player—*And they called it, puppy luuuh-uh-uh-uhve, but I guess they'll never know*—and I just met a super sweet girl with the prettiest eyes, and I feel first-kiss butterflies, and my heart racing, and, God, life is so beautiful I just want to cry. *Please, let her like me as much as I like her!*

We take Chareze inside and watch her sniff around. She doesn't seem particularly curious; maybe the freedom to roam is so new to her she's not sure of the rules. She keeps looking back at us—*Is it OK? Can I investigate underneath here?*—and after a brief exploratory expedition, scampers back, her tail wagging and tongue lolling. *Adorable.*

"Mikey, I think this dog likes you," Charmaine says, grinning.

It's true. I was raised with dogs in my playpen. Our family always had dogs. My brother and I grew up speaking Dog, and we've convinced ourselves all dogs like us. And since that's what I believe—*i.e.*, that all dogs naturally like me—it seems that most dogs like me. I live in a canine positive feedback loop; I'm programmed to recognize doggie *interest* as doggie *affection*. There are worse ways to live.

I'm fully aware of my belief/delusion. But *this* one, this little fluffy puffball, this animatronic plush toy—this one, I sense, really, really likes me.

Although she makes a Tootsie Roll-like accident, and chews on the house-slippers, and barfs up her dinner after eating too quickly, I think I really, really like her, too.

Soon I'm helpless. After two hours of orienting her to the rooms of our house—and helping her up and down the stairs, and carrying her in my arms, and smelling that singular smell—I'm irretrievably in love.

Not that I can admit it. Not yet. I'm no fool. I've been burned before, etc. Maybe Chareze is untrainable; maybe she'll never stop peeing in my office. Maybe she ain't as bright as everyone makes her out to be.

"Michael, this dog is brilliant!" Charmaine exclaims from the kitchen. "You've gotta see this!"

I walk in and find Chareze sitting on her haunches in front of Charmaine, who has her hand extended in a "stop" signal.

"Watch this," Charmaine whispers. She keeps her hand extended as she walks backward, maintaining eye contact with Chareze, who stares back solemnly, searching for meaning in Charmaine's retreating face. When Charmaine reaches the dining room, she poses dramatically, a yogini frozen in place. So's the dog.

They stare at each other. Then Charmaine drops her hand and yells, "OK!"

A mop of hairy joy bolts toward her. "Good girl! Good girl!" she says, petting Chareze with two hands. "You're so smart!"

Chareze dances a happy jig and sits down in front of Charmaine, making the game continue.

"I thought this puppy was untrained," I say, impressed at Chareze's fourteen-week-old aptitude.

"She's not trained!" Charmaine gushes. "I think she's just naturally smart."

I'm skeptical, if only because toy dog purebreds aren't exactly celebrated for their intelligence. It's not their fault; they have walnut-size brains. Their evolutionary strategy is to team up with the smartest, strongest species extant—and learn to understand the tall two-leggers better than those bipeds understand themselves. "Let's try something," I propose.

Charmaine stays in the dining room. I go to the far corner of the kitchen and sit on the floor, with a handful of dog treats between my crossed legs. Chareze keeps looking at Charmaine, waiting for a signal. I call her: "Chareze! Come!"

She turns around and looks at me quizzically. She looks back at Charmaine, who points in my direction. She looks at me again on the floor. I motion with one hand, *come here; everything's gonna be all right.*

She scampers toward me and hops into my lap. "Good girl!" I exult. Charmaine and I look at each other, wide-eyed, almost scared to speak, not wanting to break the spell.

Finally, I say, "Here, take some of these," handing Charm a few treats. "You sit over there, on the other side." I put Chareze in Charmaine's lap and walk into the breakfast nook, about twenty feet away. Then I sit down and call Chareze.

She comes running, barreling into my legs. Then Charmaine tries it. She charges at her and leaps into her lap. Then she runs back to me, then Charmaine, and what seems like a dozen more times.

We both laugh until tears are running down our faces.

At bedtime, we give Chareze a "last call" in the garden (with no results) and then stash her in a training crate downstairs, in my office, quickly closing the door and dashing up the stairs and into our bedroom, trying to get far enough away we won't hear her inevitable crying.

Too late. The puppy whimpering begins almost immediately. We stop at the top of the stairs, trading pained looks. "We've got to ignore it," I say, the voice of canine experience.

More crying. "*Ooooh,*" Charmaine moans. "Poor baby."

"I know. It's tough. But it's the best way to housebreak her. She won't go where she sleeps," I say, which reminds me of Fisher King Mike, who's out back, sleeping in Weed Hollow Cabin. He spent most of the afternoon cleaning up after the Editor, who left behind, among other detritus, a tower of eighteen *grande* Starbucks cups stacked on the floor.

"He wasn't real neat," Mike said, hoisting a broom and shaking his head disconsolately. Then he treated me to a (lengthy) disquisition on proper Guest Behavior. My takeaway: if Mike's practice is as conscientious as his theory, everything's going to be more than fine.

As for Chareze, I'm not so sure. It's been more than twenty years since I last trained a puppy, and I can feel the rust. I have no willpower. I have no *power*. I just want the super cute adorable little puffball crying in her cage to know that everything is going to be fine. Everything is going to be more than fine.

"I don't think I can do this," I tell Charmaine. "It's killing me to hear her cry."

"Me, too," Charmaine says, frowning. "But you're the one who said she's going to pee everywhere unless we keep her in her crate at night. You said they liked it."

"I know. That's right. It's true. I'm just . . ."

"You're in love. Already! That is so sweet. The guy who doesn't like little doggies."

Chareze lets loose a high-pitched wail. I feel a visceral discomfort in my chest. Charmaine and I look at each other, both of us biting our lips and scrunching our faces. "Hold on," I say. "I have an idea."

I go downstairs to my office and find Chareze sitting in her crate, tail wagging. *Adorable.* "OK, young lady," I tell her, grabbing the crate handles. "You're coming with me."

Chareze spends her first night at Vista Street in our bedroom, in her crate, crying softly, a few feet away from where we try to sleep. We comfort her with soothing tones. "*Go to bed, Chareze. Go to bed.*" Eventually, she wears herself out—or vice-versa—and the house goes quiet.

In the morning, I extract Chareze from her cell and deposit her in the middle of the garden, where she looks up quizzically. "Make potty," I tell her. "Go make potty."

Nothing. I continue to encourage her. She wags her tail, but keeps looking at me, ignoring the beckoning dirt. *Compost, compost everywhere, and not a drop to pee.* "Chareze, go make!"

Nothing. I look around. It's early. No one's up. I unzip my pants and fish myself out. "Chareze, make potty," I say, urinating on the ground between a row of bell peppers. She goes to the sound. She sniffs the soil. She wags her tail and investigates the area. Then she squats and pees.

I'm impressed, and a little taken aback. "Good girl! You are *such* a good girl!"

We go inside, where Chareze gets a good girl treat and I call my mom, in Wisconsin. I tell her about how Mom and Dad Clamor impulsively adopted a three-month-old puppy, and how we've volunteered to train it, and how she's the third house-guest in the last few days, and, oh, by the way, I think I'm madly in love with this little fur packet.

"How big is she?" Mom asks.

"Like, five pounds. You can scoop her up with one hand."

"A *little* dog," Mom says.

"Yes. Very little. And, yes, I know my feelings about toy dogs— and purebreds—are fairly well-known, but I'm telling you, Mom, this little Chareze is incredibly lovable. And—and I'm not kidding—she seems to be extraordinarily smart. Like, not just for a small dog. She's scary smart."

My mom laughs. "Yep. You're in love."

I don't tell her about Fisher King Mike. For all I know, he vanished overnight—or will soon. I do tell her about the Editor, a man she knows and likes, and she gasps. "Oh, Mike, I'm so sorry to hear that. What a shame."

My mom, a lifelong schoolteacher, with a special interest in gifted and talented children, has had plenty of personal encounters with mental illness, including bipolar disorders. She sighs. "I'm sorry, honey. I know the worst part is you want to help, but there's really nothing you can do for someone in that state. You just have to love them."

"Well, that's something. And something's always more than nothing."

"Just love him," Mom repeats. "That the best any of us can do."

When our call ends, I take Chareze out back to meet the Fisher King, assuming he's still in the cabin. It's almost 9 a.m. and not a creature has stirred, except the squirrels. I knock on the door. "Good morning, Mike!"

"Yeah. Just a second," Mike calls out. It sounds like he's getting out of bed.

I sit on the wobbly bench beside the cabin, holding Chareze in the crook of my left arm, like a hirsute football. Mike emerges from Weed Hollow grinning bashfully and rubbing his head. He smells sour. "Yeah. Sorry. Just woke up." He notices Chareze. "And this must be your mom and dad's dog."

"Chareze," I say, handing her to him. "This is Mike."

Mike holds the dog tenderly, cooing in baby talk (or another language he knows) and nuzzling her silky fur against his face. "Heh-whoa, heh-*whoa* widdul go. Hiya! Hiya!"

Chareze licks his wrinkled face. He cries out, "Oh! My goodness! Oh, my goodness!" And then he nuzzles her some more.

I laugh. He laughs. Chareze wags her tail and laps her tongue. For the first time since I've known him, Fisher King Mike seems altogether normal, just another enthusiastic dog lover in puppy heaven.

For a brief and beautiful moment, I can imagine that everything's going to be all right.

Charmaine, MK, Chareze, and Fisher King Mike.

NINE

A Peculiar Pack

M y next-door neighbor, the Litigator, is concerned. Seems
there's been a weird guy loitering on our street, smoking
cigarettes and wandering down our driveway.

"Yeah. That's Mike," I assure him. "He does indeed look weird,
but he's perfectly harmless."

It's Tuesday morning. *Terrific* Tuesdays, as they're known
around here. Tuesdays are when many of the homeowners on my
street have their homes cleaned by people who don't live on this
street. Tuesdays are the tidiest days of the week, and that's terrific.

We're standing on my front porch, the former site of the Fisher
King's bag depository. The Litigator and his husband have a lovely
eleven-year-old daughter, who they adopted at birth. They're
deeply devoted to her, and I can see how someone who presents
himself to the world as Mike does might seem not so terrific to
them. "We're letting him stay here for a couple of nights," I tell
my neighbor.

"The one you wrote the letter about. The letter of introduction.
Is he living here now? I mean, it's OK . . ."

Many wealthy homeowners in the Sunset Square area have
taken to community message boards to voice their displeasure
with the burgeoning homelessness crisis. The local correspondents

wonder why successful achievers who pay dearly to live in this neighborhood should be forced to view such unpleasantness through the windows of their luxury SUVs? Why aren't the police carting the homeless away in paddy wagons? Why isn't the Public Works Department sweeping the homeless away with industrial street cleaners? Why isn't someone with political power erasing this blight on our otherwise pristine neighborhood?

Some of the same people calling for the removal of the unsightly homeless are simultaneously soliciting donations for the recovery and clean-up of Houston and Florida in the wake of devastating winds and rains. One plea being forwarded via email has the subject line "Help Our Houston Brothers and Sisters Stay Dry!" The nice lady who wrote it proposes that our Sunset Square association send a giant box of blankets to Texas. The logic seems to be that people who once owned their own home deserve a replacement, but those who never owned their own home don't deserve one in the first place.

Another way of looking at it is that victims of natural disasters are good people like me and you who had the awful bad luck of living in the path of a hurricane, whereas homeless people camping on the street are victims of their poor decisions and, ergo, are undeserving of organized charity. Never mind that building your home in a known hurricane region might by some measures be considered a "poor decision." The underlying assumption about the homeless is that if they're living on the street, they somehow brought it on themselves. They're the perpetrators of their own demise.

Yes, they're victims of a sort. But homeless people aren't merely self-sabotagers. They're the byproduct of a toxic system founded on debased values. So long as we continue to organize ourselves around the principles of greed, self-enrichment, and "survival of the fittest," so long as we dedicate our national treasure to war-making and imprisonment instead of education and health-care, we'll continue to deposit our societal refuse on city sidewalks, where it's getting increasingly difficult not to step on "waste" of our own making. We don't really see the homeless as alternate versions of ourselves; we see them as detritus.

Poor us. And poor Joe and poor Jane, huddled in their tent on Martel Avenue, steps away from glamorous Sunset Boulevard. They didn't have the foresight to be nearly drowned in a flood. They didn't make a down payment and maintain a mortgage, so they didn't have the opportunity to watch the roof of their house get blown off by a tornado. Still, Homeless Joe and Jane need help. They need their "brothers and sisters" to care about them as though they'd been the victims of extreme weather.

I want to communicate all this to the Litigator, but I don't know how to without antagonizing. "No, no. Mike's not living here," I assure him. "Just sleeping. He doesn't use the facilities. He goes someplace else for meals and showers. We've known him for a couple of years, and he just needs a place to sleep for a few nights. Then he's moving on."

"Don't worry," the Litigator says, waving it off. "It's fine. We know you've had some interesting people living here before, so . . ." he says, chuckling. "But, OK. I just wanted to make sure everything was, you know, that you knew about this person."

"Thank you," I say. "I appreciate you looking out for us. Mike tends to come and go, but I'll introduce you two if I see him."

The Litigator leaves for work and I commence puppy boot camp, starting with property training. Little Chareze needs to know where the driveway is and where the street is, and she needs to learn to stay away from these areas, to avoid them as though they were tall monsters that made loud noises and yelled "no!"

One rolled-up magazine and about five minutes is all it takes. She gets it. This tiny purebred is only three months old and she already gets it. "Chareze," I exult. "You're so smart! Let's see what else you can do."

I teach her "down." That takes about three minutes. I teach her "roll over" in about two. And when I attempt to teach her to "heel," it takes no time at all, because, already, after two days, Chareze won't leave my side.

As we're working—or playing, depending on your fondness for repetitive tasks—I spy coming down the sidewalk the Meanest Dog in the Neighborhood being walked by the Least Friendly Person in the Neighborhood. She's a poker-faced Japanese woman in her twenties who seldom looks up from her phone yet somehow manages to circumnavigate our community without crashing into light poles. He's a miniature Schnauzer who snarls and barks at every living creature he encounters, including me, Mr. Canine Congeniality.

Chareze and I are standing on the driveway a few steps back from the sidewalk. This will be a good test. I'll let the grouchy Schnauzer and his misanthropic mom pass by and see if Chareze *sits* and *stays* as directed. I give her the signal, the "stop" hand-in-the-face. The puppy stares up at me as if to ask, *what do you want me to do next?*

Here come the meanies. The Schnauzer, pulling his owner along on one of those retractable fishing-reel-type leashes, sees me in the driveway and curls his lip, emitting a low growl. Then he notices Chareze looking at him, her ears back and tail wagging softly, feather-dusting fallen leaves from the asphalt. He stops, staring at her petite white furriness, and it occurs to me that when viewed through a particular terrier lens, little Chareze must strongly resemble a rabbit.

The Schnauzer's mom gives his leash a tug. "Po-chay! Come."

Po-chay doesn't budge. He's got his eyes locked on Chareze, who assumes the Sphinx pose and keeps on wagging. The

Schnauzer steps toward us, a persistent rumbling *grrrr* rising. "Po-chay, no!" his owner shouts.

"It's OK," I say. "He's playing." I look at his tail, a black stump the size of a tater-tot. It's wagging like a metronome set for "Flight of the Bumblebee."

"Po-chay!" she repeats. The Schnauzer isn't listening. (He never has in all the years I've observed him terrorizing Vista Street.) He's down on his forelegs, growling and yipping and jumping back. Chareze keeps wagging her tail, rubbing her nose against his, letting out happy high-pitched squeals. When the Schnauzer growls or snaps, she backs down—and then returns to cautious instigation until he agrees to play with her. When he's had enough, he snaps, she backs down—and they start the dance all over again.

"Oh, my god!" the Schnauzer's owner exclaims. "Polly, he never likes other dogs." Her English is heavily accented, strongly Japanese. I'm not sure I understood his name. Is it Polly?

"Paulie," she says, stressing the "l" sound. "Actually, Polche." She says it in three syllables, *Paul-uh-chey.* "Pol-a-che!" she says, addressing her dog. He doesn't look up from his face-washing game.

"This is not like him," she says, shaking her head and drawing a hit from an electronic cigarette the shape of an oboe. "He's not nice when he walks with me. I can't even take him to Runyon Canyon, because he might attack the other dogs if I'm there."

I observe Polche carefully. Not only is he not on the verge of eviscerating the exuberant puppy pawing at his ears, he's taking care not to swat her too hard, as though he somehow knows he needs to be careful with such a fragile playmate. He's *adorable.*

I introduce myself, and Chareze. "I'm Aya," she says. "I live around the corner."

I stifle the urge to tell her, *Yes, I know, I've tried to say "hello" to you and your dog for the past five years.* Instead, I say, "We're very glad to meet you. I think Chareze just made her first friend."

"I think Paulie made *his* first friend. Paulie, you have a friend!" Then she starts babbling at him in keening Japanese goo-goo talk. Paulie cocks his head one way and the other. *Adorable.*

I tell Aya that she's welcome to bring Polche by our house any time she wants him to play; it will be good for puppy Chareze to get socialized.

"Really? Seriously? You would be OK with that?"

I nod. "Really."

Aya smiles and nods, and I think she almost makes a little bow. She says she'll return with Polche tomorrow.

When I go to the back deck for some more doggie boundary lessons, I find Fisher King Mike standing outside Weed Hollow Cabin staring at his phone. He's wearing his Hollywood hat and earbuds, and he's rocking slowly from heel to toe. Chareze bounds toward him and punches him in the shins with her front paws. He bends down to pet her and scratch her behind the ears. He's even gentler than Polche.

"No, I was just checking my sugar," Mike says.

There seems to be a Selena Gomez video playing on his phone, so I don't inquire about his glucose levels. "Have you eaten today, Mike?"

"Yeah, yeah, that's not it. I got this and this," he holds up a liter bottle of Coke and a Hershey bar the size of an airport paperback.

I make a face. "And you got your cigarettes, too. I know. But, Mike, my brother, you need some vegetables, and some fruit."

"No, no, see, I do what I gotta do. Just trying to keep it all together, you know, since I have diabetes and, and this spinal cancer I got, it's terminal, and, and the doctors say it's six months or less, so *I have to check my sugar regularly.* OK? Otherwise I die? OK?"

"I didn't know that," I say, although I vaguely remember some terminal illness announced in 2015. "Spinal cancer?"

"Yeah, and so I got to check my sugar regularly and keep it so I don't crash," he explains.

"At least let me make you a salad. A nice, fresh Vista Street garden salad."

"Nah, nah," Fisher King Mike says. "I can't eat salad."

"You don't like salad?" I say, mirthfully.

"No, it ain't that. I can't eat salad. I don't have any teeth!" He smiles broadly, revealing two bare gums. The top gum has a lone vestigial stump poking through. "You didn't know that?"

Whoa. I hadn't noticed. "No, I didn't know that. But I don't think I knew about the spinal cancer, either. I guess there's a lot about you I don't know, Mike."

"Yeah, well, I'm not allowed to discuss certain things."

I invite him to sit down on the park bench beside the cabin. While Chareze frolics in the "dog park," the sole patch of grass in our yard, located beneath a mature blood-orange tree, I invite Fisher King Mike to talk.

"Tell me your story, Mike," I encourage him. "I'm here to listen."

"Nah, nah, it ain't interesting. She likes that grass," he says, deflecting the conversation to the puppy.

I try to redirect, but he won't bite. All of my questions earn a quick shake of the head, a chortle, and a "nah, nah." He does, however, tangentially refer to his spinal cancer, his "tumor"—on his back; in his brain; it's not clear to me—and a serious "stroke" he suffered, back when he was "much heavier." The stroke event doesn't seem to have incapacitated Mike in any way physically, and tales of his terminal illness have been circulating from the day we met, yet, still, it's obvious that *something's* wrong with him. It can't all be in his head.

"Do you mind if I smoke?" he asks, swigging Coke from a freshly opened two-liter bottle, his second of the day.

"As long as it's back here, far away from the house, and Charmaine isn't around—yes," I say. "And maybe I'll join you." I go to the back deck and grab a pre-rolled joint, left over from a series of videos called *Burnin' One, with MK Punky*, in which I recited slam poetry while sharing a doobie with a friend. (Funny, profound, ridiculous—you decide.)

When I return, Mike puts down his Camel. "Oh," Mike says, purring. "Well, let's smoke that instead."

I spark it up, take a drag and pass the smoldering stick to the Fisher King, sitting across from me. He inhales deeply, closing his toothless mouth around the tip. When he finally exhales, Mike nods, coughs dryly, and says, "Very nice. Thanks."

He hands it back to me and thereupon commences on a monologue of biblical length and complexity, spanning the globe and traversing the decades. If I once thought Fisher King Mike had a touch of the blarney, that was before I'd seen him declaiming the mysteries of the universe while smoking *cannabis sativa*. The rhetorical dam breaks. The unstoppable deluge is upon me.

I surrender. After abandoning all attempts at keeping Mike "on track" by leading him back to the main story—"You were saying? About being a movie producer?"—I sit back, relax, and enjoy the flight, during which I learn many new things about Fisher King Mike. Some of them might even be true. And I'm not sure if it makes a difference.

I learn: His full name is Michael James Bailey.

He's in his "mid-sixties."

He has a tattoo of a skull and crossbones sporting bat wings on his left arm, which he got from "some Army guys." He has another tattoo of a snake on his left leg, which he got from "some

Navy guys." What "the Marine guys" proposed to inscribe upon him he's not permitted to divulge.

He's worked "personal security detail" for people he's not allowed to name.

He's traveled anywhere you've been, including developing nations in Africa.

He used to have a "bad diet," and he once weighed more than 300 lbs. (Current weight: 124, give or take a few jackets.) How he lost the weight he's not willing to reveal.

He's terminally ill and married to Selena Gomez, and, and they haven't told the kids, not yet anyway, it ain't the right time, but, you know, there's nothing more important than family. (That part I already knew.)

There's nothing more important than family.

I see Chareze lolling in the grass beside the park bench. I hear our adopted next-door neighbor splashing in her family's swimming pool. I smell the man sitting across from me. And I wonder: Is "family" who you were born to, people you have some "blood" relation with?

Or is "family" who you decide to love?

In the aftermath of the devastation wrought by Typhoon Haiyan in the Philippines, where thousands died and hundreds-of-thousands were left homeless, almost everyone I spoke to asked the same question: Your wife, your Filipino wife—was anyone in her immediate family affected?

Everyone was visibly relieved to learn that, no, my wife's immediate family members weren't harmed by the storm. (Most of them live on a different island.) The absence of injury or property damage to my wife's closest relatives was heard as great news, a kind of silver lining to the dark cloud of death that descended on her birth country. By some sort of strange spiritual calculus, it was understood and taken for granted that blood relations are intrinsically more important, more valuable to us, than everyone else—with the exception of those who are welcomed bloodlessly into the family through adoption and marriage. Those folks are more important, also.

Our collective hearts go out to our fellow humans in the face of extraordinary suffering. We suffer with them whether we know them or not. But the suffering is so much less when the victims aren't anyone we know or anyone close to someone we know.

Feeling this way isn't wrong, or bad. It's real and true for most of us. It does, however, expose one of the fundamental problems with our prevailing value system: we're only supposed to *really* care, care more than we otherwise would, when a family member is involved. Or a celebrity—but that's another story.

Maybe how we define "family" is at the root of our troubles as a species. A narrow definition is what encourages us to form clans, tribes, mafias, religions, and corporations, organizations that are loyal, helpful, and protective of their members and competitive, dangerous, and possibly violent to everyone else. Family is the end that justifies all means necessary.

If "family" is indeed the most important organization in each person's life, then we could solve most of the world's ills simply by expanding our definition of the word. The more people we consider our brothers and our sisters, the easier it becomes to expand the scope of our kindness and to narrow the breadth of our apathy. If *every* Filipino swept away in the typhoon really was a part of our "immediate family," feeling relief at their death would seem callously insensitive.

For centuries, poets have been reminding us implicitly and explicitly not to ask for whom the bell tolls. But we go on doing it anyway, oblivious to the truth that it tolls for all of us each and every time our Filipino brother and our Haitian sister and our

Somali mother and our Afghani father, and anyone else who comes from the same exploding star, suffers the pain of being alive.

Yet, if you wish to align yourself with a mindset that no one will dispute and most will acclaim, proudly proclaim yourself a paragon of "family values." Earn a reputation as a "family man." Put "family" before self. Found a right-wing Christian political bribery machine and call it "Focus on the Family." Do whatever it is you want to do with your life, but, like Fisher King Mike, remind everyone that whatever it is you do with your life *it's all about the family.*

Ah, how we love our children and how we love our parents and our siblings (and our pets). They're more important than anyone or anything in the universe. Family: the folks we can trust and love, celebrate and forgive, rescue and remember, support and adore and abide. Family is the greatest (except for all the times when they're not).

We'll sacrifice much of our life for family and call it parenthood. We'll find extraordinary reserves of generosity for those who fit under the family umbrella. For them we'll do whatever it takes—because that's what family does for family.

But maybe our narrow definition of family is what excuses our inward-looking greed and callousness toward the travails of those who aren't made members of our group. Maybe our narrow definition of family is what has gotten us in omnipresent and catastrophic trouble, creating false divisions where there ought to be eternal harmony.

Maybe we could broaden our terms and let more souls into our exclusive club.

Modern society places tremendous importance on blood relations (even when there is none, as with legal marriage). Why? If you were able to trace your genealogy back far enough, you'd discover that you really truly are a relative of every single person on the planet. Your family is much larger than you previously believed. Adam was your Daddy. And that guy you despise? Adam was his Daddy, too.

Family, the nuclear family, is what encourages the erroneous assumption that our enemies are the Other when, in fact, they're an alternative version of us. This is a convenient misunderstanding if you're in the war-making business. Killing a stranger from the opposing team is so much easier when the enemy isn't "related" to you.

Is the new definition of family *everyone*? Is that too wide? Too impractical?

I wonder what might happen to my heart if I resolve to love "strangers" with no apparent connection to me but their common humanity. Isn't that what Jesus counseled? Take care of the least among ye—and see what happens to your heart.

"Now, see, what people don't understand is, see, old Bernie Sanders, he's running for president on his own fortune. He's a billionaire, and he don't need no help. It's like, did you hear what Newt Gingrich was saying—"

"Mike!" I interject. "Hold on!" He stops. He actually stops talking. "I have to tell you something. I've been listening to you for a long time, and now I want you to listen to me for just a few minutes. Mutual respect, OK?"

He nods, wary and curious. "Yeah. Sure."

"I'm going to talk with Charmaine about this, so it's all contingent on that. But I've been thinking: it's actually nice having you here at night, doing security and everything. We don't mind you sleeping in the cabin. We *like* it. I guess what I'm saying is, I know it can be rough out there, with your missionary work on the streets and everything, and I want you to know that you have a place you can come home to at night and know you're going to be safe. Mike, as far as I'm concerned, you're welcome to stay here with us whenever you need to."

"OK. Man, Chareze really likes playing in that grass."

"So you're going to be staying here?" I'm already reminding myself to tell the Litigator that there's been a small change of plans.

"Yeah, yeah. But like I'm saying, you know how dogs find a spot they like? Chareze. She's, she's . . ."

"We want to help you get back on your feet, Mike," I say. "I hope this might help."

"Yeah, yeah. Thanks. It will, 'cuz, see, trying to get back and forth to the Valley, and the bus not running after—well, it used to be later."

"Mike. My brother. We're going to work it out. Everything is going to work out."

"Oh, *I* know that! It's just, see, what people don't understand is, see, like what I've been saying, when you're a street pastor and you're trying to help people, and you're ministering to people, you see for yourself how tough it is on a person when nobody seems to care, and, and so, you know, you understand, you get it."

For the first time in my life, I think maybe I do.

Mike and his friend Polche, the neighborhood grouch.

TEN

Caretaker Mike

———

Charmaine's not angry. She's not upset. She's not even mildly annoyed.

She's cautiously skeptical.

We're having supper in the sunroom. Chareze is dozing on a floor mat. Weed Hollow Cabin, where the newest resident of Vista Street farmstead is presently housed, can be seen through the foliage of the back garden. Charmaine is gazing in that direction. "Boundaries. *Boundaries.* MK, I'm serious. I can't stress that enough," she says, her normal calm showing signs of uncharacteristic vocal tension.

"Absolutely."

"We need to communicate very clearly what's allowed and what isn't. Like, he's not supposed to come in our house."

"Absolutely."

"And I'm not comfortable with him doing laundry here. He can go to a laundromat."

I'm thinking: *If Mike ever has extra money for doing laundry, it will mean he quit smoking and drinking Coke.* But for now, I say, "OK."

"The problem is that even if you explain everything to him very clearly, you can't be sure he really understands what you're saying," Charmaine reminds me. "But, other than that, I don't really mind him being in the back at night. I actually feel very secure."

She smiles. She shakes her head. "You see what happens, MK? We put a Bernie Sanders sign in our front yard and everyone starts moving in."

THE NEXT MORNING, shortly after dawn, I take Chareze out to make. We find Fisher King Mike sitting on the park bench outside Weed Hollow Cabin, smoking a cigarette. He's wearing the same clothes as the day before, without the jackets.

"Good morning, Mike," I chirp.

"Morning," he mumbles.

"You sleep all right?"

"Yeah, yeah. Thanks. But I been up already. Got some of my things hung up, swept out the cabin. Getting stuff done."

"Great. You hungry?"

"I could use some breakfast," he says, instinctively reaching for a bottle of Coke on the bench beside him. "I'll get a doughnut at the church. They open at seven."

I tell him I'll make a little breakfast for the both of us. Something nutritious. "But first I've got to talk with you about what Charmaine said about you staying here."

He bows his head and nods.

"Everything's fine. She's cool with it. She just wants all of us to be super clear on the arrangement. Communication. If we can all respect each other and recognize boundaries—I think we can make this work."

"No, no. Of course. I would never," Mike sputters.

"I know, Mike. I know," I say, smiling. "I know you're a very respectful guest. Charmaine was saying how much neater you are than a lot of our friends who have stayed here. It's just important

that we have these conversations so there aren't any misunder-
standings."

"Yeah, and like I said, I can do stuff around here. You don't have
to pay me nothing. No expectations."

"We would pay you, I think," I say, unsure of how that would
work. We're not charging Fisher King Mike rent, but he still needs
to feed and bathe and clothe himself, and all those activities normally require money. Maybe we could barter. Maybe we can make
a better angels kind of arrangement, in which I take care of you
as best I can and you do the same for me.

"I could help take care of the place," Mike proposes. "There's
lots of stuff to do. I gave you that list. You know I can build a house
from the studs up, right?"

"You mentioned that."

"Yeah, so, if I got the right tools. Like I was telling you, it's
probably going to take us longer to find the right tools than me
doing the job." He laughs. "I'm not kidding."

In theory, it sounds promising. Mike will have a safe haven
from the streets; we'll have extra security and maintenance help
on the property; everyone benefits. In theory.

The last time we hosted a homeless man, our home became a
flop house, a cave from which to hide from the world. Promised
projects never got executed. Dark energy radiated from where our
guest slept with his unauthorized kittens, and the farmstead was
not altogether better off with him on the premises.

This time I know better.

I know that of Mike's many skills, staying highly organized
isn't one of them. I tell him I'll put together a short weekly list of
stuff that needs attention, selections from his handwritten master
list. He can address each issue when he's got time. (I expect much
of his day will be spent doing his missionary work.) And I'll pay
him a fair wage for his labor, taking into consideration that he's

staying rent-free in our sweet little redwood shack. "You can buy groceries with the money, and you're welcome to put the perishables in the refrigerator in the back."

He shrugs. "Fine. You know we're gonna have to go back to Home Depot, right? Your favorite place? We need a lot of stuff— I mean, if you want me to do the job right. If you want it half-assed, you can, that's up to you, but me? I don't do things half-assed, you know what I mean? You want to do it right, you need a new power drill, and I would get a bit set. I know you got one, but you need a new one, OK? And I noticed the switch in the downstairs bathroom ain't really working right. And you know some of your lights out here need to be replaced, right? I got lots of stuff to do. But we gotta go to Home Depot, OK?"

Agreed. I'll get together a preliminary project list and he'll get together a preliminary shopping list, and eventually we'll go shopping.

In the meantime, as if to demonstrate his commitment to cleanliness, Fisher King Mike busies himself with a top-to-bottom sanitizing of Weed Hollow Cabin. He removes everything from inside, except the heavy furniture, and, while I retreat to my office, disappears for an hour wielding a soap bucket, a mop, various brooms, cloth rags, and a spray bottle of mysterious origin.

To my delight—and I suspect Mike's, as well—Chareze loiters outside the cabin, lolling in the grass, mesmerized by new discoveries: a bee, two cavorting squirrels, a mockingbird. She strikes me as exceptionally curious, as though she wishes to learn the strange new world of the garden with all her senses, particularly her inquisitive nose, twitching and bellowing in the air. When Mike emerges from the cabin to dump a bucket or shake a sheet, Chareze is waiting outside for him, eager to visit.

From my office, I can't hear what he's saying to the puppy, but the pantomime I see suggests two new friends enjoying the other's company. She's wagging her tail and hopping sideways; he's bending down and offering his hands. I'm not sure I've ever seen Mike happier.

THE NEXT MORNING, per our agreement, I'm ready to go at 6 a.m. for our planned Home Depot run. Mike is missing.

He doesn't answer the cabin door after repeated knocks. He doesn't respond to verbal inquiries. "I'm opening the door!" I announce, hesitating before slowly turning the knob.

Empty. Mike's not here.

The cabin is immaculate, and all the accoutrements—the coffee maker, the clock radio, the little guest bottles of wine and soda—are in residence. The tenant, though, isn't.

I consider going to Home Depot myself, but after reviewing my shopping list, I realize I don't really know what we need. A wrench: yes, we need that. What *kind* of wrench, I'm not sure. And, really, how should a man like me distinguish between an appropriate set of drill bits and a collection of useless bolts of metal?

I'm about to go back to bed to snuggle with Charmaine and Chareze, when I hear the driveway gate scraping open.

It's Mike. A cigarette dangles from his lips. He's carrying a plastic shopping bag in one hand, a two-liter Coke in the other. "No, I was just—I was trying to save you some time so we don't have to stop at the store. I just gotta check my sugar, and we can go," he tells me, marching back to the cabin. "Just give me a minute."

"Sure," I say, relieved to see him alive and (relatively) well, but annoyed to have to wait. "As long as we can beat the morning traffic."

"Yeah, yeah, I know. But, see, if I don't get my sugar straight, we ain't going to Home Depot, we're going to the hospital."

"OK, then," I say, masking my exasperation. "Do your thing, and then let's go."

Earbud implanted, Fisher King Mike stands outside the cabin smoking, drinking Coke, and thumbing through his phone. For five minutes. Then ten. Then fifteen.

I do paperwork in my office, watching his morning ritual through the window. Twice I attempt to intervene. He waves me away with his familiar *just-wait-a-sec* gesture.

Every step I take, whether inside the house or outside in the garden, Chareze scampers beside me, attached to my heel by an invisible leash. I look down at her inquisitive face. "What's with this guy?" I ask her. "Why is he so silly?

She wags her tail and rubs against my leg. *He's gotta check his sugar, that's all*, she seems to be saying.

It's almost 6:30 a.m. now. We have to go.

"Mike!" I call to him from the back deck. "Time to go!"

He ignores me for a few seconds and then, without acknowledging my importuning, pockets his phone and retreats to the cabin. "Mike!" I shout. "Mike, what are you doing?"

He emerges with a piece of paper folded in his fingers. Wordlessly, he holds it out in front of him, flicking it about like a checkered flag at the end of a race. Then he trudges down the driveway toward Charmaine's waiting car.

"Mike, what's going on?" I ask emphatically. "Why aren't you talking? Why are you ignoring me?"

He sighs and shakes his head morosely. "No, no. The list. You said you needed a list."

Normally, I would protest and explicate and come to a mutual understanding, all the things "regular" people do when they have a small conflict. But I realize that inexplicable behavior is Mike's version of normal. Believing we can come to some sort of agreement makes *me* the crazy one. "Right," I say. "The list. Great. Now we can go."

"Right, that's what I've been saying," he grumbles, shaking his head.

After I back out of the driveway and get onto Sunset Boulevard, Fisher King Mike grunts, "Can we get some breakfast? I gotta eat something, or this ain't gonna work."

"How about *after* we do our shopping?" I propose.

"No, no, see, if I don't keep my sugar straight . . ."

"I thought that's what you were doing in the back yard for the last twenty minutes."

"No, no, see, it's like this," he says, launching into a comprehensive (and wildly digressive) explication of How Blood Glucose Works. I listen silently to Mike's imaginary version of nutrition science, a radical re-thinking of common wisdom in which the more crap you pump into your body, the better off you are. Nicotine, I'm made to understand, is an essential element in keeping everything balanced. So are Burger King Croissanwiches.

"Got it," I say, forestalling further chemistry lessons (for the time being). "We'll get some breakfast."

He shrugs. "Yeah, because, like I was saying—"

"I got it, Mike," I say firmly. "We'll grab some breakfast. And then we'll get everything on the shopping list." I reach into my hoodie pocket. "Here," I say, handing him my list. "I'm sure we have some duplicates. Maybe you should look it over so we don't waste time at the store."

He scans my handwritten inventory. "You forgot the Kilnts," he mutters. "You ain't gonna get good coverage on the white paint if you don't have Kilnts."

I hand him a pen from a shallow compartment in the driver's door. "Write it down, please."

"Nah, nah, I'll remember. I'm just saying, you gotta do a primer coat with Kilnts, otherwise you're just wasting paint. See, what people don't understand is, even if you get a good brand, like your

Behr, or, or—they say 'one-coat coverage,' but what they don't tell you is that you gotta have a good primer first. And the Kilnts covers everything. Even stains."

"OK. We'll get some."

"No, no, I'm just saying."

We pull into the Burger King. "I'll be right back," I tell Mike, popping out of the car.

He opens his door. "No, no, I'm just gonna use the bathroom."

Mike accompanies me to the counter, where I order a $4 combo special to-go: greasy sausage and cheese sandwiches for Mike, tater tots for me, and coffee for both. "And may I have a token for the restroom?" I ask the cashier, who hands me a quarter-sized gold disc, which I pass to the Fisher King. "See you soon, Mike," I say, smiling at the futile hopefulness expressed in that phrase.

"No, no," he says, the hint of a smile forming beneath his mustache. I think he sort of gets the joke.

Soon, of course, turns out to be close to ten minutes. While I wait with the bag of fried comestibles at the ready, I call home to see if Charmaine and Chareze are up and ambulatory. Based on Charm's unintelligible groan, the answer is *barely*. I tell her Mike and I are headed back to the Depot for home maintenance supplies—whenever he emerges from the BK bathroom.

"Good luck," she whispers.

It's after 7 a.m. now, and traffic is already forming on Sunset. I can feel my breath quickening and my jaw tightening. I don't resent Fisher King Mike; I resent whatever combination of chemicals in his brain makes him oblivious to the rest of the world's reality. Wouldn't we be better off, Mike and me, if I just hired a proper handyman to work on our fragile old house? Wouldn't it be easier?

Of course, it would. And it would be easier altogether if I

discontinued any interaction with him and his mental problems. But what would that accomplish? Aside from (temporary) peace of mind?

Sure, I would very much like to engage Fisher King Mike on my terms. "Normal" person terms. At this point, today at least, that's not possible. So either I withdraw from his incontinent madness or we engage on *his* terms.

Today, I opt in.

Although I'm able to suppress the sarcasm roiling in my mind and say nothing when Mike emerges, he can sense I'm not feeling very jolly. He sees me outside the bathroom door, poker-faced. My body language says *No, I will not stop at the 7-11 for a fresh bottle of Coke.*

I hand him the breakfast bag. He says nothing and shuffles to the car.

We drive in silence—aside from the sounds of chewing and slurping. The less conversation the better.

We pass The Center. We pass homeless tent encampments. We don't talk.

Apropos of nothing, Mike blurts out, "No, I was just saying, you gotta get a big bucket of Kilnts along with your white paint. They come in five gallons."

"Do we have white paint?" I seem to remember seeing a giant pail in the basement with remnants from the last job.

"Nah, you hardly got any. We gotta buy some. Maybe, like, we should—they come in five gallons."

"OK. Five gallons of Kilnts, five gallons of white paint." I'm doing the math—the price math and the time math. With Mike, the sums always seem to be more than I anticipate.

"Yeah, see, like I was saying, see, if you don't do the Kilnts first . . ."

"You don't get good coverage," I finish his sentence.

"Yeah, and, see, like I was saying, this paint's not cheap! You don't want to waste it."

"Hey, Mike, what kind of white paint are we getting?"

"It's Behr, and, and it's top of the line, and it ain't cheap!"

"Do we need to get top of the line?" I ask naively.

"If you want coverage," he snaps. "And, and, otherwise you gotta throw away what you already got down in the cellar. It ain't much, but you don't want to waste it. So, see, you gotta get the same brand, the same type, otherwise, even though they all say *white*, there's different kinds of white, and, and if you don't match them you can tell. It looks half-assed, and I don't do things half-assed."

"OK. Behr it is," I say. "Did you write down what we already have? Or did you bring the lid?" These seem like reasonable questions a reasonable person might ask another reasonable person.

"No, no, I know what we're getting," Mike replies, his irritation at my unreasonableness nakedly obvious. "It's the Behr exterior white, semi-gloss. They only got one kind."

"Great," I say. "No problem."

About this I am mistaken. I soon learn that what really shouldn't be a problem of any sort is actually a rather big problem. When we arrive at Home Depot, politely waving off the day laborers hustling jobs in the parking lot, the Fisher King and I go directly to the paint section. Pointing to a formation of plastic buckets stacked fortress style, Mike says, "There's your Kilnts."

I grab one. It must weigh fifty pounds. The label says it's called Kilz.

Mike looks on approvingly. "Yep, see, yep, that's it. That's your Kilnts."

It says "stain blocker" on it, so I think we're talking about the same product. "Cool. Now the paint and we can move onto hardware!"

I push our cart down an aisle with more walls of stacked

buckets. There: I see a silhouette of a bear emblazoned on a bucket that says—*ah-hah*—Behr. "Here we go!" I announce, a bit too enthusiastically.

Mike stands before the five-gallon buckets pensively, his arms crossed and a hand covering his mouth. He seems to be studying the label.

I read it, too. *Exterior. Low VOC. One coat coverage.* Seems we have a winner.

"This ain't it," Mike announces. "Nah, nah, this ain't it."

I read the label again, out loud: *Exterior. Low VOC. One coat coverage.*

"Yeah, I know," he says, exasperated. "But the one you got at home was red. This one is blue. This ain't the right one. It ain't gonna match. It's gonna look half-assed."

I have a good memory—good enough to have memorized enough otherwise useless information to be a contestant on *Jeopardy!* and a phone-a-friend on *Who Wants to Be a Millionaire?* I don't recall the white paint bucket in our basement having a red label. Then again, I don't recall it being blue, either. I can't picture it clearly. *Maybe* it was red. Was it red? I don't know. But what's the big deal, anyway? As long as it's the same brand . . .

Mike peers around the other paint towers, looking for our red quarry. "This ain't it," he repeats. "This one is blue."

I flag down an orange-aproned sales associate, who regards us warily. (We must present as an odd couple. *Friends? Colleagues? Lovers?*) I tell him what we're trying to buy. He points to the Behr with the blue label. "Semi-gloss? That's it right there," the young man says flatly.

Mike sputters, "This aint' it."

I explain our quandary to the associate. He suggests that the bucket we currently possess in our basement might be so old that it has a different label color. But it's more or less the same product.

That sounds extremely plausible to me. I thank him and tell Mike, "OK. We're cool. This is it."

Mike stands with his hands on his hips, shaking his head. "This ain't it. I'm telling you, like I was telling you, the one at home is red and, and this one, you can see, right? It's *blue*. OK? It ain't the right one. You'd just be throwing your money away, and, and this stuff ain't cheap. You can't return open paint. They don't do that. You gotta get the right one, with a red label. This one is blue."

"Yes, I can see that," I say, exasperated. "Hold on. Wait."

I call home. Charmaine and Chareze are still in bed, and as my wife answers I realize I'm not going to be able to describe to her which bucket among the sea of buckets in our basement I need her to find. And I know she's not going to appreciate being drawn into the Fisher King drama. I tell her I love her and that I'll be home soon. Like, in the next fifteen minutes. But then I'll have to turn around and go back to the store. I'll explain later.

"Let's go, Mike," I say with so much forced graciousness that I must sound ungracious. "We're going home."

"No, see, because this is *blue*."

I tell him I understand and that we're going home.

"No, I know, but, see this ain't the right one."

The ride home is not cheery. I seethe in silence, less angry at Mike for not *writing down* everything we're supposed to buy for the house, more angry at myself for entrusting him with list curatorship. I'm angry at myself for trying to give every person a fair shake, no matter how untrustworthy they seem to others. I'm angry for trying to treat a mentally deranged person as though he's credible, worthy of being taken seriously. Angry for being *too* open-minded. Too nice.

Mike's slumped in the passenger seat, muttering softly to himself. The question, I realize, isn't *Doesn't he understand I have better things to do than drive back and forth to Home Depot for no reason?* It's *Does he understand* anything?

The Fisher King is tuned into frequencies I can't hear, and, most of the time, I'm tuned into frequencies *many* people can hear. Most people. Almost everyone. Fisher King Mike being an exception. I've got to shield myself from the madness; I can't let my sanity be compromised by his alternate realities.

I've got to end this. This "arrangement." *The homeless handyman and the homeowner, two guys who allegedly need each other but who can't really help each other, so drastic is the chasm between them.* He might as well be speaking Arabic and I Portuguese. When it comes to reality, we're not communicating in a common language.

Stuck behind a truck at a red light, at Highland Avenue, across from Hollywood High, I know I can't continue "collaborating" with Mike. I can't waste half a day chasing common house paint.

We're breaking up.

I don't say it out loud, but it's been decided. We're done. Pick your threadbare cliché: *I can't do this anymore. It's not you, it's me.* Well, actually, it *is* you, Mr. Fisher King. You're not a bad guy— you're a lovely guy, really. But conducting anything remotely like a normal relationship with you is impossible.

I say none of this to Mike. Nothing good can come from conversing with him—except further evidence that one (and possibly two) of the men in this relationship has lost his mind. If I let this go on any longer, I'll be the one who needs mental counseling.

We get home. We march to the cellar. We find the old bucket of Behr.

It's blue. Just like the ones at Home Depot.

"No, I swear, it was red," Mike complains, aghast at the complicated conspiracy that seems to have befallen our innocent paint supply. "It was *red.* Maybe I was looking at something else. See, because before we left, this wasn't blue."

"Well, it is now. So I guess we can get back in the car and drive to Home Depot in the morning traffic."

"No, no. Hey, can I use the bathroom real quick?"

"Quick!" I wait in the car, every one of my cells pouting.

We don't talk much on the ride there, aside from me delivering a self-righteous, self-pitying lecture to Mike about what an important fellow I am, how I shouldn't be making unnecessary trips to places I don't like in the first place. How this simply can't happen again.

"I didn't mean to bother you and your wife," Mike says, slouching into himself. "I didn't mean to cause no problems. I'll get this job done—I said I would, and, and see, what people don't understand, I don't do things half-assed. I'll get the painting done and then I'll get out of your way."

I'm relieved. I didn't have to do the breakup speech. But I also feel bad. Where will he go? Where will he sleep? What will become of him?

The same questions, I realize, could be asked of every one of the 59,000 homeless people counted in the Los Angeles Homeless Service Authority's most recent canvassing. Where will they go? Where will they sleep? What will become of them?

Luckily, *it's not my problem. I'm not the one who can fix it. It's not my responsibility.*

I hear these words in my head, and I'm not admiring the person who's thinking them. Maybe these words are correct and hard to argue against, but does that make them true? When I look closely enough, when I examine the situation with as much clarity as I can muster, I think I know the answer: homelessness really isn't my problem—or your problem, or the other lady's problem—it's *all* of our problem.

And whether I like it or not, such as when a minority of my fellow citizens elects a hateful misanthrope as president, I'm part of that All. I'm one flimsy thread in a fraying fabric.

Homelessness, opioid addiction, police brutality, income inequality, institutional racism and sexism—these are all terrible stains on our society. None of us, certainly not me, can cleanse these wounds singlehandedly. Yet, without each of us—many of us? some of us?—lending a single hand, nothing happens. Change, we're often reminded, comes slowly, from the bottom up. When you're the dictator of one discrete fiefdom (yourself), you get to decide how quickly change happens. You don't have to rely on politicians and bureaucrats. You don't need permission or the proper license. You decree and enact. *I'm going to help someone today*. And then you do.

I don't reply directly to Mike's offer to decamp. I don't utter another word about the phantom bucket of Behr. Instead, I laugh out loud at the absurdity of it all, the beautiful absurdity of what's become of my life. And Mike's. I cackle like, well, a madman. Mike says nothing, lost, I imagine, in a discordant symphony of thoughts crashing into each other.

When we pass the day laborers in the Home Depot parking lot, I hear one call out, "*Pinchay gringos locos. Dos locos.*"

I don't disagree. They're probably right.

We get the paint. (Hallelujah.) We get a full complement of brushes. And tape. Miles of it. And this specialty object and that specialty fluid, and a host of other items that Mike assures me are utterly mandatory if one wishes not to be half-assed. And after one (monitored) bathroom visit, we finally approach the check-out aisle, where I learn that Mike has filled our cart with utterly mandatory items whose combined cost is more than $700.

He shrugs, "I told you, it ain't cheap." Then he laugh and laughs, right there in the checkout, while I'm swiping a credit card that's supposed to be inserted into a chip reader. "No, I'm just saying!" and he laughs some more.

We wheel the cart past the security guard and out the door,

past the glass-fronted soda cooler. "Hey, Mr. Punky, I was wondering—"

"No," I say, robotically. "Not happening."

He laughs some more. "No, I was just!"

We crawl home through the morning rush. Unbidden, Mike walks me through the necessary steps to paint a house in a way that is not half-assed. It involves Kilnts and washing and, contrary to what most people misunderstand, *no sanding*, cuz it ain't necessary unless your undercoat is in bad shape, which the Vista house ain't.

He sounds like he genuinely knows what he's talking about. His tone is confident, self-assured, a little cocky—the same tone he employs when talking about his pop starlet wife. I do my best to find his unsolicited painting lesson amusing and enlightening, even though I've heard it several times before.

As we pull into the driveway, Mike turns to me and says, paternally, "Hey, listen, don't worry. Don't worry 'bout nothin'. I'm gonna take care of this."

"OK," I say. "Thanks."

"No, because, see, you worry too much. It ain't good for you. Don't *worry*."

"Right, because, really, what would I have to worry about?" I say dryly.

"That's what I'm *saying*."

"OK. No worries, bro."

"No, no, that's not it. Hey, look, I'd love to chat with you all day, but I got lots of stuff to do. You gotta let me get to work."

"You sure we don't need to drive back to Home Depot one more time for something we forgot?"

"No, no, no. Don't. No, no." He waves me off, chortling, and begins unloading the trunk.

I go inside to debrief Charmaine and fondle the puppy. From

the upstairs bathroom window, I can see Mike prepare his tools and supplies for what seems to my untrained eye like a professional paint job. He's got buckets lined up. He's got pans laid out. He's even putting drop-cloths—those amateurish accessories—over some of the flowering plants. Then he disappears around the side of the house and I don't see him for another three hours.

Around lunchtime, I check to see if Mike wants something to eat. I find him paint-spattered and serious, chugging a Coke. Before I can finish offering him a snack, he waves me off. "No, no, I got a lot of stuff to do."

I hear, faintly, the front doorbell ringing and, for the first time since she moved in, Chareze barking—or meekly yipping, to be precise. (If it's robbers on the front stoop, they're not going to be intimidated. But still. *Adorable.*) I can also hear Charmaine calling out, "OK, Chareze! OK! Good girl!" from somewhere inside the house.

We all meet at the foot of the stairs, in the foyer. Chareze nuzzles my leg and wags her tail. "Are you expecting anyone?" I ask Charmaine.

"No. Did you hear Chareze barking?"

"Yes! *Adorable.*" I look through the blinds and see a familiar figure: It's Frank the Artist, from Elderberries. He's tall, bushy-headed, and prone to firm, long hugs, and he likes to pop in to the Vista Street farmstead unannounced, knowing he and our other friends are welcome to visit whenever they seek a serene space to write, draw, meditate, think, or do nothing in peace.

"Is it a good time?" Frank asks, releasing me from his comforting embrace. "And who is this?" Chareze is standing on his feet, wagging her tail, "protecting" the house by administering affectionate puppy nips on Frank's pants.

I assure him just about any time is a good time, and I tell him the story of Chareze, how she's not really ours—we're sort of fostering her—but, realistically, how she's probably going to end up ours. He laughs. "She's adorable."

We walk together to the back garden, where Frank has a favorite bench. Surrounded by his tools laid out on the ground like camping supplies, Mike stands with hands on hips, surveying the driveway. "Hey, the Fisher King!" Frank cries out. "How ya doin', Mike?"

"Hey," he replies tersely. He chews his lips, staring at the paint buckets and drip pans arrayed before him. This is serious business.

"Mike's been staying with us the past few days," I explain. "And he's doing some home improvement projects."

Frank looks at me, intrigued and slightly confused. *The Fisher King? Working on your house?*

"Mike's very handy," I offer.

"Yeah, look, I'd love to chat," Mike says. "But I got lots of stuff to do, so, you know, I don't have a lot of time to talk right now." He nods repeatedly. "So . . ."

"I'm just going to make some sketches," Frank says, holding up a Moleskine notebook. "I'll stay out of your way."

"No, no, it's not that, I got a lot of stuff to do."

I walk Frank back to his favorite bench. "I know it's hard to believe," I tell him, "but Mike installed that security light up there on the corner of the house. And he repaired a pipe valve. He seems to have a lot of skills. He says he can build a house from the ground up."

"He has a lot of good stories, that's for sure," Frank says lightheartedly.

"He does. But I don't think this is one of them." I explain how we started out letting him crash on the porch, and then the cabin. "And Mike has offered to sort of look after the place."

Frank nods. "He's the caretaker. He takes care of the house."

I feel the pleasant frisson of clarity shooting through me. *Yes. That's it!*

"That's it. You said it, Frank," I cry. "We're all *caretakers*. We try to take care of each other."

"Nice," Frank says, nodding. "That's gorgeous."

I observe the scene on this sunny June day: Frank on his bench, making art; Chareze in the garden, being a dog; Mike here and there, doing whatever he does to "get stuff done." It really is gorgeous, this simple tableau, and I feel such a powerful joy in my chest that involuntary tears dribble down my cheeks. Sometimes the divine perfection of life, often so mysterious and unknowable, presents itself in a child's laughter or a hibiscus flower in bloom or a million other everyday moments we manage to overlook. And sometimes, when we're lucky, we notice. And we're reminded for the millionth time that all of this—life, the cosmos, consciousness—is a kind of miracle.

I borrow a pen and paper from Frank and spend some timeless hours writing poems about the garden, and about Mike. *Caretaker* Mike.

Sitting there in the shade of a blood-orange tree, my mind is made up: never again shall I call our guest the Fisher King. He's Caretaker Mike.

And I resolve to be more patient. With myself. With everyone.

And I'm going to end the Clamor Family nonsense.

I march into the house, find Charmaine, and tell her we're going to visit her parents.

"You're going to talk to my mom?"

"I'm going to hand-deliver their adorable dog to them. I don't see how she can't talk to me—unless she wants to pretend Chareze doesn't exist, either."

Charmaine's eyes widen. "Really? I mean, it's a lovely idea. But—you know how my mom can be."

I laugh. "Yes. I have some idea."

I assure Charmaine that's it's all going to be all right—and it is.

That evening, I show up unannounced holding the cutest little puppy in the world. How could it not be all right? Mom Clamor hugs me—and immediately offers me something to eat, which is her way of saying "all is forgiven." Dad Clamor shakes my hand—and wonders if I want to play a game of chess, which is his way of saying "I'm glad you're here."

I say nothing about the year and a half of getting ghosted. That's all in the past. The Clamors have a puppy to care for now, an impossibly cute mop of fur who doesn't worry about who offended whom. Chareze has forced me to admit I really miss having a sweet dog in the house, a special friend to care for, and whatever foolish disagreements the humans have clung to, whatever sins of pride and ego—they're all irrelevant in the face of her unconditional, oblivious canine love.

To no one's surprise, the parents suggest that maybe it might, perhaps, if it wasn't too much of a problem, possibly be best if Chareze continued to stay with us for a little while longer. Until she's fully housebroken.

"Of course," I say.

We decamp with doggie toys and treats, wet wipes and baggies. It's official: she's moving in.

On the ride home, with Chareze barfing demurely in my lap, my wife looks at me differently, as though she's only now discovering she married a relatively decent fellow. Charmaine says repeatedly, "I'm so happy. I'm so happy." She shakes her head, searching for words. "Seeing the whole family together . . . talking to each other . . ."

When we arrive in the early evening, our other new boarder isn't there. But he's left a note on the back porch, printed in block letters. I find it pinned beneath a four-pack of artisanal ginger ale, the same kind The Editor gifted us in lieu of wine.

PAINTING IS DONE. GOT SOMETHING FOR MK. YOUR
FAVORITE.

He signs it:

– CARETAKER MIKE

ELEVEN

Resurrection

Four days later, Chareze is dead.

Walking home from yoga in the park, she's hit in a crosswalk by a truck running the light. I'm a couple of feet away, spared, but I might as well have been killed in that horrible, frozen moment.

It's an accident, yes. But it could have been prevented.

I failed to protect her. I failed to take care of her. She was walking by my side and she wasn't wearing a leash.

I'm responsible for her death.

Her lost life, all the human pain and suffering to come: I'm the cause. My carelessness. My over-confidence. My arrogance.

Cradling Chareze's lifeless body, knowing there's nothing to be done—I die, right there on Hollywood Boulevard.

The Michael Konik who was born in 1965 dies on a sunny July morning in 2016. All my shortcomings, my conceits and self-delusions—they're crashing down, exposed as flimsy facades hiding the broken person cowering behind them. Now the frightened little man, stripped bare and defenseless, overcome with self-loathing, shrinks inside what's left of himself, a black hole leading to nothingness, until, finally, he disappears.

He's dead. He's gone.

There are plenty of finely composed "grief memoirs" extant. Many of them find beauty in the pain of loss, and, surely, the genre is useful to many readers in reconciling profound sorrow with a joyous life. This story is not one of those. No one will be served by a pornographically detailed account of our family's particular tragedy, the terrible anguish of senseless (and preventable) loss.

But there's one essential detail to share: To go on living, to facilitate healing and somehow move forward, I vow to not let Chareze's death be in vain.

That's all.

That's how I manage the unmanageable. That's how I survive.

I vow that the new Michael will be a much better version of the old Michael. He'll be less like what he once was and more like Miss Adorable. Anything else is failure.

We knew her for only one month before her death, but Chareze Clamor touched us, changed us, as though she'd spent fifteen or more years, a whole doggie existence, as part of our family. Her entire life was five months. A puppy. She weighed maybe seven pounds, much of it hair. Chareze was a tiny physical presence. Ephemeral. How amazing—and inspiring—to realize the immense power coursing through that tiny canine body. Some would call it *spiritual power*.

Everyone loved her. Adults and children, dogs and puppies. Even the doves in our garden. Chareze projected a yogic calm and confidence; she was never aggressive and she was seldom afraid; she was ready to befriend every creature she encountered, even Polche, the neighborhood's grouchiest old snarler.

Chareze seemed determined to love the world, and the world was inclined to love her back.

Shouldn't I be more like that? Shouldn't we all?

The power of her cheerful physical presence—when it's taken away from us suddenly, shockingly, a shroud of unrelenting despair overwhelms the homestead. When I return home with Chareze's limp body, swaddled in a towel, like a baby, Caretaker Mike immediately understands what's happened. As I sob uncontrollably, trying to explain—a truck, a crosswalk—he places a hand on my shoulder and shakes his head. Soon he's sniffling and dabbing at his eyes. "I'll dig her grave," Mike says.

He buries Chareze beneath the tangerine tree in front of the cabin, next to her favorite spot. He covers the hole with bricks and a slab of countertop granite. He puts a glass candle in one corner and a tea candle in a holder hanging from the tree.

Caretaker Mike lights the candles and sits on the bench beside Chareze's final resting place. He stays there for hours, sniffling and shaking his head.

Charmaine and I both have trouble sleeping or eating for several days. I can barely talk, let alone function. Now I understand what PTSD feels like: irreconcilable shock and pain that feels like it won't ever stop.

When they learn the news, my friends Scotty and Ryan rush over and sit bedside as I moan and wail, trapped in a looping nightmare that I already know isn't a bad dream.

I know I must tell Mom and Dad Clamor, and I must do so in person. And I must be prepared for their hatred and disgust. I understand their feelings. I feel likewise. No one can hate me more than I hate myself.

The night after Chareze's death, Scotty drives us to Canoga Park to tell the parents. I'm doing all I can not to hyperventilate in the car. "Can you do this?" Charmaine asks, her eyes puffy.

We walk to their apartment from the parking lot in a trance. "I don't know."

Somehow, I do. I tell them.

Dad doesn't understand at first. He asks Mom to explain to him in Tagalog. Wailing, collapsing into his arms, Mom makes him understand. His face registers unbearable pain. And then he goes catatonic.

I say "I'm so sorry" over and over, as though the words could somehow make it all better.

Mom and Charmaine lie down on the bed, holding each other. Howling in pain.

I am the cause of this.

I will not cause this again.

I will be better.

I don't know how long we're there, excreting the misery. Eventually, sometime in the night, we depart.

On the ride back, I feel like I'm going to survive. I can breathe. If the common wisdom is correct, getting through each successive day will get a little easier.

And it does, gradually. Seeing a trauma therapist helps. Weeping helps. Talking about Chareze helps. Caretaker Mike and I sit near her grave two days after her death. I tell him that Chareze was like all the other great things in life. Not until they're gone do you fully realize their magnificence. I start crying again, "Chareze filled my heart."

"Oh, yes, oh, yes she did," he agrees. "Go ahead, let it out. You gotta talk about it, that's the only way you're gonna to feel better. The last two days—well, yeah, I've been really worried about you. I mean, when MK stops talking—that ain't like you."

"Thanks, Mike," I sniffle. "And thank you for making such a nice gravesite, and for being such a great friend to Chareze, and—you know she really loved you, right?"

"Yeah, I know, I know."

We sit in silence.

Mike chokes back a sob. "You gotta keep talking," he says, "that's the only way you're gonna feel better."

I wipe my face with the back of my arm. "OK. Well, I guess

you could say that little doggie cracked my heart wide open. That's what the therapist suggested, and I think she's right on." The act of cracking often involves pain, but it also involves widening the aperture through which kindness and compassion flow. Chareze broke my heart and gave me a bigger one.

For the past seven years or so since our friend Ella died, I wasn't ready to adopt another dog. Chareze came into our life not by choice but by chance; we were doing a good deed. Taking her in meant getting over my lifelong prejudice against purebreds and toy dogs. That wasn't difficult. Chareze convinced me no matter how small the package she bears, the delivery girl brings as much joy as any larger creature.

She taught me that love is omnipresent if you let it be.

Chareze was—and I know this is going to sound crazy—Chareze was *gifted*. She was extraordinarily intelligent, learning new behaviors and tricks on an almost daily basis. When I'm drowning in the "if only" and "should have been" phase of grieving, I fixate on the idea that Chareze was destined to become a highly trained therapy dog, just like Ella. She possessed the aptitude and the composure for the job. *Chareze would have been a tremendous therapy dog.*

"She already was a therapy dog!" Caretaker Mike says. "She was!"

He's right. Chareze didn't have a license or a cute vest, but she was already doing the work. For the month she lived in our home, she healed all of us in one way or another. She cured me of whatever neuroses prevented me from moving on from Ella and getting a new puppy. I learned from Chareze that my newly opened heart is ready (and eager) for a canine friend amid the writer's solitude. Ready to love.

As we recover from the loss, pouring ourselves in our work—I write poems about her and Caretaker Mike—Charmaine and I fantasize, wouldn't it be wonderful to adopt a puppy with some of Chareze's best qualities? *Calm, happy, confident, un-aggressive, affectionate, playful, smart.* Not one that looks like her or necessarily the same breed—but a puppy with Chareze's personality and vibe? Is that possible?

Yes. Everything's possible. The worst and the best. Tragedies happen, and so do miracles.

Searching online independently, both of us identify a potential candidate for adoption. When Charmaine asks me to check out the profile of a certain black, shaggy mongrel, it's the same black, shaggy mongrel I've been returning to repeatedly, at the end of each new search.

"You like her, too?" We convince ourselves, *it's meant to be.*

Maybe it is. Charm and I believe we've found Chareze's kindred spirit harbored comfortably in a ten-week-old mutt the adoption agency calls "Henrietta." They claim she's part *Shih Tzu,* and possibly many other breeds. Her parentage is slightly mysterious. The runt of an accidental litter, and the only black one among a bunch of tans, Henrietta grew up at Hope Ranch in Temecula, Southern California, where the rescue dogs (from pit bulls to poodles) live outdoors, uncaged. This pup likes being outside, and she likes other animals.

After one twenty-minute, love-at-first-sight meeting, we take her home.

In the car, she cuddles on my lap—and then barfs on my thighs, duly consecrating our new love. I feel reborn.

It feels so very good to be alive again.

For her soulful, deep brown eyes, we name her Billie, after Billie Holiday. Full name: Billie Henrietta Konik.

When we arrive back at Vista Street, we call out to Caretaker Mike, "Hey, Mike! Can you come up here, please? There's someone who wants to meet you." We told him we were going to Temecula to "interview" a potential candidate; we told him there was no guarantee we'd come home with a new puppy.

"Hello!" he exclaims. "Hello!" He's grinning so widely we can see his toothless gums, like two slices of pale watermelon. "C'mere! C'mere!"

"This is Billie," I say, handing her to Caretaker Mike. She licks his face, which, even with semi-regular washing, still must taste quite delicious to a puppy.

He nuzzles her, talking in a baby voice. "*Heh-whoa. Heh-whoa! Beh-wee! Beh-wee da Kid!*"

She's wagging her tail like crazy. They seem to like each other.

When we let our scrawny new friend loose in the back yard, which Caretaker Mike puppy-proofs with chicken wire and plywood, Billie quickly finds a few favorite lying down spots on her new "ranch": beneath a rose bush to nibble on; atop a leaf pile near the lemon verbena; beside the geranium pot. But her joy place, the place she returns to every day, every morning, is in a stand of tall grass beside Caretaker Mike's cabin, just across from Chareze's grave.

Love does go on. It doesn't end. Let us count ourselves lucky whenever our heart is rent wide open and love flows through us, for a minute, a month, a lifetime.

The grief ends. The remorse eventually ends. Yes, I wish I'd done better, been better, when it mattered. But I'm powerless to change the old me. I can only change the new me.

If I'm able—and I know I'm able—to resurrect a version of Michael Konik that's more like the person I wish to become and less like the person I used to be, then, I reason, Chareze's "meaningless" death won't be entirely a senseless waste.

These are the stories we tell ourselves to make it through the night, through days of sobbing and fasting, through a lifetime. Maybe they're convenient fictions, maybe they're the gospel truth.

I don't know; I just know they work. These stories work. They make sense of nonsense. They're maps; they guide us out of self-cultivated jungles and into gentle meadows that were there all along, even as we suffered.

The stories—and the clarity they offer—are always there waiting to be discovered every time we choose to be fully alive.

I watch Billie "the Kid" Konik cavorting in the garden with her new Uncle Mike, who looks happier than I've ever seen him. *Thank you, Billie*, I think.

And I think, *Thank you, Chareze. I'm sorry. I'm so sorry I didn't protect you better. I hope you will forgive me. And I thank you.*

Chareze tells me, *I only want you to be happy. That's all I ever wanted. Be happy! I don't want you to be sad. That would not please me. Take care of each other and everyone be happy.*

Caretaker Mike, Uncle Mike, the Fisher King—all the men who make this man—he's happy today. I can see it. He made a new friend. He met someone who won't judge him on his appearance, only the quality of his belly rubs. Caretaker Mike is happy.

And so is Charmaine, who holds little Billie in her lap like a toddler, all four paws pointed out and head resting on Charm's chest. We take our first family portraits on Charm's phone, and both of us cry and cry. But this time the tears taste like relief. We can feel good again. We can be well.

Billie falls asleep in my arms her first night at her new home. As I tuck her into her doggie bed—Chareze's doggie bed—I feel better about being alive.

Soon, I hope, I'll feel better about being me.

TWELVE

Birthday Gifts

⸺

I t's Caretaker Mike's 63rd birthday. Other than his imaginary family with Selena, we're the only ones he has. Us and Billie the Kid.

Charmaine, who seizes any opportunity to bake a gluten-free cake, suggests we host a small birthday party.

"The three of us? This is going to an intimate get-together."

"Well, with Billie it's four," Charmaine says. "And we can invite Aya and Polche, and maybe some of the people from the Elderberries community?"

Though he's initially reticent—"No, no, no," Caretaker Mike says, waving away the idea—eventually he assents to a small party with a limited guest list: three nice fellows with appropriate security clearances, Daniel, Caleb, and Ellington, from the Elderberries community.

And he has a special request: "You think we could have cheeseburgers and fries? In-N-Out?"

Resisting the urge for vegan speechifying, I tell him, "We'll make it happen."

Waiting in the drive-thru line across from Hollywood High School, musing on the rampant American Exceptionalism proudly on display here at the industrial meat outlet, I keep telling myself, *this isn't about you.*

And when that doesn't work, I tell myself, *you're being of service*.

Maybe it's true. Maybe I am being of service, putting someone else's desires before my own. I could certainly see how one might argue I'm accomplishing the opposite.

Either way, I do it. I bring home a heaping box of double-doubles and animal fries.

We convene the party on the back deck, the "lanai." Unbidden, each guest has procured for Caretaker Mike something useful. Aya gives him an LED reading light; Ellington, a transistor radio; Daniel, new socks. With each gift, Mike (barely) grunts "thank you" and then quickly changes the subject to an innovative metafiction no one but he understands.

Not long later, Charmaine unveils her red velvet chocolate muffins, but we don't get to sing "Happy Birthday" to Caretaker Mike. Probably embarrassed by his digestive problems, he collects a plate of (fast) food, mumbles his thanks to everyone for coming, and summarily decamps to the cabin, where, he tells us, he's got a lot of calls and messages to return.

We remainders huddle together and converse in hushed tones. "I often wonder what the real story is," I say. "He must have a family somewhere. Maybe they're missing him today." Then I realize today might not even be Mike's real birthday; maybe he just had a hankering for cheeseburgers and fries.

"Have you investigated?" Ellington wonders.

"Not thoroughly," I admit. "I'm never sure if *anything* Mike tells us is true. I mean, it's true to *him* . . ."

Later that night, after the guests have departed and the dishes have been done, I start plugging search terms into the Interweb, scattered scraps of information torn from Mike's monologues. He could be telling the truth, or he could be a kind of Keyser Söze from *The Usual Suspects*, a captivating storyteller who improvises his narrative from any available source material. But the "real" story is out there, somewhere, in the ether.

I plug in his name and date of birth. Nothing.

I try searching military records from the Vietnam era. Nothing.

I try his name plus Selena Gomez. Nothing. Nothing but many, many photos and news items about Selena Gomez, who does not appear to be a mother of two.

There are many Michael Baileys in the world, I discover. But the one going by that name living in our cabin leaves no electronic trace. If he has relatives, they don't seem to be connected by common addresses, or even cities.

Is it possible Fisher King Mike gave me the name Michael James Bailey because he knew it would come up clean when searching for arrest warrants or a criminal record? Is his name even Michael?

Who is this guy?

Caretaker Mike dines with an audience, Billie the Kid and Polche.

THIRTEEN

Female Problems

———

Caretaker Mike's ambitious project list remains a nice theoretical idea with no practical use. He can't work. He can't do anything, really. His "wife" is enduring a serious health crisis.

"It's lupus-related," Mike whispers, staring blankly at the ground.

We're standing outside the cabin. "Oh. Sorry to hear that. I was starting to wonder why we haven't seen you all day."

"This is bad. Might have to cancel the whole tour." He's shaking his head and chewing his bottom lip, visibly upset about his stricken spouse.

"Anything I can do, Mike?" I ask, hoping to move things along, hoping to shift the narrative to my version of reality.

"No, see, this is bad."

He spends most of the day, a gorgeously sunny day, sequestered inside the cabin, emerging semi-regularly to smoke and "check" his sugar. If he were one of my "normal" friends—and I'm not sure I actually have any that fit that description—I would probably say, "Bro, this is weird. Come on, man!" With Caretaker Mike I have to be careful. Contradicting his central biographical detail would be a kind of existential negation, and no one likes that. We all have elaborate stories we tell about ourselves, stories that help us believe in our individuality, our uniqueness, though we exist in a vast cosmos of anonymity. On one hand, Mike's fiction is probably more peculiar than most; yet, on the other hand, seriously, come on, man . . . am I supposed to play along with the fantasy?

Surely this couldn't all be an elaborate scheme to get out of working on handyman projects, could it?

I check the latest Selena news. Seems there actually is a problem, but it's not lupus. The young singer is checking into rehab. Again. *Hmm. This is going to be difficult to discuss . . .*

Going along with Mike's auto-immune disorder fiction won't help, but correcting the record, I've already learned a few dozen times, won't help, either, and would probably make the situation worse. Calmly and rationally insisting that Caretaker Mike's beliefs are untrue would be about as effective as arguing the meaning of "drain the swamp" with a Trump supporter. If Mike believes Selena Gomez is suffering from lupus, and that her malady somehow prevents him from doing handyman jobs—or anything else, really, besides smoking cigarettes—then it's true (for him).

What I see: A man incapacitated by worry, convinced that he's involved in a terrible health crisis an objective observer would consider imaginary.

What I wonder: How many of us nominally healthy folk are just like Caretaker Mike?

At times, Charmaine and I are, for sure. Our paralyzing fears and concerns seem "real" to us, but, then, so do Mike's (to him). Our thoughts, our beliefs, become our reality. As anyone who's tried to establish a meditation practice immediately learns, sometimes it's hard to tell who's in charge. Are we controlling our thoughts, or are they controlling us? Even with puppy Billie napping beside me as I try to write, I can't stop replaying Chareze's death in my mind, continually reliving one of the worst moments of my life. For no reason at all, out of nowhere, there's that terrible thought again. The truck. The accident. The way she was looking at me . . .

I tell myself, *I can't stop replaying this awful thought*—until the day arrives when I *can* stop, the day I decide conclusively that I must stop torturing myself.

I know that day will come for me. I'm not sure it will for Caretaker Mike.

For three days and nights, he emerges from the cabin only to use the toilet. He doesn't appear to be eating. (He does appear to be smoking.) He radiates decay and despair and foul aromas.

His self-concocted crisis couldn't come at a worse time. Seems on one of his sporadic visits to "the store" to procure Coke, Mike recently lost his phone—the one on which he "checks his sugar"—and all sorts of important people who are trying to get in touch with him can't find him and it's a big problem and his family needs him and if he doesn't get the phone someone's going to have to drive him to the Valley and, and this terrible situation requires a new phone.

For reasons that are very hard to explain to anyone who hasn't tried to have a reasonable problem-solving discussion with a bipolar schizophrenic jacked up on corn syrup and nicotine, I agree to get Mike a new phone.

I just want this chapter in his jumbled life to end, for circumstances to change. For things to be *better*.

This explanation sounds suspicious when I present it to Charmaine, who reminds me that I'm enabling negative behavior—something I wouldn't do with puppy Billie. "Just because Mike's unstable doesn't mean you have to be," she says.

Strictly speaking, no. But what about when one member of a married couple, say, the husband, finds himself suddenly suffering from allergies to common household items that one week earlier caused no reaction? Do you tell this man he's crazy, that it's all in his head? Or do you try to accept his reality, as irrational and difficult to understand as it seems? Do you help him, even though he doesn't seem to you to be ill?

I find myself taking Mike's side. "If replacing his phone will snap him out of this state, I'm willing to try."

Eye-rolling. Sighing. "You don't even own a smartphone yourself and you're buying one for someone who's just going to lose it?"

I shrug. She has a point.

The phone Mike says he "needs" is a Samsung Galaxy, which seems to me like an inordinately fancy one—although, Charmaine's right: I don't have a smartphone. I'm probably disqualified from opining on these wondrous devices, other than to commend their alchemical ability to take glucose readings from diabetic celebrity husbands.

After a few more fits of effortful rationalizing in which I convince myself this act of charity is for the best, we procure the indispensable device on a pay-as-you-go, no-plan basis. I buy the first month's load for $50. Mike assures me he'll deduct the purchase cost from future handyman earnings.

I nod and say "that sounds good," and it does, kind of. But I've already earmarked the funds for my Donations Never to Be Returned foundation. If I'm wrong, I'll be surprised.

What's not surprising is that Caretaker Mike can't seem to get his new $50 phone card to load properly onto his new $200 Galaxy. When I try to help—and I'm the last guy you want helping with your tech needs—Mike insists there's only one solution: He needs a new card and another $50, otherwise the ongoing Selena crisis will get out of hand, because no one knows how to reach him, and his family, and, and, there's nothing more important than family, and if they can't reach him, you know, it's bad. It's bad.

I attempt calmness. I attempt to be conciliatory. I offer Caretaker Mike the use of my office phone, a landline. Inside the main house.

Great idea! Generous. Kind. Going above and beyond for someone who doesn't seem to be able to help himself. Problem solved.

Silly me. Before I get carried away on a raging current of self-congratulation, the intended recipient of my largesse corrects the record. With great certainty that borders on barely contained exasperation, Mike makes me understand *only a new phone card* will do. (A landline, regrettably, does not offer access to concert videos and Instagram.) Each sensible solution I propose he dismisses as unworkable, for reasons that make no sense except to him.

I say, "no." I tell him I'm not going to do it.

He throws up his hands. "Well, I guess I'm gonna have to go walk to the Valley," and disappears into the cabin, where he sulks for the next day and a half, until Charmaine-to-the-rescue deciphers the fine print on the back of the "broken" call-card and loads the minutes on his behalf. "Let me try this," she says, punching in various digits. "Here," she says, handing me the phone after about thirty seconds of fiddling. "Should work."

I call my office landline. *Ring.* Feigning shock, Charmaine says, "I guess Mike didn't need a new card."

When we deliver the resurrected phone to him, Mike grunts his thanks and immediately connects to the Web. The news there is grim: "Selena's gonna have to cancel her whole European Tour."

Charmaine and I look at each other, not knowing what to say, what to do. Laughing isn't an option.

As a distraction from the ongoing tragedy, an attempt to pull him out of his funk, Charmaine and I arrange a Monopoly game for four: us, Aya, and Caretaker Mike. He mentioned once he liked board games, and we figure some socialization would be good for him, for all of us. Aya has only played the Japanese version, and she's tickled to see the original, with American property names. Her dog Polche, the senior grouch, starts the evening bossy and overbearing with puppy Billie, but by the end of the night they're best friends, snuggling on the floor.

They have plenty of time to bond. It's a *loooong* game, a play-by-the-rules, no-free-parking-jackpot, four-and-a-half-hour game. The brutal capitalist slog is extended somewhat by Caretaker Mike's insistence that no matter what property he lands on he's only interested in buying the green properties.

Boardwalk! "Nah, nah. Oh, no. Too expensive."

"But they pay the most when someone lands on them," Charmaine explains.

Mike chortles. "Nah, nah. That don't happen. See, what people don't understand is, you spend all your money on building hotels—what does that cost?—and then you're broke before anyone stays there."

I'm not going to argue the finer points of property ownership with a homeless man, fictional Atlantic City or otherwise. "All right, then," I announce, "Madame Banker, I'll open the bidding for Boardwalk at one hundred dollars. And if anyone doubts my seriousness, I got more paper here to back up my intentions."

The bidding goes on until Aya drops out at $300, I fold at the list price of $500, and Charmaine overpays ($600 final bid) for the property no one ever lands on. Mike shakes his head sadly—*when will they ever learn*—as Charmaine the Banker pays herself for the title card.

Every time Mike lands somewhere (other than Pacific, North Carolina, or Pennsylvania) we have an auction. He's the car. I'm the hat; Charmaine the thimble; Aya the dog, of course. After a few times around the board it becomes clear to everyone—everyone except Mike, I think—that Mike's not very good at Monopoly. Which seems about right. What would it say about the system we use to organize ourselves if people who were so bad at the game of life they end up on the streets could play the game of Monopoly, the game of acquire and acquire until you bankrupt all the others, like a champion? That would be where irony tiptoes beside heartbreak.

The object of the game—to enrich yourself and ruin everyone else—was once very different. When it was first patented, in 1904, by a woman named Elizabeth Magie, it was called *The Landlord's Game*, and it was meant to illustrate the pernicious impact of economic privilege, using dice and fake money to demonstrate how rentals inexorably impoverish tenants. (In her version, the person who started with the least and managed to double her stake was the big winner.) Indeed, when Magie approached Parker Brothers with an updated version, in 1924, George Parker rejected it on the grounds that her approach was "too political." In 1932, Magie published her game with another company. They called it *Prosperity*.

In the current iteration, only one player ultimately prospers. After a couple of hours of buying low and selling high, our homeless guest goes broke first, unable to pay a hotel bill at one of Charmaine's orange fleabags.

Before he excuses himself, I remark how fun this was and suggest that other social occasions might be a good idea. "Like, I don't know, we could see a comedy show at Nerdmelt."

He scoffs. "Who?"

"Whoever wants. You and Aya. Anyone who might enjoy a laugh."

"No, see, Aya ain't gonna enjoy it. She don't get American humor."

We all look at him blankly. "No, she *don't*! I'm just sayin', she ain't gonna enjoy herself."

I propose we do a test. "Mike, go ahead. Tell your best joke. Let's see if Aya gets it."

"No, no, no, no, no."

"OK. I will." I tell one of my favorites, about the Jewish guy who converts to Christianity to win $100. (Punchline: "Is that all you people think about? Money?") Aya nods silently.

"See? She don't get it!" Mike gets up to go. "And besides, no offense or nothing, Aya, but, no, no, sorry, I can't be seen in public with another woman. Especially not at a time when my wife needs me the most and, and, you know, I can't be there for her. And she understands, but, no, no, I can't. The photographers would have a field day. Sorry."

I turn to Charmaine. "So I guess Mike isn't going to comedy with Aya."

"No," she says, deadpan. "He can't."

Aya nods, although she's not quite able to follow the gist of our conversation.

"No, no, I can't. Can't do it. I already have enough problems to deal with. Don't need another one. No offense, Aya."

She nods affirmatively and smiles.

At least there's one lady Caretaker Mike has no problem being seen with. She's a furry black mop of hair begging for popcorn way past her bedtime. "Come on, Billie!" he calls. "Walk me back to the cabin. Good night, everyone. And good luck. Hope you all win."

If only that were possible.

Mike and his best friend, Billie the Kid.

FOURTEEN

Crisis

‎—

After a couple months with Caretaker Mike in residence, Charmaine and I feel confident leaving him alone on our property. He's inscrutable and exasperating and heartbreaking—but he's also trustworthy, never stealing, never touching anything without prior permission. (He may be the most conscientious house guest we've ever hosted.) His "leave no trace" ethos has given us the idea that we can depart town for the weekend with the main house's back doors open, allowing Caretaker Mike unfettered access to our home, where he can work on his extensive project list.

Our families and friends think we're the crazy ones. "You're letting a homeless guy with mental problems go in and out of your house without you being there?" my brother Eric yells into the phone.

"Yes."

"Because?"

I think for a second. "It's hard for me to explain why it's the right call."

"What if he . . ." his voice trails off.

What? Takes something that's not his? He's got nowhere to go.

"Eric," I tell my brother, "Mike is weird, for sure. But he's also a decent person. The way he interacts with Billie, the care he shows for our house—he's really a lovely guy, just very troubled."

My brother (and everyone else I know) is concerned that Mike's sickness will cause him to do something horrible while in residence, that I'll inherit his troubles. But I stand by my read of the situation. Leaving Mike alone with our house, all our property, our entire material life (except the car), is not going to be a problem.

"Not going to be a problem," I declare.

We're returning to San Diego, this time with Billie the Kid, or "Kid," as Caretaker Mike calls her. As I was trying to explain to my brother, their burgeoning relationship is delightful, beautiful. They're great friends. I chuckle every morning when I let little Billie out for her morning micturition and she runs immediately to Weed Hollow Cabin, where she scratches at the door, steps backwards a few feet to wait (all the time wiggling her tail and her butt, and most of her lower back), and then disappears inside when her Uncle Mike cracks open the door. She usually doesn't return for almost an hour. What happens inside the cabin, I can only imagine. (Mike's version: "Nothin'. Just visiting.") Maybe Billie is already self-training to be a therapy dog, lolling on his bed and kissing his face.

My biggest concern about leaving this weekend isn't the house. It's how lonely Uncle Mike is going to be without having his best buddy on hand to greet him in the morning and to supervise his handiwork.

There's plenty to accomplish. Per his request, we provide Caretaker Mike with an extensive "to do" list of little niggling problems to be fixed. A balky light switch. A slow drain. A rusty hinge. He looks it over with absolutely no comment. I take that to mean "this is such elementary stuff I'm almost insulted to have to address any of it."

We also leave him an extensive list of phone numbers to call in case of emergency. Plus, we have his number *and* we're going to call the office landline every morning at 9 a.m. If all goes as planned, Mike will answer the call and let us know everything is copacetic. There's no way for anything to go wrong.

I would like to stress: *A communication plan has been put into place. There is no way for anything to go wrong.*

And there really better not be. Because Charmaine is viewing this weekend as a test. She agrees that Caretaker Mike has demonstrated some level of trustworthiness, as well as intermittent moments of handyman brilliance. She also remains keenly aware of Mike's unreliability, his fantastically complicated explanations for why he can't function normally, his terrible cigarette and Coke habit. Our departure will be a kind of final exam. If he passes, he'll earn more of our faith.

I don't consider the "if he doesn't," because that's not an option.

The afternoon we arrive in San Diego, I make my first check-in call. Am I worried when I dial Mike on both his magical diabetes-monitoring phone and my office landline and he answers neither?

I'm not worried; I'm annoyed. All I want is for Caretaker Mike to keep up his end of the bargain, keep his word, follow through. Sometimes, difficult as it is for me to accept, and for reasons I can't wholly comprehend, he just can't. He's not able. This time, though, he *must*.

Charmaine and I have a spectacular day at Dog Beach with Billie, who, I learn, is determined to make friends with everyone, dog or human. I also learn that she's not a naturally inclined water dog, not like the Labradors and retrievers crashing into the surf to snatch their tennis balls and Frisbees. Instead, Billie's more of a sand dog. She likes running in it, rolling in it, wiping out after a game of circular chase in it. I watch her frolicking, so joyously *alive*, and a wave of tears catches me off-guard. I don't know if they're from sorrow for Chareze or gratitude for Billie the Kid, or a combination. But they come, and then they go, and afterward I feel cleansed and a wee bit better about all I've done and haven't done.

Mildly elated, newly refreshed, I call Mike again. He doesn't answer.

The next morning at 9 a.m.: no answer.

That afternoon: no answer.

He's busy working. He's engrossed with his tasks. He's doing everything in his power to take care of our home like we've been trying to take care of him. He's fine. Last time we left he didn't answer my call, either. Everything's all right.

This is what I tell myself to drown out the persistent voice in my head morosely whispering, "Trusting this guy was a bad idea."

He's *fine*.

All weekend I call periodically. No answer.

I don't tell Charmaine. She's got a concert performance to worry about; she doesn't need additional stress, especially over theoretical "what ifs." I'll deal with Caretaker Mike's inscrutable choices alone. *This has happened before*, I remind myself. There's an explanation for Mike's silence. I can't say exactly what at this moment, and it might not make sense to a rational thinker, but there's got to be an explanation, and it will all be clear soon.

On Sunday afternoon, we head for home, with Billie snoozing in Charmaine's lap. About an hour south of Los Angeles, while we're plodding through Anaheim, my phone rings. It's Mike!

He's in a hospital emergency room somewhere in the Valley.

For reasons only he understands, Mike left the house without identification, money, or keys. Just walked away, like he wasn't planning on returning. For reasons only he understands, Mike left the keys to the house and driveway gate (and all his other possessions) inside the cabin, and the house completely unlocked and open to uninvited visitors. How he ended up near Tarzana, how he was admitted to a hospital, we'll never know.

He tries to explain why he put our home at risk. He tries to make me understand why he couldn't do his projects, why he couldn't stay on site until we returned. Nothing he says makes any sense. Telling him I don't understand only incites another meandering monologue filled with contradictions, impossibilities, and fabrications. Whatever has happened—and I really can't say with certainty—Mike's tenuous grip on consensus reality has slipped. He's lost his connection to himself. He's lost.

But now that we're back in town, he wants to return to Hollywood. He wants to come "home" to Billie and the cabin and a couple of kindhearted Samaritans who seem to have great difficulty saying "enough is enough."

Mike tells me, "I need you to pick me up. In the Valley." He wants me—someone, anyone—to rescue him from his bad decisions.

I want to be helpful and kind and Christ-like, but I'm furious (mostly with myself for being such a fool). "Absolutely not," I tell him. "I'm not going to be your chauffeur, Mike. You managed to get wherever you are. You managed to leave our house unattended and unlocked. And now you'll have to manage to get yourself back. Or find someplace else to sleep."

Chastened by his lunacy, regretful for having trusted an untrustworthy man with my home, I've finally learned my lesson. No more.

"No, no, see, what people don't understand—"

"No, Mike," I interrupt him. "I'm not picking you up. Charmaine isn't picking you up. We're done. You're on your own."

I stress that he's still welcome to sleep in Weed Hollow Cabin, that we're not kicking him out and onto the streets. But we're not going to be his livery service.

I hang up and begin apologizing to Charmaine for my poor judgment. "It's over," I assure her. "We're done." She's surprisingly accepting, possibly out of relief at finally having the disruptive force known as Mike—the Fisher King, Uncle Mike, Caretaker Mike, Michael James Bailey—out of her life.

Normalcy, that's all we want at this point. A somewhat normal life.

For Mike, and tens-of-thousands like him, a somewhat normal life means hustling. Constantly hustling. In order to survive on the streets for any amount of time, you develop a set of skills to keep yourself alive, including an ability to persuade others to help—with food, with clothing, with money. Unbeknownst to Charmaine and I, while we're traversing the final stretch of freeways leading home, a desperate Caretaker Mike calls his Monopoly buddy Aya, crying and screaming, begging and bullying her into shuttling him in her car from the Valley to Cedars-Sinai hospital, a renowned medical facility fifteen minutes from our house. He tells her he'll die if she doesn't get him. He tells her we're out of town and unreachable and it's an emergency and we left her number in case of emergencies and this is an emergency and he's going to die if she doesn't help and she's got to help him because his life is in her hands and there's no other choice unless she wants him to die.

His plea is delivered in English, Aya's second language, the one she sometimes struggles with. What our Japanese friend hears sounds like a genuine crisis, not the rantings of a seriously ill man.

Before consulting with us, she drives out to the Valley to save him.

On the way to Cedars, threatening to use Aya's Honda Element—a white, fur-lined, pink hub-capped Hello Kitty-themed vehicle—as a toilet if she doesn't comply with his wishes, Mike forces her to stop at a 7-11 for Coke and cigarettes.

We know all this because Aya calls us crying, utterly flummoxed at what to do with the sick man stinking up her car, yelling at her to do what he tells her. She says she dropped him at the emergency room and drove away, shaken and disturbed.

Now we're even more furious at Mike. We (I) can't apologize enough for getting Aya involved in our (my) poor decision-making. We (I) failed to inoculate her from the virus that is Mike the Deranged, and now he's infected another innocent bystander. His dysfunction has spread, and I still don't have an antidote other than strictly quarantining the malefactor.

We must insulate ourselves in a protective layer of circumspection. We must avoid contact with volatile Mike. That's the new strategy.

Our house, miraculously, is just as we left it. No damage. No thievery. And not a single project completed—or commenced—in our absence. Just an empty house missing its caretaker.

We're relieved. We're emotionally exhausted. We're done.

For the first time in many months, Charmaine and Billie and I are the only ones home. We have our lives back.

I wonder about Mike, but I don't worry. He's under the supervision of medical professionals. He's the system's reclamation project now.

After spending a night undergoing a battery of expensive diagnostic tests—various MRI scans, blood work—all of them negative, the doctors as Cedars-Sinai inform Mike there's nothing more they can do for him and order him discharged. With nowhere to go but Skid Row, L.A.'s version of Dante's lowest rings conveniently located beside gleaming downtown skyscrapers and freshly gentrified warehouses districts, he summons what must either be courage or oblivious audacity and calls my office phone—the one he never answered while we were away.

"Hey, I'm out. I got no money or a bus pass, so I need you to pick me up. Take me back to Vista Street."

"No," I say, flatly. "I told you before, Mike. We're happy to give you a place to live, but I'm not going to be your chauffeur, especially when you decide to leave the property when we're expecting you to be there." I'm angry, but I'm careful not to kick someone when he's down. The last thing Caretaker Mike needs now is to be told what a fuck-up he is. "Our position remains the same: You're totally welcome here, but no rides."

Instead of arguing, Mike hangs up.

Then, without our knowledge, he bullies another mutual friend, Daniel the Gentle, from the Have Seeds House, into ordering Mike an Uber to deposit him back on Vista Street.

Daniel calls to deliver the news. "Hey! I just got an emergency call from Fisher King Mike, from the emergency room at Cedars."

I brief Daniel on how Mike ended up there, apologize for getting him involved, and ask that he not approve Mike's request.

"Too late," Daniel says. "He's already in the car. I was just calling you to give a heads-up that he's arriving."

Now I'm really steaming. I want to look Mike in the eyes and make him understand how much distress he's brought to our small community of caring friends. I want him to understand the consequences of his behavior. But I've known him long enough to realize he can't understand any of this, not fully, and if he can, he's somehow powerless to stop himself from making one compounding mistake after another. Choose your metaphor: child, puppy, addict. Mike's all of them.

And in some ways, he's me, too. We're all fragile; we're all imperfect; we all want to be loved. We all make terrible mistakes that we later regret.

When Mike shows up at our doorstep that evening around 7 p.m., he's as remorseful and humble as I've ever seen him, his eyes downcast, his shoulders slumped, as though he were bearing a tremendous backpack stuffed with sorrow. I know the feeling. I've *known* the feeling, and not so long ago. I had to face my wife and tell her Chareze was dead. I know what it's like to fall, to fail, to face the world defenselessly. And I know the healing power of acknowledging your failures.

He says, "I've made some bad mistakes."

I know what that feels like.

"I've let a lot of people down in my life, and I know I let you two down."

I know what that feels like. It's a horrible feeling.

"But I ain't gonna let you down anymore." He nods and stares at the ground. "Also," Mike says, "I realized during this whole incident that I'm supposed to be the Caretaker of this place, but I can't take care of nobody else if I don't take care of myself."

Yes. That's how I feel.

"So I'm gonna start doing that. Taking better care of myself."

Charmaine is the first to speak. "That's a great plan, Mike."

"Yeah, no, cuz I gotta do better at that." He nods, he stares. He says, "Do you think I could get a hug?"

We three embrace, with Billie teetering on her hind legs, jumping on our shins.

Charmaine and I agree to let Mike stay another night.

FIFTEEN

The Charmaine Regime

———

The next morning, Charmaine gathers us all on the back deck. "I have an announcement," she says, sounding uncharacteristically officious. "I need you two to listen carefully."

I smile. "Listening!"

Mike looks down and says, "Yes, ma'am."

"OK," Charmaine says. "Thank you for your attention. Uncle Mike," she says, attempting to make eye contact, "I've been thinking about your situation—our situation—a lot, and I think I have a plan that will work for all of us." He continues to look down, seemingly terrified to meet Charmaine's gaze.

She inhales deeply. "Mike, this incident, this latest incident— we can't have anything like that happen again. We can't . . . we have to do better. Now, I don't want you back on the streets, or in a hospital. But I also don't want our home put at risk in any way. I don't want your problems to become bigger problems, you know what I mean?"

He nods silently, cowering.

"So, I've decided. You can stay. We're not going to kick you out. But from now on, from this point on, you're going to have to follow *my* rules, not MK's. You understand, Mike?"

"Yes, ma'am," he mumbles.

"I don't want you to worry about where you're going to sleep, Mike. The cabin is available to you. But only under one condition. I'm going to be in complete control of your diet and wellness. You're going to follow my program. You're going to get better, and I'm going to help you. But it's going to require you letting me manage your diet and your treatments. All your meals. All your vitamins and supplements. Your bodywork. No exceptions. Do you understand what this means, Mike?"

He nods affirmatively, but she can sense he doesn't fully comprehend her dictum.

"What this means, Mike—and MK, I need you to support me on this with no exceptions, none!—what this means is a total change in your lifestyle. What this means is no more Coke. No more cigarettes. No more anything that isn't good for you. We're cutting gluten out of your diet. We're taking out lactose. No more processed sugar. No more anything harmful."

I expect Mike to explain to Charmaine that she doesn't understand his rare form of diabetes (the one that requires three liters of soda a day), his complicated strategy for keeping his blood sugar "straight." But he stays silent, looking down, nodding.

"It's going to be rough at first, very rough," Charmaine predicts. "But I'm going to help you get through this, Mike. You're going to feel better. Everything's going to be better."

She places a comforting hand on his shoulder. "We care about you, Uncle Mike. So does Billie! And we just want you to be well."

He nods, attentive but mute.

"And so, for now, until you've earned back our trust, things are going to change." Charmaine looks at me, as though her declaration is meant for my consideration, not Mike's. "For now, we're not going to give you money for the jobs you do. I'm sorry, Uncle Mike. You've shown us you can't handle that yet. So, instead of money, we're going to compensate you by providing your room, your clothing, your meals, and your healthcare. That's the plan."

Her deal is non-negotiable, Charmaine tells us. It's her way or the highway—and he's welcome to leave any time he wants. "Mike, I want to stress, this isn't a prison. You're absolutely free to go. But as long as you're living with us, those are the new rules. They're not meant to punish you. I really just want the situation to be better. For all of us."

He says nothing, staring down.

"Mike, do you understand?" Charmaine asks.

"Yes, ma'am."

"MK, do *you* understand?"

"Yes, ma'am, I do," I reply, smiling, quite enjoying being the good cop for a few minutes, watching Charmaine be the meanie.

"We're all going to take care of each other," she announces. "We're all going to get better."

Caretaker Mike finally speaks out. "I'm going to do what you say," he pledges. "I'll do my best. But do you think I could get some help with my follow-up appointments at Cedars? I don't have any way to get there . . ."

"Yes, of course," Charmaine says. "Of course, we'll help you with your appointments, Mike. MK can go with you. Right?"

"Oh, yeah. Sure," I say.

Mike nods. "And, and, do you think I could just finish my last pack? I only got a couple of cigarettes left?"

"No," Charmaine says flatly. "You've had your last cigarette on this property. And your last Coke, and your last Monster and candy bar and Wendy's. That's the old way. We're not doing that anymore. We're not going to let you poison yourself."

He doesn't try to correct her "misunderstanding" of his unique medical situation. He doesn't reiterate how he's terminally ill with a spinal tumor. To my astonishment, Mike simply nods and says, "OK. Yes, ma'am."

"It's a new beginning," Charmaine announces, perhaps as much for my benefit as Mike's. "We're moving forward."

Stifling tears, Mike grunts his thanks, and shuffles off to the cabin, his shoulders slumped in abject defeat, our jolly puppy trailing behind him.

"You're so mean!" I joke with Charmaine.

"Hey, man. Tough love!" She sighs. Then she repeats her entire Game Plan to me, as though she's fearful I'm the one who won't be able to comply with her directives. "I'm serious, babe. He follows the rules or he's out. I'm not kidding."

"I know," I tell her. "That's why everyone around here is so scared of you."

"Including Billie?"

"Well, maybe not Billie. Because she doesn't drink Coke."

Charmaine excuses herself. "I've got a menu plan to write!"

I go to the cabin, where Mike hands over a stack of medical records generated during his two most recent emergency room visits (the Valley and Cedars). He gives me and Charmaine permission to review them in preparation for his planned follow-ups. Then he says, "I ain't feelin' so hot. I gotta go lie down," and retreats into the cave-like darkness inside Weed Hollow.

Papers in hand, I walk upstairs to Charmaine's office, where I find her wearing a pair of sexy librarian's reading glasses, staring intently at something she's typing on her desktop computer. "I'm writing up Mike's meals and supplements," she announces in a voice that doesn't invite interruption. "We're going to cook for this guy."

"Great," I say reflexively, not considering what that might mean in practice. "And I'm going to accompany him to all his appointments, to his doctors."

I place Mike's medical records on her glass desk. "When you get a chance . . ."

As a highly trained physical therapist, Charmaine reads medical records like I read *The New Yorker*. She looks away from her typing and picks up the first page of the stack, a form from Cedars-Sinai.

"Oh, my god," she murmurs. "Did you see this?"

"No. What is it?"

"His real birthdate." She's shaking her head and covering her mouth.

According to his hospital records, Mike's not sixty-three, he's *forty-three*.

We look at each other, wide-eyed, simultaneously understanding for the first time just how ill, how deeply damaged, our unexpected guest really is.

"He certainly *looks* like he's old enough to have served in Vietnam," I say.

"This guy needs a lot of help," Charmaine says, continuing to look through the records, shaking her head. "I don't know, MK. I don't know. He might be, I don't know, not *healable*. I'm not really sure we can help. I mean, we can *help*, but I don't know about him ever getting completely better."

When it comes to matters of wellness, Charmaine usually *does* know. That's why people pay her to treat them. Her palpable uncertainty with Caretaker Mike makes me frightened for him.

And it makes me wonder even more who out there in this vast world is looking for him. Who's thinking about him? Who's missing him? Who knows the real person hidden beneath all those layers of delusion and denial?

Who is he?

I grab a notebook and a pen and decide to be a journalist again, gathering the facts, following the narrative trail, figuring out the story. Encyclopedia Konik is back on the case! I harvest useful new data from his medical records—actual birthdate, authentic Social Security number—and start poking around seldom-visited precincts of the internet, piecing together Caretaker Mike's true biography like a homemade quilt.

His real name really is Michael James Bailey.

He's forty-three.

He has no verifiable military history.

He seems to have only one confirmed family member, a woman named Brenda, relationship unknown.

His last known address was in Fort Walton Beach, Florida. This was more than five years ago.

The street he lived on back then, in an apartment, was exactly one block from a local road called Hollywood Boulevard.

Now he's here, still exactly one block away from the street of dreams.

I still don't have a clear picture of Michael James Bailey's backstory, but I sense that the elaborate fiction he's created about himself might also include some verifiable facts. Some truth. The borders get blurry and jumbled in his mind and, *voila,* he'll tell you he's been living in California, one block from the real Hollywood Boulevard, forever. Maybe his new wife Selena Gomez is merely a better, more glamorous version of Brenda—or maybe Brenda is his daughter, the young daughter he now believes he raises in Calabasas, alongside her imaginary brother, on the estate. Or maybe none of this matters. What's important is that Michael James Bailey has a past. That past included family, a residence, a place he might one day return to. A life not on the streets.

Something happened. I'll probably never know what. The forty-three year-old-masquerading-as-a-sexagenarian sleeping in our cabin, enigmatic and mysterious though he may be, needs someone to help him get back to whoever he was when he had a residence in Fort Walton Beach.

It might as well be me.

The next morning I accompany Caretaker Mike (Bailey) to Cedars-Sinai, where, in an unwelcome flashback to our absurd Home Depot misadventures, he manages to lose his green folder of hospital paperwork, the one with all of his records in it, while I drop him on the curb and park the car.

It seems impossible: I've been gone for less than five minutes. Yet, somehow, merely by exiting the vehicle and standing on the sidewalk in front of the medical towers, Mike has lost track of his dossier. It's vanished.

"Mike, that's ridiculous!" I snap when he breaks the news. "When I let you out of the car, you were holding the folder in your hands. How can you tell me it's gone? These things don't just evaporate."

"I don't know, I don't know," he replies glumly.

It occurs to me that Mike might have ditched his records in a desperate last-minute attempt to avoid going to his appointments. Why he'd do such a thing is hard for a healthy person to understand, but at the moment it seems slightly more plausible than a laminated folder spontaneously combusting—or being abducted by aliens, or whatever's happened. Maybe he just doesn't want to get well.

"Mike, I thought you wanted to go to this appointment. I thought you wanted me to help," I remonstrate. "But I can't help you if you don't want to help yourself."

"No, no, it's not that."

We're standing in a shady plaza between two tall medical buildings, each one filled with hundreds of doctors and nurses and technicians, all of whom have dedicated their working life to aiding the unwell. Rivers of humanity flow past us, people wearing scrubs and white coats, people in wheelchairs and wielding canes. Mike, wearing his best denim pants belted high over his hip bones, stands still in the middle of the motion, shoulders slumped, eyes downcast. The world's on the go; he's stuck.

"OK, look, maybe we don't need your paperwork," I propose. "Just tell me the name of your doctor, or the room number. We'll just show up."

He can't remember. Not exactly. But Room #302 rings a bell. I check the listings in the lobby of the East tower. Seems there's a dermatologist in that room. I run across the plaza and check the listings in the West tower. No luck: gynecologist.

I'm struggling to contain my frustration. Once more I'm furious at Mike for being so brazenly dysfunctional, but I'm more furious at myself for again allowing him to draw me into his self-concocted disaster. "Mike, do you want to get better?"

"No, no, it's not that."

"Because I can't help you—no one can help you—if you won't do the most basic stuff. Like hold on to your medical records."

"Like I was telling you, I had 'em in my hand, and, and, I don't know . . ."

He must have thrown them away. There's no other explanation. I start searching the trash bins around the plaza, fairly certain I'm going to find Mike's folder stuffed beneath discarded Styrofoam cups and soiled paper plates. He watches, shaking his head, saying nothing, while a uniformed security officer eyes me, as though I'm planting explosives.

"Just looking for some paperwork that got thrown away by mistake," I explain.

The guard nods.

"In fact," I say, "I'm wondering if you saw a green folder. It had my friend's medical records in it."

"Nah," he says phlegmatically. "But I'll keep an eye out."

I spare him the fantastical tale of how a seemingly solid object vanished. The clock is ticking. Mike's 10 a.m. appointment is a minute or two away, and I can feel that I'm about a minute or two away from a tantrum, something cathartic and cleansing, something to release me from the mental chaos enveloping me. I exhale heavily. "I don't know what to tell, you, Mike. I wanted to take you to your appointment, but if you won't hold up your end of the bargain . . . I can't do it. I'm sorry, man. I can't do it."

He nods but says nothing.

"Come on," I say. "We're going home."

We start back toward the parked car, passing the crosswalk where less than twenty minutes earlier I dropped Mike on the curb with instructions to wait for me in the lobby. Steps away, behind a low hedge of flowering bushes, lying on the dirt like a discarded sandwich wrapper, Mike's green folder glints in a Caravaggio-like ray of sunlight.

I part some branches and extract it from the vegetation. Inside are all of Mike's records, perfectly intact.

I look him in the eye, waiting for an explanation, a providential sign, some clarity. He says only, "I don't know. I don't know. It was in my hand, and, and, I don't know!"

Suppressing the urge to lecture my addled companion, I review his appointment confirmation: He's supposed to be seeing a Dr. Hong in room 203—in a totally different building than where we're standing (the one where he adamantly insisted he was booked). It's a brisk five-minute walk away, on the other side of the block, but we're already late for Mike's appointment. I call the number listed and get a fax machine. I try again; same result. On the verge of frustration tears, I try the listed fax number instead. A nice lady answers. She tells me it's all right if we're a little late; we might just have to wait longer. But, sure, come on over.

"Thank you!" I say, with what must seem to her to be inappropriate enthusiasm. She can't know how elated I am that another Caretaker Mike/MK catastrophe seems to have some chance at salvation.

"Let's go!" I say to him, summoning my conception of a motivational high school football coach. "They're going to hold your appointment, but we gotta hustle!"

"OK, yeah, because I thought it was in this building. Doesn't the paper say—what's the address?"

"It's in a different building," I say, forestalling discussion. "Follow me!"

I take off to the north, Mike trailing. The plan is for me to go on ahead a little and get him checked in, save a little time. It takes me only about thirty seconds to realize that this is not a good plan. As I'm power walking to the auxiliary building, endowed, I infer, by some wealthy benefactor named "Spielberg," I look back to check on Mike, who's huffing and puffing like he's just finished the anchor leg on a 4-by-400-meter relay. He's leaning against a bus shelter. From my vantage point, about fifty meters ahead, he appears to be bumming a cigarette from a waiting passenger.

I sprint back to where I just came from. "Ay! Mike! Come on, man!"

"You go on ahead," he says with a theatrical laboriousness one associates with mountaineering movies.

No way, I tell him. No cigarettes. No check-my-sugar breaks. We'll just keep moving. "You're doing great, Mike," I say. "It's literally just around that corner. Which I know, because I already walked up there." I pat him on the back and give him a gentle push. And we're off.

The intervening minutes—and there are only a few—are filled with Mike declaring he won't be able to make it, Mike declaring he needs to use the bathroom, and Mike wondering if we could take a break. I get the sense Mike is dreading his doctor visit, hoping to avoid it. But on we trudge. And just like when I completed Colorado Outward Bound School as a teenager, climbing 14,000-foot peaks and running a marathon at altitude, we put one foot in front of the other, one step at a time, one step closer to where we want to be, and eventually one of those little steps lands on home.

The check-in desk! Our summit.

While Mike uses the toilet, I do the initial intake, apologizing for our lateness.

"No problem. Are you the caregiver?" asks a pleasant young man behind the desk. He's wearing scrubs, which makes me want to ask, "Are you the doctor?"

I think for a second and tell him yes. "Yes, I am. Michael Bailey's caregiver." I hand him my identification, which he copies into a form. He hands it back with a clipboard. "Please have the patient fill this out and turn it in, and then the doctor can see you."

"Thank you!" I say, again with perhaps a bit too much enthusiasm. For once things seem to be going right. So long as Caretaker Mike emerges from the restroom—and I recognize at this point in our relationship the very real possibility that he won't, for any number of unimaginable reasons—our morning escapade won't have been a complete waste of time.

Yes! There he is, shuffling into the waiting area, back hunched, eyes on the floor. "Mike, Mike!" I call out, walking toward him. "Good news," I tell him, guiding him to a seat near the water cooler. "We're not too late. Doctor's going to see you."

He nods. "Oh, well, yeah."

"Here," I say, handing him a cup of water. "You need to stay hydrated. Especially since you're not drinking any Coke."

"No, no, it's not that."

He fills out the paperwork without my help, printing in block letters. When he's reached the last page, he hands the clipboard to me. I bring it to the desk. Everything appears to be in order. And now we wait.

"How did you like the oatmeal Charmaine made you?" I ask, attempting conversation. The first morning meal of the Charmaine Regime was a breakfast bowl of oatmeal, roasted seeds, dried berries, a dash of cinnamon, and stevia in place of sugar.

"No, no, it was all right," Mike says unenthusiastically.

"How you feelin'?"

"No, I'm fine," he says. "That walk took it out of me, though. Longer than I expected."

I'm about to remind him that he used to walk around Hollywood all day, miles at a time, when another scrub-clad, clipboard-toting assistant appears in the waiting area. "Michael Bailey?"

We follow her to an examination room. "I'm the caregiver," I whisper to her.

"Oh, I thought you were the patient," she says. Everyone's a comedian in this town.

She deposits us in a spacious, immaculately adorned examination room—well done, Mr. Spielberg!—where we wait for the doctor. She takes Mike's temperature (normal) and blood pressure (supposedly very high; today surprisingly normal) and I can see by the look on her face that she's wondering what's the relationship between me and Caretaker Mike (besides "caregiver and patient"). Are we husbands? Brothers?

I suppose you could say we're friends.

She leaves. Mike and I wait together, looking at the anatomy charts on the wall and the antiseptic supplies on the counter. "Funny how your green folder just disappeared like that," I say, feeling lighthearted enough now to joke about our preposterous delay.

"No, see, like I was telling you. I had it when I got out of the car, and, and, I must have put it down somewhere."

"While you were scrounging for cigarettes, no doubt."

"Noooo, no, no."

"Yes, yes, yes. Mike, come on, bro. Nothing else would distract you as much."

He's saying no, but he's grinning, and for a second I really do feel like I'm this peculiar guy's friend.

There's a knock on the door. In walks what appears to be a teenaged girl on the brink of adulthood. It's Dr. Hong—still completing her residency at UCLA med school, I'd guess.

"Hello, Mr. Bailey," she says, adjusting her horn-rimmed eyeglasses. "How are you feeling today?"

"No, no, I'm OK," he says. "It's just that, you know, and I told the doctors, I've got a lot of stuff going on. Spinal cancer, brain tumor, heart condition, and, and, the diabetes."

He prattles on, cataloguing his ailments while Dr. Hong listens patiently, murmuring assent as she flips through a ream of papers and cross-checks information on a computer monitor. "Uh-huh. Uh-huh," she says as Mike delivers one of his epic, mostly nonsensical, monologues. I stifle the urge to interject, to apologize, to help her understand that nothing he's saying is true. To each of his fanciful claims I subtly shake my head. *Nope. Not really. Nuh-uh.* Dr. Hong, though, seems to be ignoring me and focusing on her patient, who's unburdening himself of accumulated suffering, real and imagined, to someone who will listen, someone he can sense really cares.

As much as I appreciate her kind bedside manner, I'm wondering if the young doctor fully comprehends Mike's real malady, the unnamed monster invading his mind. Does she know what she's dealing with here?

"And, and, like I was telling the doctors the other night, if I don't keep my sugar straight then I have a risk of a stroke right there," he insists.

Dr. Hong nods, she reads, she listens. She clicks through a few more forms on her computer. Then she smiles.

"Well, Mr. Bailey," Dr. Hong says, catching my eye. "I've got great news for you. As you know, we ran a complete battery of diagnostic tests, and I've got all the results right here, and according to all the tests, everything's negative. That means all the illnesses you had when you came to the emergency room the other night? They've gone into remission."

Mike nods and shrugs.

"It's all negative. No spinal cancer. No heart disease. No diabetes. You might say it's kind of a miracle," she tells him.

"That's great!" I jump in, validating and affirming. "Mike, you're cured!"

She hands each of us her card. "You can make a follow-up appointment in a couple of weeks, if you'd like. In the meantime, whatever you've been doing, keep doing it," Dr. Hong tells him. "It's working."

"Amazing!" I exclaim. "He stopped smoking cigarettes and quit drinking Coke," I add, as though I'm revealing the magical source of Mike's dramatic reversal. "My wife's making veggie smoothies for him."

Dr. Hong nods. "There you go."

"Huh," Mike says. "The cancer went away?"

Dr. Hong thinks for a second, choosing her words carefully. "The cancer—well, we couldn't find any trace of it in your blood work." She catches my eye again. "We can continue to monitor the situation. But for now, I'm happy to say you're completely cancer-free."

I'm on the verge of applauding. "Truly miraculous! And his blood sugar?"

"Well, it's a little high, but he's safely out of the range of a diabetic. Pretty much normal."

Mike's smiling now. Nodding and smiling.

She offers to show him the results on her screen. He demurs. "Do you have any questions, Mr. Bailey?"

"No, no, that's . . ." He nods some more.

Dr. Hong shakes our hands and excuses herself to attend to another patient. We both thank her profusely. Me especially.

When she's gone and we're alone in the room together, I throw my arms around Caretaker Mike and squeeze him hard. "I'm so relieved, Mike," I tell him. "It's a miracle, truly a miracle."

He hugs me back a little. "Yeah, yeah, it's good. Good news. Good news."

I smile at him conspiratorially. "It's *great* news. Miss Charmaine is going to be very happy when she hears your report."

"Oh, yeah, well . . . No, I was just sayin', it's like I told the doctors the other night."

I don't remind him that what he told everyone at Cedars-Sinai was a tragic story of terminal disease. I just keep affirming. "This is great news. You're getting better! You're getting better!"

"No, no, see, it's not that."

"Yes, Michael James Bailey, it *is* that," I say.

We head for home, where Charmaine has another green smoothie waiting for us.

SIXTEEN

Thanksgiving

———

For two weeks, Caretaker Mike barely emerges from the cabin except to retrieve meals and use the bathroom. Frequently. About four times an hour. It seems every time I look out the window, I see him speed shuffling from the cabin to the casita, his adult diapers peeking out over the waistband of his sagging pants.

Charmaine's not concerned. "He's detoxing," she explains. "It hurts. It's physically painful when all those poisons are leaving your body."

"And mentally painful, I'd imagine."

"That, too. This is going to be a rough time for Mike."

But how much rougher could it be than sleeping on bus benches? Finding a public toilet? A shower? If Charmaine's rigorous detox program proves to be a magnitude worse for him than the streets, I assume he'll take the path of least resistance and end up back there. But having a vague idea of what he's managed to escape by taking up residence in Weed Hollow Cabin, I'm betting on him staying the course.

What's not to like? Charmaine prepares three meals a day for him. They're all nutritious, tasty, and easy to digest, and they all adhere to Charmaine's remove-the-toxins regimen. Boiled potatoes; steamed rice; grilled chicken. Some green vegetables. A lot of broth and soups. And supplements: B-complex vitamins, D3, Omega-3, Vitamin C, and a complete panel of amino acids and probiotics to help restore his ravaged digestive tract. Billie and I deliver Mike's meals (and pills) to him on a tray, solitary confinement inmate-style. When I meet him at the cabin doorstep, he barely speaks to me, hardly acknowledges my presence.

Me: "How ya doin', Mike?"

Him: "Nah."

I don't try to make small talk or provide comedic relief. His suffering is palpable. I can see it: He has a light rash on his face and arms. I can smell it: His body is like a fetid swamp disgorging itself of toxic sludge; he's someone you'd be forgiven for wanting to avoid.

Billie, whose olfactory preferences include dog droppings and decomposing animal carcasses she can roll on, is the only one who visits Mike regularly, for hours at a time. I have no idea what she and Mike do inside his dark cabin, but she always comes back to the main house unbothered, wagging her tail and wiggling her hips. Charmaine tells me these visits must be like therapy sessions for Mike, someone to keep him company, someone to listen. Someone to distract him from the agony of being alive without the "life-giving" support of Camels and Coke.

As much as I'm enjoying the relative tranquility afforded our household by Mike's descent into mute acquiescence of his circumstances, I find myself missing his impromptu monologues, his fantastical tales. Well, maybe "missing" is an overstatement. But I've grown accustomed to Caretaker Mike's low-grade mania, his peculiar energy. In the few months that he's lived with us, I've grown accustomed to seeing him shuffling around the property, tending to various handyman tasks, staring at his phone, swigging from plastic bottles of soda, puffing on a cigarette, delivering soliloquies.

That's all over now. Charmaine has decreed: never again. Never again will Michael James Bailey be the version of himself who first found shelter on our porch, not as long as he remains under the roof of Weed Hollow Cabin.

My hope is that he's not becoming a worse version.

Whenever we do chat, whenever I make eye contact with him, I see a man enduring unspeakable pain. Much of it is physical; much of it, I can feel, emanates from a place with no corporeal containment. Call it his soul, his heart—the intangible place where we harbor the invisible energies that make each of us individuals. Wherever that space exists in Michael James Bailey, I can feel it breaking apart, crumbling. The old Mike is disintegrating in slow-motion. One version of him is dying.

I've been there. Maybe you've been there. It hurts.

It *hurts.*

It hurts so bad you don't think you can endure another second of the agony.

But then that second passes and you're onto the next, and you're still alive, and you realize, *I can survive this. I can get through this. I don't know* how. *But I can. And I will.*

Mike shares nothing with me and Charmaine that would provide insight into his thought processes, his methodologies. He suffers in silence, in solitude.

But he sticks with the program religiously, never leaving the property for surreptitious corn syrup infusions, never violating Charmaine's protocols.

Except once. On an early morning a week into the Charmaine Regime, I find him on the sidewalk near our community library, pathetically canvassing the curbside for discarded cigarette butts. Instead of scolding, I put a hand on his shoulder. "We gotta stay strong, Mike," I tell him. "You can do this."

I'm ready for his usual rejoinder, his proclivity for meeting reasonableness with nonsense. *No, see, what people don't understand is . . .*

Instead, he nods and gives me a quick hug. "I know," he says. "I know." Then he excuses himself for another bathroom visit.

We never speak of cigarettes again.

About three weeks into Mike's detox, Charmaine and I are standing in the kitchen, looking out the window overlooking the back garden as we make smoothies in our blender. A crockpot of beef stew (for Mike and Billie) gurgles in the corner, just below Mike's store of dietary supplements, aligned in soldierly formation. The delivery system is in place; the recipient isn't. "Have you seen Mike, lately?" Charmaine asks, peering through the garden vegetation. "He usually comes out pretty often for a bathroom run."

No, I haven't. And she's right. Seldom does half-an-hour pass—and usually far less—before Mike re-emerges from Weed Hollow and dashes to the Be Well toilet. It's been many hours. This is strange.

"And I haven't really seen him on his phone lately," she adds.

"There's a good explanation for that." I tell Charmaine that Mike's last phone card ran out of minutes and, per her instructions, I declined to give him money for a new one. "I didn't want to be the cause of a terrible diabetic incident," I joke. "But I also didn't want to get in trouble with the wicked witch."

"So now he's going cold turkey on the phone, too," Charmaine muses. "Radical."

"Yep. I don't think Mike's very happy at the moment."

Who would be? He's excised everything from his life that previously made his life seem worth living. He's gathered all his addictions—the ones we know about, anyway—into one poisonous bundle and simultaneously dumped the whole lot into a trash bin. What's left? A middle-aged man with the body of an unwell senior; a man with no money, no property, no family; a man without love in his life.

Bleakness.

"You know we're this guy's family now," I blurt. "We're the only ones who care about him. You, me, and Billie. We're the only ones who take care of him."

"We have to," Charmaine says.

"I mean, you're cooking all of his *meals*."

"I have to. It's the only way he's going to get better."

We sign no papers. We undergo no vetting. But on that September day in 2016, Charmaine and I realize that we've unintentionally adopted a homeless man named Michael James Bailey, forty-three, last known residence Fort Walton Beach, Florida, one block from Hollywood Boulevard. Can't tell you much else about the fellow except that he's awfully nice, a gentle person with what you might call "a good heart" if he didn't have an imaginary heart condition.

"Do you want me to go check on Uncle Mike?" I ask Charmaine.

Just then, on cue, there he is, ambling with what appears to be a mild spring in his step down the stone path leading from the cabin to the casita. Billie dashes out to greet him. As he bends down to pet her, we can spy a little plumber's crack between Mike's bony butt, which barely holds up the waistband of his boxer-brief underwear.

Charmaine nods appreciatively, as though she's thoroughly enjoying the show. "*That's* a good sign," she says, nodding more.

I look at her, smirking, thinking of a response that somehow ties together homelessness with the Thunder from Down Under, when Charmaine flashes me a look that says *Don't you get it?*

"What?" I say, not getting it.

"It's working," Charmaine says, smiling. "Our program is

working. Mike's not going to the bathroom as much. And I just got pretty good visual evidence that he's not wearing diapers."

Outside of a clinical setting, continence, or a lack thereof, isn't an easy topic to discuss with anyone, especially hypochondriacs with extraordinarily fertile imaginations. But I tell myself that our home has gradually become a kind of clinical setting, and I'm part of the team that makes the clinic function. I intercept our sole patient on his way to the facilities. "Hey, Mike. Good to see you. How you feelin'?"

"All right," he says. "All right."

"Doesn't seem like you need to use the bathroom as much," I say.

"Nah. Not as much."

"So you're able to, you know, enjoy your meals . . ."

"Oh, yeah."

"No more diarrhea?"

"No, not really," he says. "I'm all right."

"That's great!"

"Yeah. But I sort of gotta go now," he says, giggling. And with an amusing formality, "Would you please excuse me?"

"Oh, right! Sorry."

He tromps to the casita; I return to the main house, where Charmaine's standing by for my report. I tell her Mike has indeed regained his continence. And maybe almost as important, for the first time in nearly a month, I heard him laugh.

She thinks this is all promising. "If his body is able to hold and absorb nutrients, I'm going to expand his food selection a little bit. More veggies he can eat without teeth."

Charmaine thinks now that Mike's body is functioning properly—or more properly than it has in years—we should also make sure to work on his mind and spirit. "It's got to be holistic," she insists. "So you be in charge of the laughs."

I've performed in some tough rooms and to some tough crowds, but never to anyone simultaneously quitting sugar, smoking, and the World Wide Web. Someone suffering from crushing depression. With no support system other than two strangers and their incredibly cute puppy.

Now, see, that's what people don't understand: the power of a puppy.

Over the next few days, I make it a point to never confront Caretaker Mike unarmed. My method: I knock on the cabin door. When Mike answers, palpably grouchy, I hand him a squirming Billie package of fur. "She wanted to visit her Uncle Mike," I tell him.

"Hey, Kid! Howya doin'? Didja miss me?" Billie wiggles her assent.

"How *you* doin', man? Talk to me."

"No, I'm all right. I'm all right."

"Good. Good."

"No, 'cuz I know there's a lot of stuff to do around here. Lot of chores."

"No, no, it's not that," I say in a fairly good impersonation of Mr. Michael Bailey, and we both laugh. "It's *not* that," I say.

"No, because I fully intend. I'm going to get to that list. I just gotta get my head together."

And his body, and everything else. I tell him to take his time. He can go back to being Caretaker Mike when he's taken proper care of himself.

As if to prove to me—to himself?—his usefulness, his intrinsic value to our micro-community, Mike begins to tackle home improvement projects without being asked over the next few weeks. He rises very early, with the sun, and has all the potted plants watered before I've made his instant oatmeal and my first cup of coffee—which I'm not supposed to share with Mike until

Charmaine declares him cured of his caffeine dependency. Then he moves into the workshop cellar and does what I imagine are wonderfully useful and manly tasks, emerging periodically with some tool or another to repair or restore or refurnish, to address some issue or another that requires someone wonderfully useful and manly.

All day, with time out for lunch and doggie breaks, until the sun sets, Mike putters around the property, making it demonstrably better.

Broken latches: fixed. Stained walls: cleaned. Renegade weeds: removed. Overgrown bougainvillea: trimmed. Slow drains: cleared. Incrementally, slowly, almost invisibly if you're not observant, our tired old house starts getting better.

Fortified with organic vegetables from the garden and a new-found sense of purposefulness—he now finds pride in introducing himself to visitors as "the guy who takes care of this place"—Care-taker Mike incrementally, slowly, almost invisibly, starts getting better.

Unlike nicotine or sugar, you can't simply go cold turkey on insanity, though. Quitting "crazy" isn't possible. The shedding of mental disturbance happens with the sneaky gradualness of climate change. Each day, it seems to me, Caretaker Mike gets infinitesi-mally but measurably more well, more "regular." He starts to give what Charmaine calls "appropriate responses" to questions, instead of entertainingly random rants. He makes eye contact during conversations. He understands and appreciates jokes.

I'm seeing it unfold in slow-motion: He's healing himself.

Michael James Bailey is consuming no pharmaceuticals; he's seeing no doctors. We're helping, for sure. We're facilitating. But Caretaker Mike is healing himself.

Maybe the truth is we all ultimately act as our own healers, no matter how many or few helpers we have. Maybe we all have the ability to make ourselves well. Maybe all it takes is determination and a little (a lot of?) encouragement. In Mike's case, he seems to have made a conscious and willful decision to flip the binary switch in his mind from "ill" to "well." That doesn't mean the change happens instantly, of course. A better metaphor, perhaps, is topographical. Mike seems to have decided to walk down a different path, one that's leading toward something beautiful. The path he's on isn't lined with manicured sod and daffodils. It's plenty thorny, and it's anything but a straight shot. But it's leading to the right place.

Then there's the encouragement factor. Caught in a marvelous positive feedback loop of improved continence, improved nutrition, and newly discovered personal achievement, his energy level and general industriousness spike upward. He gains weight. His posture gets straighter. His ability to conduct a cogent, sensible conversation devoid of references to pop starlets and private jets returns.

He bathes regularly and grooms meticulously, asking for supplies like cotton earbuds, skin lotion, and hair conditioner.

He segregates his work clothes from his "regular" clothes.

He announces lofty project goals—"I'm gonna reorganize the storage shed"; "All that bougainvillea above the cabin, where the rats live, I'm gonna take it down"—and achieves them without complications or delays.

And he does all this without a single cigarette (formerly two packs a day), Coke (two-to-three liters), or candy bar (large, children's charity size).

I never imagined I would feel this way about "Fisher King Mike," but this version of him is an absolute pleasure to have around. A delight.

And I'm not the only one who thinks so. We have a few friends over for a weekend afternoon hang-out, including some of our crunchy pals from the Elderberries/Have Seeds community, the ones who introduced us to Mike in the first place. "Yo! Mike!" I call out from the back deck across the garden. "We got some folks here who want to say hello to the Caretaker!"

Instead of hiding in the cabin, waiting for the world to go away, Mike stops by the back deck for a quick *hello-and-how-are-you* before excusing himself to the cellar workshop. "Can't stay. I gotta lot of stuff to do," he reports apologetically, snagging a few tater tots for the road. "Like I was telling MK, this house needs a lot of work."

While he's still in earshot, I begin reviewing all the home improvements he's accomplished of late, stopping myself when I start sounding like a real estate agent pitching his hot new listing. "Let's just say that man right there, the one with the baseball cap, is tremendously talented," I tell everyone. "And it's all starting to come out."

He shakes his head, laughing, and descends to his workshop. To someone meeting him for the first time, let's say a neighbor we've invited to the party, Caretaker Mike would probably seem odd, eccentric, slightly off. To the kind young people gathered on our porch, all of whom are *not* meeting him for the first time, he suddenly seems alarmingly, impossibly *normal*.

He understands jokes. He's polite.

Wide-eyed and smiling, Gentle Daniel whispers, "He's like a different person."

Caleb the Canadian says, "I think that's the first time in my life I've had a conversation with Mike that didn't involve Selena Gomez."

"I know this is hard to believe," I tell our friends. "But he hasn't mentioned her—or their kids, or anything—for more than a month."

Charmaine adds, "And we don't talk about it. It's like it never happened."

Caretaker Mike reappears outside the cellar door with a hammer in one hand and some small rectangles of wood in the other. "Park bench. Needs a little bracing," he announces.

"This guy is so talented!" I crow, pouring on the positive affirmation.

He waves his hand theatrically. "Stop!" He chuckles. "I'm just trying to do my job."

Then he goes and does it directly, *hecking* and *schmecking* without pause, leaving out the improvisational speeches highlighting his various claims to fame.

"Wow," Daniel says, shaking his head. "I'm still processing this."

To Charmaine, Mike's turnaround makes sense. "When all you're feeding your brain is Coke and fast food, of course you're going to lose your mind. His incontinence, everything going straight through him—his gut wasn't absorbing anything to feed the brain," she tells us. "It can't survive on nothing. You heal the gut, you heal the brain."

Whether you're an obscure artist living in a cramped studio with no windows or a homeless person living beneath a freeway overpass, a lifelong poet dedicated to haiku and villanelles, or a vagrant with no immediate family, when you go through life feeling useless, meaningless, a net-negative to the society you live in, of course you're going to lose your mind. It can't survive on nothing.

On some level, we all need our singular existence in a vast cosmos of anonymity to be recognized. We all need to feel useful somehow. We all need to feel visible.

For the first time in what I assume is a long time, I can tell Mike is feeling all these things.

And he doesn't need diapers.

After wishing our guests farewell—"Good to see ya, good to see ya," he tells everyone—Mike asks if Miss Char and I have a minute.

"Sure. What's up?" Miss Char asks.

"I wanna show you two something," he says, motioning toward the casita. "Come on, Kid!" he calls to Billie. "Come on!"

We four walk down the driveway to the casita, Charmaine's healing space.

"They ain't attached, or nothing. I just got 'em balanced up there for you to get an idea of what it would look like." Above the entrance, leaning on the door frame, Mike's placed rustic wooden letters painted in different shades of green and blue.

The blocks say:

BE WELL

IT'S THANKSGIVING MORNING, exactly two years since we first met the Fisher King on the streets of Hollywood. Even if, like me, you're the kind of person who tells himself that anything's possible, that the only limits on the life we live are the ones we place on ourselves, you'd require extraordinary powers of imagination—and perhaps some consciousness-altering substances—to have seen this coming. Two years ago, I couldn't have envisioned the homeless man with five crucifixes around his neck, the one wearing three jackets (one of which has inscrutable messages scrawled on it in magic marker), merrily ensconced in our kitchen, chopping vegetables with a butcher's knife and chitter-chattering about his culinary history with my Filipino mother-in-law.

They're cooking up a storm together—and it was Mike's idea. So transformed is he that Charmaine and I gladly invited Caretaker Mike to attend our family Thanksgiving celebration. He accepted immediately—and insisted on helping cook. "I was a line chef, you know," he said. "Seasons. Fine dining chain. Rotating menu."

We thought he was reverting to his usual defense mechanism, hiding his insecurity behind a façade of grandeur. Now we're watching him handle a knife, slicing potatoes into perfect cubes, and I'm thinking he might be telling the truth.

"See, what people don't understand," he explains to Mom Clamor, "there's a right way to sharpen a knife. There's a right way to slice a carrot." He proceeds to demonstrate. Mom is suitably impressed.

"Oh!" she exclaims, laughing. "That's professional!"

"No, see, 'cuz if you use a dull knife, see, that's when you get in trouble. Dull knife is dangerous." He seems to know what he's talking about, and it occurs to me that I haven't sharpened our kitchen knives for, oh, I don't know, seven or eight years.

Reading my mind, Caretaker Mike says, "See, these here are dull. But I'm gonna sharpen them right up." While he and Mom prepare a smallish turkey (for the non-vegetarians visiting us), gluten-free stuffing, yams, gravy, and all the other fixings, Mike periodically plucks a fresh blade from the rack and waves it back and forth over a stropping iron—hey, we have one of those!—like an orchestra conductor. By mid-afternoon, when guests from the Clamor family start to arrive, Mom and Mike have prepared a Thanksgiving feast for fourteen *and* rehabilitated our entire set of cutlery.

He excuses himself to change, and when he returns I can see he's freshly shaven and self-barbered, his mustache clipped uniformly and his sideburns neatly trimmed.

Before we all sit down for supper, Mom pulls me aside in the kitchen. "Mikey," she says. "He's so nice! I like him!"

I hug her. "Me, too, Mom. I really like him, too."

When we all congregate in the dining room, before the feasting, Charmaine asks everyone to share what they're thankful for. We go around the room—"Family"; "Being here with my loved ones"; "Good health"; "All this delicious food"—and when it gets to Mike, who's sitting at the far end of the long table, next to his cooking buddy, Mom, he bows his head slightly. But instead of staring at the floor, Caretaker Mike looks up, he looks around the room.

"I'm thankful to be part of this gathering, and to Mike and Charm and Billie for, uh, for, for taking me in." He nods and looks down again.

When it gets to me, I'm almost too overwhelmed with gratitude to participate. Without getting impossibly maudlin and weird, how can I put into a brief toast my new understanding of all I have to be thankful for? Which, basically, is *everything*. The beautiful and the ugly. The tragedy and the comedy and everything else. All of it. I never wished for a man like Michael Bailey to come into my life . . . or maybe I did wish for exactly this. I don't know. I'm only certain that somehow I've ended up knowing a challenging person who forces me to be a better version of myself. Caretaker Mike gave me that opportunity, and I'm thankful. I say, "I'm thankful for everything," and leave it at that.

Very soon after everyone has overloaded their plate and commenced to masticating, Mike quietly excuses himself and retreats to the kitchen, where it sounds like he's doing dishes.

Charmaine leans over to me. "Is Uncle Mike OK?"

"I think he's bashful about eating in front of other people."

She tells me to go check on him.

I push through the swinging door between the dining room and kitchen, where I find Mike at the sink, scrubbing pots.

I put a hand on his back. "What a tremendous meal! Compliments to the chef."

"No, see, I told you, I used to do this for a living."

I want to know when, where, the whole story. What came before? What came after? For now, I say, "I can tell. You're a pro."

"No, no," he says, and then he turns off the water and gives me a giant hug. "I'm gonna go to the cabin. Been a long day."

"I understand."

"But I want you to know, I really am thankful."

I look him in the eye. "I know, Mike. And I am, too."

Then we go our separate ways, somehow traveling on the same path.

SEVENTEEN

The Turn

———

Do you believe in karma?

Do you believe all our actions and energies, our intentions and thoughts, eventually return to us in the form of reciprocal actions and energies?

Does it happen instantly, John Lennon-style, or in another lifetime?

Is it all imaginary?

Is karma merely a concept, one of those comforting myths that salves our addled minds, helping us bumble onward, storytelling 'til the end?

I used to think so. I had myself convinced that everything inexplicable and mysterious about life could be ascribed to randomness, to the infinite panoply of results produced by a universe in chaos. I was certain that any correlation between good deeds and subsequent rewards—or the converse, *i.e.*, wickedness leading to eternal punishment—was a convenient fiction meant to encourage badly behaved humans to behave a little better.

You reap what you sow; it all comes back to you. These sounded like clever control mechanisms to me.

My late father Eugene was, in addition to being a former United States Marine, a staunch Newtonian. He'd frequently remind me and my brother that every action has an equal and opposite reaction (he'd also remind us if you want a job done right, do it yourself, and to keep our rooms neat). Whenever my dad would reference the 3rd Law of Motion when I was a boy, I figured he was invoking science, the exquisite beauty of physics, to help us understand how life unfolds. *Every action has an equal and opposite reaction.*

Now I think maybe my dad was talking about karma.

Concurrent with Uncle Mike's transition to good health, to a truer version of his authentic self, our household is struck by an avalanche of slightly delayed karma, as though some omniscient arbiter of righteousness—known as "God" in some versions of the tale, "the universe" in others—has decided we somehow deserve all the goodness in the world. The truth, in my version of the tale, is that we *all* deserve all the goodness in the world, each of us living miracles the recipients of divine blessings. We don't have to earn this goodness; it's our birthright. Yet—and there's that karma thing again—when we believe our values, thoughts, and actions are in perfect harmony, when we know we're successfully manifesting the new and improved versions of ourselves we wish to someday become, the goodness seems to flow like water.

I can't say if this phenomenon is caused by karma or the ghost of Isaac Newton, if it's a hybrid of the natural and supernatural, or something else altogether. But I'm sure it's real.

On the Monday morning following Thanksgiving, after Billie and I come home from hiking and yoga, Caretaker Mike's cutting timber with a table saw. Several months ago, this would have been impossible (and alarming), but I've become gradually conditioned to start viewing the impossible as the highly improbable. So, sure, why not? If he says he knows what he's doing, I'm inclined at this point to believe him. Still, the sight of the toothy circular blade whirring viciously between his hands reminds me of a James-Bond-meets-his-end torture scene. But Mike pushes the boards through the blade calmly, with the kind of concentration I associate with chess grandmasters and vascular surgeons. Everything's going to be all right.

Everything *is* all right.

I feel it. I know it. *Everything is all right.*

Then, as though he knows he's being watched, as though he's reading my mind, Caretaker Mike shuts down the saw and rises from his hunched position. He pushes yellow safety goggles to the crown of his head and nods at me. "Don't worry. I'm working on something. No, see, because Charm mentioned she'd like a bench for outside Be Well. Like another park bench, for the clients."

Before I can reply, Caretaker Mike says, "Everything's all right."

I tell him I was just thinking that and leave him to his creativity.

When I return to my desk for another day of writing, another day tip-toeing the tense high wire between artistic imperative and artistic irrelevance, I'm confronted by twin internal voices. Most creative people hear them. They remind you that you've got a responsibility to honor your abilities and, also, that those hifalutin abilities are possibly irrelevant to the society you live in. This is why we need encouragement, all of us. We need to be filled with courage.

I've seen it work with Uncle Mike.

I've seen it work with myself.

Encouragement.

Before I commence to writing poems I reckon few people will read, I check my email. I see from the subject lines of several of the messages in my inbox that I've gotten a few more form-letter rejections from the earnest publishers of obscure literary journals. I can tell, because they all read "RE: Your Submission to [whatever publication you once dreamed of seeing your work in]." I've gotten about a million of them. They're generated by a computer robot, along with the pleasant and, yes, mildly encouraging, rejection letter contained therein.

I click on one that says: RE: Year 14 (62,000 words). The book's been offered, considered, and returned unwanted for more than seven years.

When the message loads, I can see it's much longer than the usual rejection. Words cover the whole screen. So accustomed am I to having this comic, heartbreaking novel, maybe the best work I've ever done, rejected like a gangrenous cow on the slaughtering line, I'm already instinctively wondering why these particularly pretentious editors need a magnum opus to tell me *Year 14* isn't "quite right" or "not a good fit" or "doesn't meet current editorial needs."

Then I read the first line:

Hi MK,

I really love YEAR 14, and would like to talk with you about making it the next book from Barrelhouse Books.

I read it again. And then the next line:

I guess the first thing is to confirm with you that it's still available, and then to make sure you're cool with us publishing it, under our usual terms.

I read both lines once more to make sure I'm not misunderstanding, and then I scream.

The sound issues forth from the darkest, deepest place inside of me, the cloistered cell of feeling locked tight by rigid muscles and rigid thoughts. Imagine a joyous noise somewhere between an orgasmic wail and a cosmic sigh. I mean to say "yes!" But what comes out is, "AAAAAAAAAAAAAAAAAAAAAAAAHHHH-HHHHHHHH!"

Billie jumps out of her bed and wags her tail nervously, her ears pinned back. Caretaker Mike rushes up the porch steps to the doorway of my office.

I have tears streaming down my face. "Nothing's wrong. Nothing's wrong," I tell him, falling into his arms like a drunken lover. "Something wonderful happened."

"No, see, because I heard you yelling!"

Sniffling, laughing, breathing heavily, I try to explain. "Mike, I've waited so long for this day," and immediately collapse into paroxysms of pure happiness. I feel buoyant, as though a crushing yoke has been removed from around my shoulders.

He pats my back tenderly. "You had me worried there!"

"Sorry," I sniffle. "Didn't mean to . . . it's just . . . good news, Mike. Good news . . . I was starting to lose hope." And then another epic sigh escapes my chest.

He nods and releases me. "I know. I know. You're all right."

"Oh, yeah. I'm all right. I'm better than all right. I'm . . . I'm so . . . *happy.*"

"Then I am too," Caretaker Mike says, smiling, flashing me his gums.

I return to my office to re-read the acceptance and call Charmaine, who's out and about in Beverly Hills, performing physical therapy on well-to-do ladies. The last line incites another crying fit.

Thanks again for sending the book to us. Reading through nearly 400 submissions was kind of a bear, but such a great pleasure to come across a book I really loved.

Without pausing to think, I dash back outside. "Mike!" I yell, bounding down the stairs to the entrance of his workshop. "Mike, I gotta tell you something!"

He emerges from the cellar and meets me on the stair landing.

"Mike," I say, looking him in the eye. "I love you. I just need you to know. *I love you.*"

He chortles nervously. "No, no. Don't . . ."

"Come here," I say, drawing him into my embrace. "I love you, Mike."

"Well, no, yeah, OK, thanks," he mumbles.

"I love you. Billie loves you. Charmaine loves you."

"*Loveyoutoo*," he blurts, breaking our hug. "I got some work to do. Lotta stuff needs to get done around here." And then he slips away into his lair.

Just a few days later, before the high of having *Year 14* accepted for publication has worn off, before I've had a chance to frame the touching, hand-made "Congratulations" card from Charmaine and Billie, another email arrives in my inbox. This one says that my poem "Salmon," the one I wrote about Caretaker Mike painting the back deck railings orangey-pink, has won a national contest and will be printed as a limited-edition broadside.*

The next day, I learn that my poem "Guru," about listening to Caretaker Mike's rambling monologues, has been accepted by a literary journal out of Virginia.

The day after that, two more poems about Mike—the Fisher King version—are accepted by the University of Arkansas' annual anthology.

Then the *Suisun Valley Review,* a venerable journal from Northern California, takes "Adoption Story," about Chareze's death and Billie's arrival.

Then, as if every publication extant suddenly wants something Caretaker Mike-related in their pages, the feminist journal *Minerva Rising* decides to publish my poem "The Homeless Metaphor," even though I'm a male.

And then, finally, as though the universe wishes to smother me with happiness, the way a father kisses and snuggles his daughter until she laughs so much she can hardly breathe, I learn that my *Report from the Street: Voices of the Homeless* has been chosen to inaugurate a new series of social justice chapbooks. "Report"

---

* See Appendix.

contains eight monologues, each one in the voice of a different homeless person—but all of them, I realize upon rereading, have been inspired to some extent by the formerly homeless man living in our backyard cabin.

I can't say what the correlation is, or if there even is one. But something *positive* is coursing through the Vista Street farmstead, anointing each of us who live here. Something good.

It doesn't dawn on me immediately that *Something Good* is the title of one of Charmaine's best-selling albums. Nor do I initially connect Caretaker Mike's freshly manifested energy and industry with my freshly manifested publishing success. The coolly analytic former professional gambler still lives in me, and I'm tempted to explain away the concurrent results as parallel events, delightful coincidences, and nothing more. Yet, you mustn't be wildly superstitious to feel an unseen force at work—call it "the force," call it whatever. Is it karma? We can't really point at "humidity" and says "that's humidity." We can only point to manifestations of humidity. I can't really point at Caretaker Mike's renaissance or my poetic awakening, I can only point to manifestations of rebirth.

They're everywhere.

For the past two years, Charmaine has applied her gifts to healing—her patients and herself. Her private practice has grown; so have her skills. But Be Well Therapy probably wouldn't have been possible if she hadn't turned away from her first love, music. Burnt out from touring, hustling, grinding, and filled with a latent rage at the "business" that co-opted her art, Charmaine stopped making music. She recorded a ravishing album, *The Better Angels*, in 2015, and did a few concerts, but gone were the manager, the publicist, the radio promoter. Gone were the impromptu visits to our piano, performing for no reason but the joy of singing. Charmaine was in a musical funk.

Call it coincidence, or call it fanciful nonsense, but after opening her heart to Uncle Mike, Charmaine's heart seems to have opened again to the world of music. Energy flows to her, finds her.

Out of the blue, like an acceptance letter for your beloved novel, Charmaine's asked by a famous pianist-arranger she's never worked with to record an album with him for release in China. A week later she's invited to take one of the starring roles in an original Filipino-language musical and film being staged in Napa, California. Then, only a few days later, another bolt out of nowhere: Charmaine is offered the female lead, an Erin Brockovich-ish lawyer who fights for elderly tenants, in a new *English*-language musical, no audition necessary. The author says the part was always meant for her.

Something Good, from 2010, contains a groovy track called "Flow," about water. It's Vista Street's new unofficial soundtrack. *Something good* is flowing through our household, through all of us. Maybe that something is love. Allegedly it has great powers. *Every action has an equal and opposite reaction*, and when your action is making love, creating love, being love, according to Isaac Newton and my father, your love invites an equal amount of love into your miniature universe.

Michael James Bailey, the man Charmaine and I used to affectionately call "Mr. No," is now a manifestation of love energy. He's adding a new (and shockingly healthy) spirit to our unorthodox family, imbuing everyone and everything he touches with a faint patina of fairy dust. I don't mean that he only brings us good luck. As he transforms himself, Caretaker Mike literally transforms our home. And he does it efficiently, sensibly. He dispatches tasks that only a few months earlier would have taken him weeks to complete with stunning alacrity. After getting Charmaine to sign off on the color, Caretaker Mike empties, cleans, paints, and reconstructs the dining room in one highly focused day.

By himself. "Needed to be done," he informs us matter-of-factly.

The next day he unilaterally decides to clean the fireplace bricks, removing decades of carbon stains we'd convinced ourselves were permanent. The day after that—one intensely concentrated day—Mike singlehandedly empties, cleans, paints, and reconstructs the entire living room, the largest space in the house. It was weary and smudged. Now it's cheerful and bright, radiating peach-colored light.

Room by room, each with a different vibrant color, he gives our house what might be called an "extreme makeover," except he's using non-toxic organic paint. Pink, lavender, yellow, burgundy, green, melon—every wall and door on the property receives a new sheen from unexpected regions of the color palette. When he's done, it feels like we're living in Key West, or the south of France. Every room is warm, funky, giddy, light.

People in the neighborhood call it "the happy house." Children like it.

Thanks to Caretaker Mike's careful, constant attention, our home now resembles a glowing rainbow. It's an accomplishment I'm fairly sure I couldn't have managed—at least not without a few years to figure it out. *He's done it in less than a month.* But Charmaine is worried. "I think Uncle Mike is entering another manic phase," she confides, reviewing his latest paint job, the upstairs bathroom (chartreuse). "I don't think it's normal for someone to be able to do all this so quickly."

"Maybe he's just showing his true potential," I propose. "Maybe we all are."

With each home improvement triumph, Mike's self-esteem grows. Now he's eager for visitors, eager to show off the results of his hidden talents. Instead of hermiting in the cabin when guests arrive, he hangs around the back deck, ready to be bumped into unexpectedly while performing his refurbishments, eager to receive the plaudits and wonderment his work inspires.

He's unfailingly modest and dismissive of praise, but we can tell Uncle Mike no longer likes being known as the crazy guy from the streets who's married to a celebrity and owns a private jet. He no longer references his job as a "street pastor." He has a new role, with a new uniform, and he wants everyone to see it and know it. When Caretaker Mike goes to his job each day, "commuting" from Weed Hollow Cabin to the cellar, he wears his "work shirt," an old green hand-me-down with a couple of holes in the back.

On the front it says, "Achiever."

EIGHTEEN

I'll Be Home for Christmas

It's the end of December, when life suddenly becomes
Merry—and thoughtful and considerate and generous, which
is why, perhaps, so many people consider Christmas the very
best time of year. It's when people like me and you who live in
comfortable houses volunteer at soup kitchens on Skid Row and
feel a wee bit better about the pernicious imbalances in our
diseased society.

For folks like Caretaker Mike, for homeless people who have
no family and few friends, the "happy holidays" can be crushingly
painful, an omnipresent reminder of loss and regret. As December
24–25 draws near, we can feel Mike retreating into silence, con-
structing a protective shell around his pain. His normal
loquaciousness gradually recedes. His smile is less frequent, less
bright. He doesn't joke; he doesn't laugh.

Michael Bailey has lived with us in Weed Hollow Cabin for
nearly six months. Throughout his residency he's received zero
visitors, hosted zero guests, maintained zero friendships—other
than with his housemates and Billie the Kid, who clearly considers
Mike her un-official, official Uncle. We all do. Without prompting
or pondering, Charmaine at some point stops calling him "Caretaker Mike" and exclusively starts calling him "Uncle Mike." He's

as much a member of our family as someone who was born into it, or married into it. Or adopted into it.

He's our peculiar, lovable, weird, entertaining, sweet Uncle. Every family has one, right?

We need him; he needs us. That simple fact—being *needed*—changes everything. So does human contact.

We know our Uncle Mike needs to socialize, to interact with people other than the trio of creatures who live in the main house. He needs to practice his rediscovered conversational skills, his penchant for interaction. "I think we should invite Uncle Mike for Christmas," Charmaine announces one morning over breakfast.

"Sure," I agree. "We'll put up a stocking for him on the mantel."

"No, I mean, more than that. Not just Christmas dinner and presents. I mean, let's invite him to spend the entire holiday with us."

"Like, move into the main house?" I'm concerned.

"No!" she cries. "Oh, no. Not that!" Charmaine means he ought to join us for the cooking, the gifting, the conversing. "He's part of the family. He should participate. In every way."

With Mike's mental illness in a state of abatement, I no longer consider such a plan foolhardy and practically complicated, if not impossible. I think it's a great idea.

We three walk into the back garden, where Mike is watering the plants. "Hi, Uncle Mike," Charmaine calls out. "Good morning!"

"Morning," he replies. "No, I was just taking care of these roses."

"Hey, Mike, you know how you helped my mom make Thanksgiving dinner?" Charmaine says. "We want to invite you to spend Christmas with us. We could sure use your help in the kitchen!"

"Really? That would be nice," he says, turning back to the plants. "But I don't have any money to give presents or nothing."

We assure him it's not important, but he seems fixated on the idea of participating like a proper American, displaying his affection with made-in-China consumer goods.

I could loan him some money. I could purchase gifts on his behalf. Or we could just skip that part of the festivities.

"No, no, no," he says, categorically dismissing each proposal. "You don't come to a Christmas party without gifts."

"We can make an exception," I say reassuringly.

"No, he's right," Charmaine cuts in. "Christmas is about giving. But, Uncle Mike, if you really want to give us the best gift ever, all you've got to do is show up and be yourself. That would be a wonderful present, and I know everyone—my mom, my dad, the cousins—everyone would appreciate a gift like that."

"Yeah?"

"*Oh*, yeah," Charmaine says, nodding with great certainty. "The best!"

"Hey, Kid, are you OK with that? Huh, Kid?"

Billie signals her assent with a well-timed yawn.

"OK, then," I announce. "Seems like it's a plan."

Mike buries his free hand in his pants pocket, as though reminding himself that it's empty, bereft of dollars and cents. "I don't know. I'll think about it."

As the calendar creeps toward the big Day (and big Eve), I offer again to spot Mike some money, to take him shopping for presents. But he tells me, "No, no, you don't gotta."

"I'm happy to do it."

"Thanks. But it ain't necessary."

"No problem. Just want you to know, if you need a hand, I'm here to help."

"I appreciate that," he says, looking me in the eye. "I really do."

FOR REASONS I'VE never fully grasped, the Clamor family doesn't wait for Christmas Day to open their gifts. (The ones from

Santa? Who hasn't yet departed the North Pole?) They do everything on Christmas Eve.

On the afternoon of the big night, Mom Clamor and Uncle Mike reprise their kitchen klatch, while Dad Clamor and I play chess. DJ Charmaine has selected a French children's choir singing carols, extracted from her procured-at-flea-markets-and-garage-sales vinyl collection. When I'm instructed to pause the game and go light some candles in the living room, I spy beside the piano a growing pile of wrapped gifts, including a few I've put there myself. Three of them stand out. They're wrapped in the Sunday comics. Although my mom used to do the same thing when I was a child, these presents aren't from me. They're from Mike.

When we congregate in the living room to celebrate the birth of baby Jesus by exchanging the modern equivalents of frankincense and myrrh, Uncle Mike tries to stay in the kitchen, doing dishes. I don't want to force him to participate, but, on the other hand, people want to give him gifts. He's got to be present to get the presents. Fortunately, Mom Clamor declares that there shall be no gift opening unless Uncle Mike joins us. It's an ultimatum.

So in walks Mike, technically inside the room, hovering at the periphery.

"Mike! Sit down!" Mom says, waving at an arm of the couch. "Sit, sit."

Smiling bashfully, he mumbles, "No, no," and dutifully takes his perch in the middle of the room, beside his kitchen buddy.

Motioning at a bright red box, with a pink ribbon, Mom says, "This one's for you. Mae, could you?"

Charmaine hands it to Uncle Mike.

It's a shirt. A nice new one, in a box.

Then, on the next round, he gets a zippered hoodie.

And then a winter jacket!

Receiving each gift, Mike seems appropriately grateful,

repeating his thanks and appreciation. When he tries to apologize for not having gifts for everyone, Mom will have none of it, and, therefore, the subject is mercifully closed.

Finally, only the comic-wrapped packages are left (and they're pretty big—could be anything). Mike says to the handful of nieces and nephews and cousins scattered around the room, "I'm really sorry I wasn't able to get you a gift."

"It's OK!" "It's OK, Mike." "No problem."

"No, I'm just saying, I didn't, you know, I wasn't . . ."

"Don't worry!" "It's OK!" "No problem."

"No, so I did bring gifts for, uh, the *immediate family*," he says, smiling, glancing at me and Charmaine, smushed together on the other end of the couch. "And that includes you, Kid!" Billie taps her tail demurely. It's her first Christmas.

"Actually, Char, the biggest one there? That's for Billie."

Charmaine removes the paper on Billie's behalf, and we all gasp and mock-scream. It's a doghouse, painted white, with window holes. On top, painted in yellow outlined in green, it says: BILLIE BOX.

"I figure we could put it in the corner out front, the one next to the gate, where she likes to sit."

"Oh, Mike!" we gush. "It's beautiful." Billie sniffs it approvingly.

"Well, yeah, thanks, I was working on it down in the basement. Wanted it to be a surprise. Hope the Kid likes it."

Charmaine is beaming. "She *loves* it. I can tell."

"Well, yeah, thanks. It's just some old plywood. Like I was telling Mike, we gotta lotta good boards down there, projects we can do and so forth, and, and, anyway, I made you something, too. It's the one with the 'C' in the corner."

Charmaine picks up the package, about the size of a jumbo loaf of bread. She peels back the comics. "Aaaaaahhhh!" she squeals.

It's a miniature bench, with tiny Basset hound legs, for toilet visits. She's been asking for one. Mike's version is sanded to a fine sheen and stained dark, like mahogany. For all I know it *is* mahogany. It's a little work of art. She goes to hug him, and he reciprocates, resting his cheek on her shoulder.

I'm last. "Here you go, MK," Charmaine says, gently sliding the package across the wood floor.

"Something I thought you could use," Uncle Mike says.

It's a compact, two-level bookshelf, constructed of various scraps, painted white.

"For your books," Mike says. "You put all your books on the top shelf and all the you know, collections and what not, the poetry, you put the rest on the bottom. You know, a shelf for your work. I measured. It'll fit right there next to the fireplace. And there's plenty of space for *Year 14*, and more if you ever write another book."

I hug him. "This is one of the best gifts anyone's ever given me," I say.

But not quite. The best one comes after Christmas dinner.

The entire family gathers in the (freshly painted) living room to sing carols around the piano. Charmaine breaks the ice/intimidates the rest of us into awed silence, by going first. Eventually the rest of the congregation, led by Mom Clamor, joins in, cycling through all the classics, with Charmaine providing workmanlike accompaniment on the keyboard.

"Mike! Uncle Mike! Sing, sing!" Mom demands. "Come on. Sing with us!"

"No, no, no," he demurs, waving her away.

"Everyone sings in this family!" she reminds him.

He doesn't argue.

Uncle Mike rises from his seat and stands in the middle of the crowd, beside the piano. He regards the audience. He nods. And then the former Fisher King, the former bard of the bus shelter, begins to sing.

He holds himself like a star, upright, open, expressive, like someone accustomed to being in the spotlight, someone supremely comfortable with performing. Living in the moment.

His eyes clenched in concentration, Uncle Mike sings, "*I'll be home for Christmas*," his voice wavering with pent-up emotion. He sings in tune. He sings genuinely. It's a lovely rendition.

Charmaine glances my way from her seat at the piano, her elegant fingers finding the chords from memory. Her eyes are shiny, welling with a thousand feelings.

So are mine.

From now on, it seems, our troubles will indeed be miles away and our days more or less merry and bright, just as promised in our favorite carols. Because Caretaker Mike really is home for Christmas.

And it isn't only in his dreams.

NINETEEN

New Year, New Mike

⁓

C aretaker Mike begins 2017 in solitary confinement.
After cooking a delicious New Year's Eve dinner for
the family—he insisted on being chef for the night before
retiring to bed before midnight—he won't come out of the
cabin. He doesn't want to talk. And he doesn't want help. It's
like he's detoxing again, but this time nicotine and corn syrup
aren't the malefactors. Mike seems to be ridding himself of
painful memories.

Charmaine and I can only theorize. We don't really know, and
Mike's not saying. Perhaps, we reason, his new awareness—of
himself, of his new reality—has shocked him into despair. Maybe,
we conjecture, he's shamed by the past indignities he's brought
upon himself—and upon the family and loved ones who must be
out there somewhere, wondering what's become of their lost
Michael.

Maybe he's just lonely, sex-starved, crippled by unrequited love.
Sad about everything.

Charmaine figures more autonomy might lift Uncle Mike's
spirits. Although she's convinced that giving him money is still a
bad idea, Charmaine thinks allowing him increased independence
will improve his general attitude and boost his self-esteem. "I

know this sounds backwards," she explains to me, gazing out the kitchen window at the garden and cabin outside. "But I think we should start doing *less* for Uncle Mike."

Her idea: Helping too much might be hurting him. Swaddling can be comforting, but it can also be constricting.

"Mike's a grown man. He needs to start taking care of himself," she says. "He'll feel better about himself if we don't treat him like a patient in a hospital. He needs some freedom."

Charmaine announces—decrees?—she'll no longer prepare and serve Mike's meals. He's going to do that himself. "Come on," she says. "He's a trained chef!"

We supply him with a microwave, a toaster oven, and copious supplies of nutritious staples: potatoes, rice, and "soft" vegetables, like cooked peas and carrots. He's got eggs, peanut butter, and bananas. He's got a freezer full of chicken thighs. And lean beef patties. He's got autonomy.

Still, Caretaker Mike remains morose, and, I'm guessing, paralyzed by regret, lamenting the bad relationships and bad choices that brought him to the streets of Hollywood.

He doesn't eat much, doesn't do much. If his holiday surge of energy and productivity was indeed the "manic" part of his bipolar diagnosis, then this surely must be the "depressive." Nothing seems to interest him much, nothing rouses or arouses him. Not even Billie the Kid.

Have you been to this dark place, where you've got yourself believing no light will ever enter? Where everything that once gave you pleasure no longer pleases?

I have, and not so long ago.

You don't have to be suicidal to know despair; you just need to live long enough, and the shadow will eventually catch you. The trick—and it really is a neat little trick, nothing major—is to redirect your focus, take it off of woes and misery and put it on the light, wherever the faintest sliver can be found. Change your thoughts, change your feelings. Change your reality.

Ultimately, that means learning to love.

Love yourself. Love others.

Love.

It's simple. And complicated and challenging and sometimes excruciating. But, really, once you decide to do it, it's simple.

Love. Make it, create it, give it, share it, live it, be it.

Watch what happens.

As I stand at my desk looking out on the garden, I can feel sadness emanating from the Weed Hollow corner. It's palpable, like a fog.

I need to burn it off, be the sunshine. Be the light.

With Billie leading the way, I approach the sinkhole of dismay. "Yo, Uncle Mike," I call out, knocking on the cabin door. "I need you."

I hear rustling. The door cracks. Out of the gloom comes, "Uh-huh?"

"I need you."

"What for?"

"Nothing in particular at this very moment. Just in general. Wanted you to know, I realized—Miss Char and I were talking about it: You're not only very much welcome here you're *needed* here. We *need* you. Thought you should know that."

"OK. Well, thanks."

"Hey, can we talk?" I coax him out of the cabin and onto one the park benches outside it. We're in Los Angeles, but it's January, and there's a pleasant nip in the air that reminds me of my Wisconsin boyhood, raking leaves, playing in creeks, throwing a football with my dad during halftime of the Packers game. I wonder what boyhood memories Michael Bailey cherishes—but I've learned by now that uninvited interrogation will get us nowhere. He doesn't need my questions. He needs my love.

"Mike, I've listened to your stories," I tell him, smiling wryly. "A *lot* of stories. Now I want you to listen to one of mine."

"No, no, I understand how much you and Char have done for me. Without you two . . ."

"That's true," I say. "But, see, what people don't understand is . . . how much you've done for *us*."

He shakes his head *no-no*, but I plow onward, undeterred. I try to make Michael James Bailey understand how his care for our home—and our puppy!—has transformed our lives. How he's helped us become better versions of ourselves.

"Look, I didn't know you until a couple of years ago," I remind him. "And you didn't know me. But, I'm certain you weren't always the guy I met at Elderberries. Right? Well, if you would have met *me* twenty years ago, ten years ago, even five years ago—I wasn't the MK you know now, either. I was very 'successful' according to the rules of game, but I don't think I really approved of myself fully. I was happy most of the time, but always unsatisfied. You understand? I was a big winner but I was also sad about something. And I think that something was *me*. I think I was sad about myself, about not having my values and thoughts and actions in harmony. Well, now they are. And I *like* this version of me. I *like* caring about other people. I like being generous. And kind. And, I guess what I'm trying to say is: I give you a lot of credit for helping me become this version of myself."

He nods and shrugs.

"Mike," I say, "you're one of my best friends. I'm really glad we met."

"Yeah, yeah, so am I."

"I consider you my friend. A real friend." He doesn't reply. "Mike, do you consider me your friend?"

"No, no, it's not that, I'm just sayin', no, we gotta nice arrangement. You help me out, I help you out."

"I see our relationship as way more than *a nice arrangement*," I tell him, suddenly feeling like a jilted boyfriend. "You don't consider me your friend?"

Poker-faced, he says, "I don't really have any friends."

It hits me like a kick in the nuts. I want to sob, I want to lecture. But instead I say, "Yeah? Well, neither do I. And you're one of them!"

He chuckles a little.

"Whether or not you acknowledge it, we *are* friends," I insist. Then I assure Michael James Bailey, the former Fisher King of Hollywood, that not only are we friends, we're something more, something like complementary particles that bind together, improving the lot for both. We have a symbiotic relationship, and those are usually the best kind. "I know I've helped you get better. And you've helped me get better. Like you say, we've helped each other. And I just want you to know I'm thankful for you, Mike."

"Well, yeah, thanks. Me, too."

"And I love you."

He nods, but doesn't respond. He chews his lips.

"You don't have to feel the same way," I assure him. "But you do need to hear what I'm telling you: I love you, Mike. You're my friend, my brother, my family. And I love you."

"Thanks," he says. I can feel he wants to say more, volumes more. But he only shakes his head, lost in private thoughts.

I'm about to get up to go back to my office when he says, "You been telling me that, and it's been a long time since anyone said that to me."

"I'm sorry about that, Mike."

"My grandparents," he says. "I was raised by my grandparents, and, and let's just put it this way: They weren't good people."

I say nothing, hoping he'll continue, tell me everything. But all Mike says is, "Been a long time. Been a long time." He looks at his hands. "Long time."

I'm heartbroken for him. But I try to stay positive. "Well, the good news is you won't have to wait long to hear it again. I love you. Got it, bro?"

"Yeah, yeah."

"And so does Billie and so does Miss Char—and probably more people than you even realize. We all love you."

"OK. OK."

"I'm not going to stop telling you, so you better get used to it." He waves me off. "No, no. Stop."

I hug him. "Whether you realize it or not, you're my friend and I love you. That's all I've got to say. Goodbye. See you soon. I'm going."

I turn to leave. Sure, I'm hoping Mike will reciprocate. But when he doesn't I'm not devastated or deeply disappointed (OK, maybe I'm a little disappointed). I'm elated and content—because I'm learning, just starting to understand the life-altering power of compassion.

Unlike, say, an EpiPen or a Naloxone injection, love infusions don't necessarily produce immediate results. Love is more of a time-release capsule. Uncle Mike doesn't immediately emerge from Weed Hollow singing a joyous tune. Indeed, the next morning he hibernates in bed until 11 a.m., and his mood remains aloof, slightly surly.

A few days later, though, the fog begins to lift. As the sun rises, I open the back door to let Billie relieve herself. "Morning!" he calls out to me with a crisp salute, already doing something or other in the workshop at 7 a.m. "Lotta of stuff to do. Couldn't wait for my assistant. Hey, Kid! Howya doin?" Caretaker Mike is back. A version of him is back—but this one is so unrelentingly can-do and optimistic you'd be tempted to call him a new man.

Over the course of the next few months, he treats the entire property—every square inch, inside and out—as his handyman playground, reinvigorating our century-old home, turning it into a marvelous showplace of happy colors, a pink-and-purple fairytale playhouse. It's so beautiful and tranquil and peaceful that I'm tempted to become an urban shut-in, perfectly content to never leave the bubble of tranquility.

All of our neighbors start hiring him for odd jobs—painting, wall-mounting, landscaping. With his pay, Mike buys himself new boots and shirts and saves the rest. When we make a Home Depot run, he ignores the soda cooler, and on the way home he dismisses the idea of a Burger King stop (even though I have coupons). "Too much sodium!" he explains.

My friends become his friends. Scotty and Ryan—and all the other lads who come by—make it a point to get their Uncle Mike time, trading stories, sharing laughs. (They also appreciate the hand-rolled doobies he makes for them from what he calls his "special blend," which, from what I can gather, is a proprietary mix of buds that have fallen on the floor of the cellar during the drying process.) Scotty, with his strong Long Island accent, lays a hand on my shoulder and tells me, "Mike's a great guy. I would hang out with him even if I didn't know you."

His raconteurship might not be as fantastical as in the Selena days, but Mike still likes telling stories, "bullshitting with the boys," as he puts it. Everyone—even Charmaine—likes hanging with Mike, just as the laws of attraction planned it. Even the animals, and not just Billie the Kid. In June, as his one-year anniversary of Vista Street residency approaches, our adopted Uncle Mike comes to my office window, waving for my attention. I step out to the back deck. "What's up?"

"I know you're busy," he says, "but c'mere. I wanna show you something."

Billie and I follow Mike down the stairs into the garden and back to Weed Hollow cabin. "Hey, Kid, be nice," he says, holding her collar and pointing to a patch of calla lilies across from Chareze's gravesite.

I look down and see a tiny baby squirrel, about the size of a large mouse, trembling in the reeds. It's beyond adorable. So small, so cute. "Is it OK?"

Mike explains, "That windstorm last night? You heard that, right? Well, I think the nest got blown out of the tree"—he indicates a towering palm on the other side of the fence—"and this little guy is the only survivor. Chris," our neighbor, "told me he had to fish a few of them out of his pool."

"Oh, no! How awful."

"So I don't think this one has a mom no more. He comes to me. Doesn't run. I been feeding him. Mostly birdseed and some dog treats. Sorry, Billie." Our mutt is sniffing the area with great interest and zero aggression. The baby squirrel doesn't seem frightened, just dazed and confused.

"They look like they could be friends," I remark.

"No, no, they already are." Crouching down, he pets Billie with one hand and offers some sunflower seeds with the other to the squirrel. "Here you go, Ollie," Mike says. "Everything's gonna be all right."

"Ollie? Like Oliver?"

"Yeah, and, and if he turns out to be girl we'll call her Annie. Two most famous orphans of all time." He presents his open palm to Ollie/Annie, who politely eats one black seed at a time while Billie watches, wagging her tail and whimpering softly. For all the trauma this little rodent has endured, he seems calm now, undisturbed, like he understands somehow that the tall, toothless creature feeding him snacks will eventually nurse him to health and usher him into adulthood.

"Welcome to your new home," I tell the squirrel.

"See, Billie?" Uncle Mike says, beaming. "This is your baby brother Ollie. You gotta be nice to him. He's the newest member of our family."

TWENTY

The End?

———

"I think I'm ready to move on."

We've been waiting to hear these words for almost a year and a half, most of that time quietly doubting they'd ever be uttered. But as 2017 draws to a close, Caretaker Mike calls a Family Meeting—Billie invited, Ollie not—to discuss his future. The conclave in our breakfast nook comes at a good time. For the past few months, Charmaine has been wondering out loud what's next for our adopted Caretaker.

Is there a next? She asks, "You don't see him living here forever, do you?"

No, that's not something I desire. But I can also envision various scenarios where we'd be compelled to offer permanent residency. If Mike needs me, I'm prepared to take care of him, housing him as long as he wants a place to sleep that's not a bus bench. Unless he suddenly became dangerous or aggressive, I know I'll never cast Mike out on the streets. He's my friend. And like every person walking this planet, on some level he's my brother.

But now it's moot. He's discharging himself. Leaving us.

Am I relieved? Excited? Yes, a little, maybe. But then why do I feel so sad, on the verge of despair?

"It's like I was telling MK," he explains, "I've been talking to a caseworker at The Center, and, and he thinks I could be eligible for some housing subsidies and so forth. They're gonna help with the applications, all the paperwork. Food stamps, GR, and I think Social Security, 'cause I have a number, I'm already in the system."

"What's 'GR'?" I ask.

"General Relief. Welfare."

"You can get that?" Charmaine asks, skeptical.

"Well, yeah, if the paperwork gets done right. And you can't do it unless you got a California state I.D. and a real Social Security card. Not just the number. The *card*. So that's the next thing we're going to work on. They're helping me. I think they're going to take me to the office, the Social Security office, and help me get one."

So far, none of this sounds to me like one of Mike's tall tales. But I'm curious: how does he plan on getting official identification? Doesn't that come from the DMV? "Is The Center going to help you get a driver's license?"

He grins. "It ain't necessary. They already did." He reaches into his back pants pocket and fishes out his wallet. "We already got it!" Mike flashes his laminated I.D. card at me and Charm like a pilot at TSA security.

"Let me see that!" I say, reaching for it. Mike lets me grip the shiny rectangle, but he doesn't seem to want to let it out of his grasp. "I'll be careful," I assure him.

Charmaine inspects the card over my shoulder. "Nice picture, Mike," she comments.

"No, no, no."

The card looks totally authentic to me, but I'm not sure I'd recognize a forgery anyway. Apparently, Michael James Bailey has fallen through the cracks in the system again, only this time he's defied gravity and fallen up instead of down. "Nice going," I compliment him. "You got yourself a driver's license!"

"No, no, it ain't a driver's license. It's a *picture I.D.*, which, like

I said, you gotta have if you want to qualify for services. I already got a driver's license. Used to have a CDL, too. Not many people have that."

"CDL?" I ask.

"Commercial Driver's License. You need to it operate certain vehicles. I used to drive trucks cross-country. Got to see just about every state that way."

Is it true? Does it matter anymore?

I go to hug him. "I'm really proud of you, man," I say, holding him tight. Charmaine comes around the other side and sand-wiches us in her embrace, with Billie wiggling below, trying to get into the scrum.

"Well, it's gonna take some time," Mike tells us. "There's a lotta steps."

"It's a process," Charmaine offers.

"Yeah, and the process, you know, it can take a few months, from what I understand."

"So you're not leaving immediately, right? Like, not today?" I blurt.

"No, no, no, I mean, if that's still OK."

"Of course!" we assure him.

"Could be thirty days, could be a few months," Mike explains. "But, like Miss Char said, the process is starting. So . . . Eventu-ally, I'm gonna have my own place."

We ask him where? How? Does he have a vague idea or a concrete plan?

"Oh, it's all arranged," Mike informs us. "I already seen it."

Charmaine catches my eye. This is sounding more and more like a Fisher King-era fantasy. He tells us he was shown a studio apartment in a three-story, thirty-unit building in Silverlake, known for its hipster coffee shop culture, where every other cre-ative young person moving to Los Angeles dreams of living.

According to Caretaker Mike, the building is managed by HUD—the federal Department of Housing and Urban Development—and it's meant for people like him, folks known as "chronically homeless." He tells us his new place has its own little kitchenette and a private bathroom, with a shower. "Let's just say it totally exceeded my expectations," he reports. "Much bigger than I expected."

Mine, too. Which is why the next morning I reach out to Nathan Sheets, the director of The Center, who knows we've been looking after Michael Bailey while he mends. Although privacy laws prevent Mr. Sheets from furnishing any personal details whatsoever, he assures me that the general picture Caretaker Mike painted is more or less accurate. "Everything is on track for him, possibly even the fast track."

When I relay the information to Charmaine, she's elated. Finally, she'll get her healing space back. She'll no longer have to share her Be Well casita with a (nice) man from the streets.

I'm happy for her. I'm happy for us. But mostly I'm happy for Michael James Bailey. He's getting his life back.

AS 2017 SLIPS into 2018, Caretaker Mike spends fewer mornings at home and more at The Center, where he sees a caseworker who's helping him navigate the confusing bureaucracy of Los Angeles social services. There's not much to do around Vista Street; Mike's completed every project on his list, and dozens more, leaving his personal mark all over the property. The veggie donation table out front gets a new hand-painted sign; the walkway to Charmaine's Be Well practice gets a trellised archway. All that's left is the cellar workshop space, still cluttered with tools and building materials, still a symbol of the chaos that once (still?) disturbed his mind. He assures me he'll get to it sooner or later, but Mike's main priority at the moment is getting his affairs in order.

One afternoon, when he returns from his twice-a-week appointment to talk with a counselor, Mike knocks on my office window, seeing if I'm busy.

"Yes, sir," I say, greeting him at the aperture. "How may I help you?"

He chuckles. "Well, actually, here, I got something for you." He hands me a little hand-rolled joint. "My special blend. From downstairs."

"Thank you," I say, accepting the gift. "I'll enjoy this later. I'm writing now. Working on a book about you—and me, and Billie."

"Oh, yeah?"

"Is that cool?"

He nods. "No, no, that's fine. Good luck. I hope it's a bestseller."

"I hope it's enough of a seller that you and I could do a book tour together, talking about our experience. The Mike and Mike show. Readings, maybe a Q & A. People will want your auto-graph."

He chuckles. "No, no . . . Look, before that happens, I gotta ask a favor. I ain't had any money to speak of for a while now, and, and, I'm gonna get more than I've had all at once, and I'm afraid I'm not gonna be able to handle it right. Manage it. So I was wondering if, you know, you could help me out a little? Make sure I don't do nothin' crazy?"

"Like buy cigarettes? Sure, Mike."

"No, no, no. You know what I mean."

I think I do—although nothing about Caretaker Mike's behavior over the past six months has triggered any alarms. He seems to be a thrifty shopper and a careful saver, and his major monetary "leaks"—supporting Big Tobacco and Big Sugar—have been nicely patched by my wife, Dr. Hardcore. But the "new" Mike was very recently the "old" Mike, and that guy, I recall, certainly had a problem with fiscal management, among other issues.

"You know I'll help however I can," I tell him.

"Thanks," he says. "Me, too."

A WEEK LATER, I wake to find an unsigned note from Caretaker Mike left on the back deck table:

CENTER IN THE MORNING

APPOINTMENTS IN AFTERNOON

Then I go about my business. It's another beautiful day.

It's February 14th, Valentine's Day. Charmaine and I celebrate "this special holiday" by treating it identically to every other day on our fully booked romance calendar. We giggle and carouse and behave like insufferable teenagers, but the tuxedo and gown stay in the closet. It's just another day, another beautiful day.

Around lunchtime, Charmaine asks me if I've seen Uncle Mike. I mention the note he left; and then I go about my business again. At some point, Billie ambles through the garden and scratch-knocks on the Weed Hollow Cabin door. No answer. She backs up and tries again, wagging her tail. No answer.

We all go about our business.

Typically, Mike's home from his outings by 2 p.m., 3 p.m. at the latest. Around 4:20 p.m., the time when Mike's Special Blend is most appreciated, I realize he's still gone.

When I report the news, Charmaine's openly concerned. "Should we be worried?" she wonders. "Do you think there's a problem?"

"No," I reply, trying hard not to worry. "He's getting used to more independence. Making his own decisions. I'm sure he's fine. Now, if he's not here by nightfall . . ."

We wait. We attempt unsuccessfully to go about our business. Uncle Mike's not home by nightfall.

Over dinner, theories abound, and they cover both ends of the

Good-Bad spectrum: He's on a shopping spree; he's been abducted. He's moved into his new apartment; he's relapsed. Alcohol is involved; Valentine's Day is involved.

We don't know, and, of course, that's the hardest part.

After dinner, Billie and I search the cabin. Other than his wallet and money and crucifixes, all of Mike's personal items and clothes are where he left them, spewed haphazardly about the cabin. He's planning on returning, that's clear.

Bedtime, I check again. No Mike.

What should we do? Go looking for him? File a report?

Who would we call? What would we tell them? *I'm trying to locate a homeless person with no permanent address or phone number who lives with my family in our backyard cabin.*

"Let's see if Mike comes home tonight," I propose. "If he doesn't, I'll call The Center in the morning."

Neither of us sleeps well. I listen all night for the tell-tale scrape of our metal driveway gate being opened, but it never happens. At daybreak, I tiptoe out to the cabin with Billie. We knock on the door: No answer. We go inside: No Mike.

Back in bed, Charmaine asks, "Did he leave a note or anything? In the cabin?"

"Nothing. Other than the one I told you about—his appointments—he didn't give me any information about where he was going. But don't worry. I'm following up. As soon as they open, I'll get in touch with The Center."

At 8 a.m. on Wednesday, the time when dozens of clients from the streets of Hollywood converge there for coffee and compassion, I call The Center and leave an explanatory, beseeching voicemail. Then I email, copying Director Sheets: "URGENT: Michael Bailey Missing." In my note, I stress that in the nearly two years Michael's been living with us, he's never failed to come home before sundown.

I wait. I call again. I wait.

I wait some more.

No word from The Center. No word from Caretaker Mike.

I'm not "very concerned" now. I'm very worried. I don't understand what's happening. I hold onto the hope that *nothing's* happening, and, therefore, maybe I'm fretting over nothing. I keep telling myself, *Mike's OK, and soon we'll all laugh at the misunderstanding.* When someone vanishes, though, the not knowing, the mystery, becomes a visceral pain, gnawing at you, gradually consuming all your energy and spirit. An airplane over the Pacific disappears from radar; a child fails to come home from school; a pedestrian vanishes in a vast urban jungle—when a loved one goes missing, a restless fugue state of anxious expectation begins.

When I report the news to Charmaine—no news—she looks stricken. "Do you think he's OK?"

I tell her the truth: I don't know. But I'm hopeful, and I'm trusting all the great survival skills Mike's developed out of necessity will serve him well in case he's in trouble. Mike's smart; he's resilient; he's resourceful. And he has our phone numbers.

I remind Charm, though we could imagine a thousand possible reasons why he hasn't yet called, we have to acknowledge the small chance that Mike just doesn't want to talk with us. Maybe he's perfectly fine, carousing with a new friend, a lady friend. Maybe he got a motel room. Maybe he hired some company. Maybe . . .

The phone rings. I see on the caller screen, it's The Center.

A kind, empathetic person who understands the complicated relationship we have with Michael Bailey, call this person the Source, sidesteps various rules and regulations and tells me exactly what's happened.

Michael came to The Center yesterday morning and asked repeatedly for psychiatric help. He said he was having "very dark thoughts" and he needed help. We explained to him that the way the system works, if we call for help, a PET—a Psychiatric Evaluation Team—would be sent. We told him he'd be taken to a police station and they might restrain him for his own safety, and after getting evaluated he would probably be admitted to one of the County's emergency psychiatric facilities for overnight observation. We explained all this and Michael was very adamant. He said he understood the procedure and he wanted help. We couldn't determine if he had an actual plan to harm himself, but he did express suicidal thoughts. So we made the call.

The PET came and determined he should be further evaluated. Like I said, he was probably taken to a police facility and then transferred to a psych hospital. Which one I don't know. They won't tell us. They won't tell anyone. This is where the privacy laws come in. He could be any number of places.

They usually keep patients on an emergency hold for forty-eight hours before we hear anything. We can try again in the morning, but I have to warn you we probably won't know anything for some time. They won't let the patient make any outgoing calls when they're on a suicide watch, because they don't want to trigger anything. So we just have to let the medications work, and when the situation has straightened out, we'll probably hear something. But it's got to come from Michael.

I'm really sorry to tell you all this. I know you and your wife have been great friends to Michael, but there's really nothing more I can tell you, other than I understand how upsetting this is. Really, I can't count how many times I've been working with people for weeks, months, years, and they just vanish. I guess I've gotten used to it, working in this field. But I know it can be painful and it's not easy to accept.

No, it's not. But I'm not at the acceptance stage yet. On so many levels, for so many reasons, I'm heartbroken. (The thought of Mike in handcuffs, drugged with powerful pharmaceuticals keeping him on "an even keel," devastates me.) But I don't have time for feelings of regret and remorse. I have to follow the leads and find my lost friend. I'm a seasoned journalist. I'm Encyclopedia Konik. I can do this.

The Source sends me a list of all the psychiatric hospitals in Los Angeles County. Dozens. Five of them have been highlighted with the annotation "This is where I would look first." I spend most of the day making calls, sounding officious as I can, acting as though I know where he is. *Hello, my name is Michael Konik, calling on behalf of the Homeless Center in Hollywood. I'm trying to locate a Mr. Michael Bailey, date of birth July 26, 1971. He would have been admitted to your facility yesterday.*

Most of the nice people on the other end of the line look through their files and regret to inform me they have no record of him being admitted. Some of them tell me that even if he were there—and they won't say he is—they wouldn't be able to confirm or deny the fact. All of them assure me that if they see him—and it's always conditional, *if*—they'll surely give him the following message: *Please call Michael and Charmaine; they're worried about you.*

How many calls like these do they get every day from frantic families looking for their troubled child, their mom, their dad? When someone wants to get lost in Los Angeles, it takes more than amazing grace for them to be found. They have to want to be found.

At the end of the second day of Mike's absence, the Source has no new information. The County of Los Angeles isn't talking. The cabin remains empty.

Charmaine and I tell each other reassuring stories with unequivocally happy endings, and manage to get some sleep, still alert for a welcome scrape on the driveway.

We don't expect fresh news over the weekend, and none comes. Storytelling continues.

On Monday, I resume contact with The Center, where Director

Sheets tells me, "I can't say where exactly Michael would be staying, but from experience in these situations, usually folks come out in a clearer head space having gone through psych evaluation and gotten the meds they need. Of course, this often wears off, but we're hoping we catch him in that window of clarity, and we can proceed with a proactive approach through his mental health provider."

Then he reminds me all further information must come from Michael Bailey.

That's the last I hear from The Center.

Monday passes. Tuesday passes. On Wednesday, while I'm morosely recounting Caretaker Mike's week-long absence to my friend Scotty, I realize that all my feelings of failure and fear are the product of looking at Mike's situation through my prism instead of his. Scotty actually thinks it's *great* that Uncle Mike asked for help and got it. "Imagine if instead of walking away and getting help he had stayed and done something horrible on your property."

Yes. He's right. How strange it hasn't occurred to me, never considering it for a second, believing nothing horrible can ever happen in our little Eden, so long as we all drink our smoothies and take care of each other.

Scotty was there when we lost Chareze and he's here when we've lost Mike, and both times he's helped me see the good and beautiful side of a situation that at first appeared to be only darkness. For the rest of the week, I start to adjust to Life Without Him, purposefully tweaking my attitude, telling myself that it's nice to have more privacy, nice to be able to walk around my garden as naked as Adam—as if that happens with any regularity.

It's all good. Mike's getting help; he's . . . somewhere. We're here . . . waiting.

For a moment, I fixate on the idea that Mike "owes" us some

clarity, a sense of closure. But I quickly realize that the cosmic ledger is beautifully balanced: I can't say for certain who "saved" whom, or if anyone was saved at all. We were *there* for each other. Present. Every time I look at the empty cabin, I feel a twinge of sadness. *He's gone—but it's all good.*

It's all good, sure, yes, OK. But this is the part people don't understand: Michael James Bailey has become one of my closest friends. When you don't have many of them to begin with, losing one is crushing. To combat what feels like creeping depression, I tell myself the Buddhists are right: *everything* is impermanent, that change, for better or worse, is the nature of existence. Michael James Bailey is a human *mandala*, a sublime work of art that takes many hours and days to create and seconds to lose. Like Chareze. Like all of us.

But I miss him. I miss his smile. His laughter. His love for Billie and baby Ollie and, maybe, I feel, me and Charmaine.

She's delighted to have the casita back to herself, but on Friday, when it's clear something has shifted, the energy in and around our home fundamentally changed, Charmaine tells me, "I miss Uncle Mike."

"I do, too."

Charmaine frowns. "And so does Billie."

ALMOST TWO WEEKS from the day Uncle Mike walked away from Weed Hollow Cabin and into the caring hands of emergency psychiatric workers, I'm working at my desk when there's a knock at the front door.

EPILOGUE

— ⁓ —

At first we don't talk.

When I open the door and see Mike on our porch, the same porch on which he once slept—wearing clean new clothes, his mustache trimmed and hair combed, I break into sobs and hold him close. There's so much I want to tell him—I'm relieved, I'm angry, I'm overjoyed—but I can't speak.

I don't have to. All the feelings pour out of me (and onto Mike's shoulder). He pats my back. "I know. I know."

Billie races out the door, cry-barking. She smashes into our legs, jumping on her hind legs, wiggling madly. Sniffling and snuffling, I croak, "We were so worried about you."

"I know," he says. "I knew you would be. That's why I came back. To check in. Update you on what's happening." He picks up Billie and brings her to his face, which she kisses maniacally. "Howya doin', Kid? I missed you, too."

He seems calm.

"Mike, all this time, where have you been, man?"

"I'm staying in a shelter downtown. Skid Row. It ain't pretty."

"But the cabin is here for you. I don't understand."

He tells me a long, complicated story involving appointments with doctors and counselors, a story that sort of makes sense and

255

sort of doesn't. He confirms what I learned from the Source: He had "a lot of dark thoughts." He needed help. And now he's getting it.

So, does he have to stay in a shelter to qualify for permanent housing? Not really. Are all his social service helpers located downtown, in the heart of our city's largest homeless encampments? No, actually, most of them are closer to Hollywood, near The Center.

I still don't understand. Why wouldn't he just get on a bus and come home to Vista Street? Why wouldn't he call?

More not-quite-clear explanations, more quasi-believable tales.

Then I see a pack of Camels sticking out of the inside pocket of his jacket, and I think I get it: Michael Bailey would rather face the indignities of sleeping in a loud, dangerous, discouraging homeless shelter than face the indignities of someone telling him what he can and cannot eat, what he can and cannot smoke.

"I see you're back to cigarettes," I say flatly.

"Yeah, well, you know. It's tough down there."

I don't press. I know he hasn't come here to be judged and criticized.

"Hey, how's Ollie?" he asks.

"Growing up. I think his testicles are starting to show."

"Stop!" he sputters.

I invite Mike to see for himself. We go to the back, but all the squirrels are a few houses over, feasting on a helpless avocado tree. Waiting for Charmaine to finish with her Be Well client, Mike and I sit beside Weed Hollow Cabin, on the park benches. As he commences to recount the awful things he's seen in the past week—thievery, assault, rampant drug use—Miss Char emerges from the casita, beaming. "I *thought* I recognized that voice!"

She joins us beneath the blood-orange tree. "Tell me!" she says.

It's a tough story to follow, but Charmaine listens patiently to

Mike's recounting of his travails, nodding and smiling, encouraging him to talk. If she's eager to inquire about gluten and lactose, she doesn't show it. All Charm asks is what kind of medications Mike's taking.

"Just something for anxiety, something to help me sleep at night. And an anti-depressant."

Charmaine nods. "I see." She won't say it now, not in front of him, but I know she's thinking we've lost Mike to the dark side, where toxins in his food and pharmaceuticals (and cigarettes, and who knows what else) attack his body, leading to nothing good. He's back on the road to a leaky gut and a leaky brain.

When he excuses himself to use the bathroom, I turn to her and sigh. "We tried."

She smiles. "Yes, we did. And now he needs to be free."

MIKE SPENDS THE night in the cabin. The agreement is he'll stay with us when he needs to be near his Hollywood appointments, and when he needs to be near downtown he'll stay at the shelter. Most of his clothes and possessions will stay here. This is still his home base. *Home.* Haven't countless books and movies reminded us there's no place like it?

The next morning it's February 27th, my late father's birthday. He would have been 81. It's also the last day we ever see Michael James Bailey.

He's gone.

He slipped away early. No note.

Most of his stuff is still in the cabin, including two books inscribed for him by the house author. It sure looks like he's coming back, committing to the game plan, ready to return when it's logistically convenient, knowing he's always welcome.

But he never does.

In May 2018, after nearly two months without any Uncle Mike

contact, I reach out to the caseworkers at The Center for an update. They remind me that because of regulations they can't share client information without the client's permission, even under these circumstances. "What Michael *has* said we can share is that he's doing very well," I'm told. "And that he's still on track for the studio in Silver Lake."

The next week we clean out Weed Hollow Cabin and store Uncle Mike's personal items in the shed. On June 1st, we welcome new guests: a friend of Charmaine's going through a divorce, and his eight-year-old daughter.

Two months later, after they find their own apartment, we take in young Maxwell T, twenty-two, a fledgling jazz pianist and the brother of my chess buddy Ellington. Max happens to be super handy. He enjoys house-painting. Power tools don't intimidate him.

He's also recovering from a serious motorcycle accident. Healing.

We call our newest resident Caretaker Max. His first major project involves cleaning up after his disorganized predecessor, transforming the Aegean Stables of our cellar into a proper handyman's workshop. During his initial canvassing of the space, digging around beneath a pile of sandpaper, Caretaker Max discovers an old Altoid tin left behind by Caretaker Mike. It contains a couple of crinkly hand-rolled doobies, filled with Uncle Mike's Special Blend.

I'm saving them for the day my fantasy comes true.

IN MY FANTASY, I'm working at my desk, perhaps on the book you're reading today.

There's a knock on the door. Billie's barking and squealing like crazy. It's Mike!

He smiles when he sees me. He has teeth! He looks terrific!

He wants to know if Charmaine and I and the Kid would care to visit him. He wants to cook us dinner—at his new apartment.

He tells me he's been waiting a long time for this day, all those lonely nights in our backyard cabin, dreaming about having a place of his own. Now it's happening, and, see, what people don't understand is he couldn't be more thrilled.

He tells me he's doing great, better than ever. He's creative and productive and helpful to others. He's happy.

He tells me all is well, and I can see it's true.

He wants to know how I'm doing.

I tell him all is well. And I can see it's true.

Michael James Bailey, February 2018. (Thomas Schaefer)

APPENDIX

Poems inspired by Caretaker Mike

Salmon

Salmon sounded acceptable somehow
when he put it like that, when the man no one ought to trust suggested
"Salmon" would be the perfect shade to rehabilitate the tired white
    railings
delineating our back deck, drawing a perimeter around our privilege.
Never mind everything around the garden is green.
"Forest Green." "Seaweed Green." "Apple Green."
We sagely avoided "Summer Sage," and paddled past "Caribbean
    Coral."
The person with our dream job, she who names paints,
described a particular shade of orangey pink we found hiding in the
    basement.
Called it "Salmon." No qualifier. No evocations.
    And that's the one we spread like cream cheese shmear
    on pliant posts and pickets, two zealots convinced
    this bold new color choice was simultaneously funky
    and inexplicably in harmony with the general scheme of Nature.
When the paint mottled dry and looked like "Salmon" in the same
    way salmon in a can
looks like a simulacrum of salmon,
maybe vaguely the mind color you picture when you read the word
    salmon,
we discovered that our tired white railings had in fact been dappled
with a concoction called "Evening Peruvian Ivy"
and all our calculations and confabulations, all could be forgiven,
    eventually,
a comprehensive catalogue of our misdeeds and misnomers
splashed over and obscured
and one day blissfully forgotten.

—A winner of the 30 West Broadside Contest;
published in *Naugatuck River Review*

Guru

The wise man spoke
I listened with big ears and open heart
Everything made perfect sense until
He mentioned offhandedly that he was married to
The hottest woman on the planet
A singer 38 years his junior
She was away on tour and he was very sorry to say
His wife would not be joining us tonight
On the glamour corner of Sunset Boulevard and No More Hope
    Street
Where I found him at the bus shelter
Orating sagely and eating donated cheese

                 —Published in *The Fredericksburg Literary Review*

Grief Ends When You Decide

When the homeless handyman sleeping in our backyard cabin
failed to emerge that marine layer morning, we brought
coffee and day-old doughnuts to rouse him from pop starlet dreams.
Yelling and crying, yes, of course we did, upon discovery, for we loved
    him
as we love our pets.
His passing shrouded an unsurprising surprise over Eden, a
loss anticipated and unwanted—which is what he said about himself.
No family or friends. No identification in his new jeans. We imagined
burying him in the garden,
beside the puppy dog he interred there just the week before. Eternal
    friends sharing
their viscera with the insect world
teeming furiously, silently, in the dirt.

Her death was an accident. The worst kind, the preventable kind.
His death is a question, and who could say if it was preventable?

—Published in *Applause Literary Journal*
(University of Arkansas)

Matrimony

Betrothed to an all-night train
gone off the tracks, unbound by rails or gravity,
seldom on time. Presently scheduled for no return
on the days she needs everything arranged
just so, without random number generators. Without a pulse
bullying the blood. That mean old bigot who taught Biology
used ersatz bits of Yiddish
for comic effect. Comic relief from chemical revolts
epicentered in high school hallways, where
the nuptial dream began.
Yeshikta! It means "history," this teacher said.
Now he's somewhere. Alive or finished.
Yeshikta!
In the fantasy her man was rugged and terribly self-sufficient.
A modern shaman uncorrupted by the corporate extortionists.
In the fantasy, he was home
when she dreamed him. Properly coupled.
Now they're moving furniture into the middle of the street. Setting
up tents and zeppelins. Ready to fly.
Already beginning final descent.

—Anthologized in *Voices Israel*, 2017 edition

Adoption Story

The dog was easy. The homeless man somewhat less.
We adopted them both.
The dog, the shaggy little mutt, was living on a rambling foster ranch,
so we're not going to say "rescued."
Altruism was hardly involved, not when a sweet puppy would lick
    away tears
still fresh from the death
of another sweet puppy,
a sweet puppy I loved completely and protected poorly.
When she was struck by a truck
in a crosswalk, close enough I could have dived on her,
I died with her, instantly ghosted by grief.
All my illusions, all my lies,
shredded in gnashing teeth of self-recrimination
It was my fault. It was my fault!
I cried until dehydrated. Because it *was* my fault.
And then we found Billie, three-months-old, looking for a friend,
and she saved me.
A rescue after all.

Now she scampers through the autumn garden,
crackling Sycamore leaves beneath
her bounding paws, turning prematurely grey already, at five months.
She's on her way to visit Uncle Mike.
Fisher King Mike they call him on the streets.
Current name: Caretaker Mike.
He lives in our cabin, the backyard cabin
tucked into a corner of tangerine and gardenia,
the little wood cabin once used for trysting and hosting friends and
    vagabonds.
Weed Hollow Cabin: Uncle Mike calls it home.

Modest, yes, but palatial
compared to a bus shelter or a park bench.
"What people don't understand," he'll start his story,
the kaleidoscopic starburst of improbable tangents
that somehow, miraculously, all returns home
to Weed Hollow Cabin, where Uncle Mike adopted
a woman, a man and a puppy,
who mistakenly thought it was they who were adopting,
and made these confused angels his family.
Altruism was hardly involved, not when a sweet puppy would lick
     away tears
still fresh from the loss
of another sweet family,
a sweet family Mike loved completely and protected poorly.
When he left them, whenever he left them,
wherever that was,
he died with them, instantly ghosted by grief.
All his delusions, all his lies, every alternate narrative
silencing the persistent soliloquy of self-abnegation
It was my fault. It was my fault!
And then he found Billie, and Charmaine and the other Mike,
looking for a friend, and he saved them.
A rescue after all.

—Published in *Suisun Valley Review*

REPORT FROM THE STREET:

Voices of the Homeless

The Homeless Metaphor

If we're speaking practically, solving problems
then yes, go ahead, you can identify and analyze all the reasons
why 40,000 human beings are living on the streets of Los Angeles
Mental illness Domestic violence Bad choices over and over
Me? Mental illness, for sure
I had the crazy idea I was going to be somebody
Go ahead
Solve the homeless problem . . .
We'll wait
I'm like world-class at that
I should work in a restaurant
I'm such a great waiter
While you're figuring the finer points of your rescue plan I'm going to
    look at the
situation metaphorically, not historically or rhetorically or euphorically
Just the way it is
Try to count all the poems that are written and books that are
    published and
paintings that are painted
Try to count all the unheard songs all the essays ignored
behind every door Muted Voices without an audience
without anyone to pay attention
The unsuccessful, the virtually anonymous and the unliked
There's going to be a certain number of failures in a system set up like
    a pyramid
Authors unread Love unrequited
Useless words, useless people
Everyone here, everyone on the street is a poem
no one will ever read

Take Care of Each Other

The sign I carry says "Take Care of Each Other"
because that seemed to be the distilled essence of my essential
    message,
the guiding mantra
the reason why I was put here
so far as I can figure.
People find it funny in a darkly satirical ironic melancholy way
that someone who looks like she can't take care of herself
walks around downtown all day
or sits in silent meditation with her sign turned outward leaning
    against a wall
urging the world to accomplish the impossible
while her mission quest crusade is for vacant toilets and showers,
impolite fluid receptacles
reminding us we're all human, even the losers without a place
to wipe away
the stench of living.
I'm used to it by now, the invisibility.
They turn away.
But I watch their eyes, the corners, and sometimes I see them
reading my sign.
Often they chuckle snigger swallow down a true and powerful feeling
suppressing
a sense of connectedness
when confronted with the end
of the line, where all your capitalist dreams go to die.
Those are the moments I know I'm doing something good with my
    life.
I'm getting through and I'm getting by.
That's marvelous. And I am dumbstruck with gratitude.
There are days, I confess, that the only thing I seem any good at is
being ignored.

Being disconnected from the grid and from someone to care for.
I'm an expert at that. Have been for some time.
I grew accustomed to irrelevance long before the street.
Nobody listened then so you can understand
I don't really expect anyone
to listen now.
My story is just as boring and horrifying as everyone else's:
bad choices, etcetera you don't want to hear it believe me because it
    will heartbreak you and
then it will send you off on a there-but-for-the-grace jag that will
    make you feel better about
your life of Netflix and artisanal cupcakes and treadmills but somehow
    it won't make you
feel deeply enough to consider why you take better care of your dog
or your gerbil
than you do the woman sleeping in a tent beside the freeway.
Maybe I could walk your dog. Maybe that could be my career
my Lifepath
my way of earning a rightful place in your highly celebrated society,
somewhere near the bottom, of course, yet
officially part of the game
still an eligible receiver of illegible messages transcribed for future
    broadcast.
I would be helpful, not an unpleasant manifestation of the system's
    waste products.
May I walk your dog? I no longer have useful references and for that I
    apologize but I
believe you'll nonetheless find me eminently qualified to walk your
    dog to the organic pet
food store so that we can both try sample biscuits
and she can move her joints and then her bowels while you're away
doing more important things than spending time with your best
    friend.
She deserves it. You deserve it.

Someone to simply *be there*. Like a security guard.

Someone to look after your prizes, the stuffed animals you won at the carnival thanks to

hard work and perhaps a little luck and more hard work.

You are a winner. You earned what you've got. And now you've earned my service.

May I, madame?

May I, sir?

Or do you think, would it be better

to grind me up,

to reform me as appetizingly crunchy pellets and

feed me lovingly

by the handful

to the fluffy just-shampooed creature you care for most?

Although I smell unpalatable to you, I am high in protein and loaded with nutritious

disappointments

that dogs and cats and some confined birds find delicious.

Please consume what is left of me. The body and the blood. Let me be your Jesus. Let me walk

your dog.

If I can take care of you in this way, like the sign says,

maybe you could take care of me?

Or someone else you don't know.

Or someone you do.

Let's call it even and everyone is happy.

That's all I've ever asked for.

Take care of each other and everyone is happy.

People Watching

People watching. Observing people. That's my thing, what I'm best at.
People watching. The endless parade. Colors and curves.
Mesmerizing, really, how they slither by my sidewalk manor.
From where I lie, like my man Buddha, propped on an elbow, in transit
to Nirvana
mostly ignored, almost invisible,
accepting it all, receiving your energy messages—
from my disadvantageous vantage point
there appears to be
a surplus of pain in this world, in all our lives.
Mine included. And yours, I can tell.
So although the pavement won't never nohow erase
my memories of mattresses
all foamy and cushiony and made for snuggling,
I don't envy your misery,
the demon that compels you to keep climbing
the hamster wheel to nowhere.
On the coldest and wettest nights
yes of course I wish for a proper roof.
But I suspect
how can you really know?
I'm in the right place,
in some version of where I'm meant to be.
You should do what you think is best.
You should keep running, running to wherever you think you're going.
Meanwhile I look up at the blue and the clouds and I see an airplane
crawling across my no-cost movie screen. I see
a slave ship going somewhere
I know I'll never visit.

List of Grievances

Actually, no, I would not like to list my grievances
as you say. My grievances. No I would not.
Please don't misunderstand. I'm glad the Sociology Department is
    sponsoring your outreach.
Your reaching out. Talking to us. Thank you. *Arigato.*
Yes. Yes. I speak 14 languages, including Tagalog, Malay, Vietnamese,
    and a dialect of
Martian.
So I say to you: *nyet.* No. *Urk.* I would not like to list my grievances
    because
I'm against lists. I'm against listicles. I am fiercely opposed to bucket
    lists.
Top ten. Top five. List of the Top 100!
Comprehensive list of All the Things You
Should . . .
You're too young. This was before.
Listmania began I think it was in the '70s. The best-selling book was
a pulpy airport paperback prayer manual called
"The Book of Lists."
There were follow-ups.
And now all anyone wants is to organize chaos into quantifiable lists.
    Don't you
find it all a bit demoralizing?
I do. And, yes, I would like a granola bar and a bottle of water,
    although
bottled water is a terrible choice if you're concerned about the
    environment.
I'm very concerned about the environment, which I know must sound
    surprising
coming from someone who lives in the litter.
Top three things you can do for the environment. Top four things you
    can do for the homeless.

You want me to list my grievances? Like number seven
I hate not having my own
private jet.
Number six I hate having to pay my ex-wife Salma Hayek alimony.
Number forty-four I hate when I can't get the remote to work on my
    home theater. I mean
I could go on, but, no, really, I do not wish to list
to make a list
of millions of particles
when all you really need to know is the atom.
The essential.
The indivisible truth.
Indivisible. One nation, indivisible. One nation, under god, indivisible,
indivisible
one nation
under god
indivisible
with liberty and justice for all. Indivisible
with liberty and justice for all.
Indivisible. With liberty and justice
for all.
I have no grievances. I have no list of grievances. I have only pride to
    have been born
an American.
I have been at liberty to pursue one version of happiness
and when you look down this alley of boxes and tents
you can be sure that justice has been properly served.

I'm Praying for You

Nice lady says to me, *I'm praying for you.*
Even though I'm thinking
If you're able to talk with God, ask him why he allowed this
what I say is:
I'm praying for you, too.
I pray for you.
For all of you. All of ya'll.
I pray for you, that you don't end up here. Like this.
I pray for you. Yes. Yes, I do it so you don't have to, so you can avoid
  the bother.
The wasted energy.
So much wasted energy, that's what this is about. Misappropriation of
  energy and resources.
Poor distribution. A failure to distribute properly. That's all.
We appreciate the sandwiches and the bibles and the positive
  thoughts.
Ya'll mean well, I know.
But it's too late. Your prayers are squandered on me.
I'm never leaving
unless the angels come in the dark and spirit me away on feathered
  backs
because what you can't understand until you been there—
and don't worry, I'm praying for you—
living like this
immersed up to your chin
in filth and disease and a kind of relentless omnipresent pain
someone with a home and a car can never understand and will never
  feel,
thank you, God,
I'm talking way beyond physical, a pain in the *soul*—
without help I won't rise above

278

these undignified circumstances,

this tar-paper swamp

yanking me back to the ground every time I try to fly.

No one ever does. No one escapes. No one that I'm acquainted with.

There's no help for the lowest of God's children.

Literally, we are helpless. We have no help.

No help, no hope.

No hope. Around here we call it Nope.

This is the Land of Nope. Thank you for visiting. We pray you have
    enjoyed your brief tour

under the rug, where the mistakes are swept.

It's like going to the zoo, right?

No cages or enclosures here,

but you

you're always on the correct side of the divider,

the voyeur

gazing greedily from a safe-dangerous distance.

Me and the other Nopesters, we're on the wrong side of the glass.

Same side as the zebras and monkeys.

But charity is what makes us human I've been told, and I want to be
    charitable

and righteous and a better person than I was yesterday, and I want to
    be

as generous as you are.

I want to gift you my willingness to listen empathetically.

Big ears. Big heart.

I reckon your prayers must be beneficial

to someone

who is not like us.

The person who prays is a pray-er and what they say is a prayer. The
    recipient is the pray-ee

unless the prayer is secretly meant for the pray-er.

So keep praying, my friend. Someone might feel better soon.

Trust me, beautiful person: You don't know what the bottom is.

Trust me, exalted soul,
when you hit bottom, the street bottom, you don't bounce back. You're
    stuck.
Static.
Implanted into inertia
yet constantly unsettled and debased
trudging head-down on a forced march to next night's no place.
Trust me: even though time goes slowly on the street, when you ain't
    doin' nothin'
the clock doesn't move much, yet life
ends quickly.
Is that what you call a paradox?
On the street
your body breaks and ages in fast-motion, while all the events of the
    daily decay
go slowly.
Imagine an invisible antagonist, stepping on your back,
grinding you into sidewalk graffiti,
unwilling to relieve the pressure
booting you down
until
you're completely out of sight.
Unfindable. Officially lost.
Unlikely to reappear.
Buried.
You can't climb out of a hole if you don't have hands or feet.
So that's where you are and where you shall be and everywhere you are
    that is where you are
forever.
I think that's Zen. But me I'm a sort of relapsed Christian.
And I'm praying for you, friend.
I'm praying for you, nice lady. I'm praying to God for you.
I can't do it out loud around here because folks conversing with
    nobody, talking to the air—

that's crazy.
And if your discussion becomes too loud or impassioned
they throw you in a paddy wagon and transport you to a hospital and
    give you pills
to put an end to dialogues with imaginary friends.
So like Falstaff I must exercise discretion in my valor
when I pray for you and for all the people like you
who didn't drown and have not yet sunk.
You don't have to thank me. It's the least I can do, and also the most.
You can't save me but maybe I can save you and
my life will have been worth something more than nothing.
No, no, I am not insulted that you wish to pray for me.
I'm grateful, truly I am, I'm grateful that you talked to me as though
I'm still a human being worthy of human discourse.
Quite refreshing. Your prayers are refreshing, like a drink they
    advertise on TV, with just a hint
of lime.
Please pray for that, too.
Spritzers from the heavens for all the thirsty ones.
And a clean pair of socks.
Go ahead. Pray for all the wishes you can think of. The children. The
    whales.
And don't worry. Don't you worry.
I'll be praying for you.

Mental Illness

I'm not the one that needs help. I'm not ill.
You. Your appetites are aroused
over and over again.
Your passions, your appetites are fed
and aroused and fed
again. Until you no longer distinguish
punishment from pleasure. *That is*
what the Queen wants!
You're taught to worship power. You're an obedient slave. You under-
     stand power.
You once had some. And now you serve. You're a slave and you will be
     punished
and you will find it
pleasurable
because it's not the punishments that perfect you
it's the master.
The one who wields the whip. The one you don't question.
The one you love for loving you.
Go worship your master. Go eat your money.
Stay away from me, please. Everyone in this community,
this encampment under the freeway,
has chosen to live here
voluntarily
for a reason.
Me? I was escaping mental illness, mental sickness, diseased minds.
I came here
fleeing you and your fellow zombies. Your insanity.
Must come with owning a house. You lose your mind. You have no
     consciousness.
I pity you, friend. You're unconscious. Comatose.
You're asleep at the wheel while the minivan filled with your church
     soccer team

veers off the road into a ravine.

Your appetites are aroused and fed. That's all you know. That's all you
care about.

And you know that's the truth

painful as it may be.

Doesn't hurt me, not at all. But I could see how having a street person

a homeless person

call you on your bullshit

might be upsetting for a second or two of revelation,

until you go back to looking at your phone.

I'm not cutting down the Amazon, bro. You are.

You. Even if you never held a chainsaw you cut down the trees

with your appetites, your need for meat, your need for cheap meat.

Your need

to eat five meals a day.

You put people in cages for wishing to communicate with the spirit
world

through visionary plants.

You murder strangers in Afghanistan for reasons you never considered.

You sleepwalk. You're not really there. You can't be blamed for nightly
mayhem.

I'm sorry you're sick, I really am.

I'm sorry you're unwell.

I'm afraid

I can't help you, friend.

I can't cure your insanity.

No matter how much I meditate and observe the breath going in and
out

I can only cure one soul at a time.

Observed

How kind of you to include me in your annual census.
I'm afraid
I don't have any cookies to offer you. Or a place to sit down that's not
    the ground.
Apologies, nice man. *Mea culpa*
if you prefer the language of my former Church.
How kind of you to take note of my presence on this December night.
    And you even
brought a What is it? A toiletry kit? Oh, that's useful *and* symbolic.
Do I have to answer your questions to get it?
Just kidding. Joking only. I'm so happy to talk with you.
To be seen.
Until you arrived I was only a theoretical probability. Until you
    observed me
I might not have existed.
Like the moon. Or electrons. But when you came out here tonight
    with your clipboard and
your thoughtful grooming gifts
I was reborn. My existence was confirmed.
This is all basic simple
Heisenberg uncertainty principle. The way of the universe. We all need
    someone to see us
in order to exist.
But the act of viewing fundamentally changes the content of
what we're seeing.
Come on, this is all obvious elementary roots of modern physics crap
    that
I'm sure you flew past years ago
on your SAT crash course
riding your rocket ship
riding your particle wave to the top of the food chain.

Now you're a particle! Now you're a wave!

You remember all this?

Now you're confirming the high probability that

93 trillion trillion trillion atoms have coalesced into the approximate
   form of

a human male. Here on the corner of two streets

in the Toy District.

Where amusements are sold! Isn't that amusing to muse upon?

Now

according to Schrödinger's math

thanks to you and what I observe to be a pen

making check marks on a form

Now I count. I made the count! I'm part of the population.

I'm part of the problem without a solution and therefore I count. I'm
   down for the

count. I'm down but not out. I'm down, dog.

I'm a down dog dharma dude.

I count like Dracula. I'm a statistical lacuna filler.

Like the man said

I'm worse than death but I ain't no killer.

Now I matter. I *am* matter. I'm a radio wave passing through

two apertures.

Thank you, man. Thank you, Heisenberg. Thank you, universe. Thank
   you, God.

Please note for the record that the respondent was not

being facetious.

He means what he preaches. I do.

I do. I do take this woman to be my lawfully wedded wife. I do.

I did. I said

I do

to two different ladies back in the day. But no. Stop.

Stop.

Mea culpa once again I must say.

Sorry, man. I understand the point of this charade is

to collect numbers

not stories.

I won't bore you with mine if you won't deplore me with yours, you
dig?

Before you glide away to the next tick on your tally

I want to say that you taught me a lesson today that

in a strange way made all the despair and depravity feel

almost beautiful and certainly miraculous.

You did. Thank you.

Yes, you did. You taught me, man. You didn't

say I do

but you did. You taught me. You taught me that

the reason why all of us must talk to plants

in your garden or your windowsill or when they brush your shoulder

is so they know that

someone is watching over them

caring for them

observing them into being

tending to them. See what happens? You talk to a living creature and
now

it has been manifested by your gaze and it knows

it has a purpose. Life has meaning, some meaning. No matter how
humble or grand.

I mean

I am here to be a tapestry thread.

I am here to be where I belong.

I am where I belong.

I belong.

Very comforting when the sun dips below the bank building.

I'm like any cabbage. Or cauliflower. I'm like a cockroach. A cocka-
doodle rooster. A hen.

An egg. An eggplant.

There's the lesson you taught me, man.

When you speak to her the eggplant knows she must grow

for reasons grander than species propagation. Talk to her.
She knows one day she'll be a feeder. She knows
her life is part of a higher life that somehow she intrinsically
    completes.
Her tapestry thread now woven closer to perfect harmony.
You see how it works? You get what I'm saying?
Man, you talked to me. You affirmed my existence
and you helped me learn
a transcendent and eternal truth. A great lesson.
I thank you for that
I thank you for
helping me understand that right now
right now
here in the Toy District
right now and until someone else with a lanyard round their neck
    confirms
my existence
at this moment that we're sharing right now
my life has a *purpose.*
You taught me this and I am genuinely glad to be alive. I'm grateful.
I am a tapestry thread.
I am a one-celled plankton in your sea of data.
I was microscopic until you made a dot in a box, a slash through a
    letter.
I'm a check mark that represents more than we can discuss at this
    juncture.
I'm a check mark representative. I serve this street
in the House of Representatives, one integer representing many
    constituent digits.
Put me on your census. Will me to life.
Because I am useful and I have a purpose and now we all know
I'm part of this masterpiece.
I'm forever.
I'm the moon.

I'm here now
I'm gone.
I'm the airplane jet condensation trail reminding you
pollution can be beautiful.
I'm only here when you look.

The Next Witch Trials

When the witch trials return to this fair land
as they do periodically and without warning
you're going to pick me to be the catalytic converter
the fuse sparker.
When you need someone to be the first accuser
you're going to want me then.
My name is Sarah. Just like the beggar witch of Salem.
I wasn't there in Massachusetts or 1787 Philadelphia or at Salem II in
    the
1800s but I remember
the McCarthy hearings from the '50s and I saw a play by the Miller
    man who married Marilyn
Monroe
for a spell
of enchantment.
And I lived and worked in Manhattan Beach
yes, I did!
in the '80s
and I was there when the last witch trial erupted in America
at the school where I had a job teaching English
the language of Shakespeare and Joyce and yes and oh yes and and
and it was my first job out of school . . .
I was so young and now I'm so old . . .
Now I think I must be almost 70 and
once
for a time
I was a respected member of society and
I was a respectable member of society.
That's my long day's journey into night
neatly summarized.
The little witches didn't think I belonged. You didn't think I belonged.
Believe the children. I know all about it.

Believe the children.
Believe the grandmother.
That's my slogan.
Believe the grandmother. She can divine witches among us.
You know
you are aware that no one was convicted of anything, right? We were
    all of us
everyone acquitted
of everything.
Every ridiculous charge. We got a begrudging pseudo apology to
    accompany our tainted
innocence.
But you don't have to be guilty to be ruined.
Just ask the other Sarahs. Or Tituba or all the faceless blameless slaves
    who confessed
in order to be saved.
Ask the deaf lady drowned in a well
her wild animal screams confirming suspicions of the secret spirit
lodged in her untrustworthy female breast
now safely put to rest.
The schoolgirls who testified to fantastic fly-aways on airplanes
taking them to where our Satanic rituals were allegedly conducted
these girls were broomless
very different than blameless
mind you
yet still they could author aerial adventures
like those Salem girls on their pitchforks.
Believe the children.
Believe the children
because they can fly.
There's a fine line
I have found
between magic and mental illness.
I have found the fine line.

I have found out that
I have been found to suffer from various maladies
I have a diagnosis.
Most of us do
in this encampment beneath the *porte-cochère*
do you know that word, dear? It's my pet name for the 101 overpass
overhead. Above my head. Above our heads. Concrete that's hard to
    sleep on
and harder still to fully comprehend.
When the witch trials happen again
they'll be triggered by a kind of viral
highly contagious form of mental illness.
The California schoolgirls and the Salem witches had a disorder.
The symptoms correspond with what Freud called *hysteria* and
what they now call *conversion disorder*
which is when powerlessness manifests itself
as a disease.
Most women have it. A sickness in every cell membrane.
A society rotting inside every uterus.
The original witch-killing Puritans sought to see the devil
and so it was the devil they saw.
The current iteration of Puritans
the ones who put me here and the ones I know who frequent the finer
    soup kitchens
prefer to express what can't be said comfortably with language
in passive-aggressive acting out
we sometimes call *fits*.
History has shown us that *fits* of all manner get heard more than mere
    words
In times when those without power become profoundly ill
from profound lacking.
Look around you. That's Mike. With the dreadlocks. The one
    screaming and chopping.
He is most definitely

possessed

of great confidence

in his ability to conjure ghosts.

He's yelling and heaving imprecations at the Devil

yet you would not be wrong if someone asked you to point to the man
    on this street who most

appears

to be mentally ill.

Believe the grandmother. She can divine witches among us, and Mike
    is a witch.

And so am I.

This was not the vocation or avocation or hobby I envisioned.

I was going to be a teacher. God meant for me to teach. I was teaching
    when it happened.

You know the mother who started the mendacity boulder rolling down
    the hill was sick, right?

The one who said her girl had been molested.

Disturbed.

She was disturbed.

It's in the trial records. She was paranoid schizophrenic, this Johnson
    woman.

And according to the doctor who signed my papers apparently I am
    now, too. I inherited

her sickness.

I was society's sponge sopping up the mess.

This is my thanks. This here is my thanks. Urine stench. Constant
    itchiness.

You are welcome. You are most welcome.

Welcome to my world. It's been awfully lonely without you.

Witches have special powers you know.

That's why we're more frightening than the average woman

who of course has always been and shall forever more be terrifying

by dint of being

a woman. Witches can see what you prefer to think

292

is not there. All the evil devil Luciferian Mephistophelian

energies hastily consigned to other people's nightmares and then
     safely out of sight

like the clothes clogging your closet

the hand-me-downs that can't be handed down

any lower

the sweatpants from a sweatshop you dump outside the mission in

a brown paper bag.

To me and to Mike and Robbie and Chris and I daresay a plenitude
     of perpetual bystanders

here on the sidelines of life

we see quite clearly whatever you're rushing to escape

in your climate-controlled armored rolling fortress

impotent as protection from what you accept. Now isn't that fright-
     ening? Isn't that mortifying?

All the time you're doing whatever you're doing or you think you're
     doing

perfecting your perfect life by increments

we're watching. We're unpaid observers for the UN. We're stringers for
     the AP.

We

don't need a subscription to the *Times*. We cannot be made to pay

for grammatical errors and a general absence of

credibility. We see

what's going on

like Marvin Gaye. We're doing our job. Watching. Clairvoyants of the
     present.

Visionaries of the visions

you and your family amply provide.

Ginsberg said Dylan blew everyone's mind

except Leonard Cohen. Then Cohen blew everyone's mind. Except

not really mine. Those words and stories he used so gorgeously are
     omnipresent

swirling in a milky star soup

circling my pointy black hat for eternity

because there is no time

there is no time

for quibbling over genius. The ordained Buddhist monkpriest would
say so himself.

He would affirm and encourage.

What Sarah sees now is what Sarah saw then and what she will see
when the trials come again.

From my precarious perch on the finest of lines between magic and
mayhem

I can report from the street

what you speed past each day in your SUV is simultaneously

preventable and inevitable.

That you see is the tragic flaw in our flawless society

in our systemically septic social system.

Someone has to live here like this.

Might as well be the witches. They have more conversion disorder
powerlessness disease in

them than

the Jews and

much less money to fight back when you come belt-looped with
plastic zip ties

to round us up like livestock.

Although you can't tell at this stage of my decrepitude . . .

Now I avoid mirrors

but I once was quite beautiful . . .

I once was quite beautiful and I had a lover

a deeply delicious boy of a man

a magnet to draw me

to trace my outlines. My lover

he told me I must be a witch. You must be a witch

he told me. Because I can't get you out of my head.

What kind of concocted potion did you feed me

what doll did you pierce
he asked me.
Why do my thoughts return to your eyes your smile your curves your
    skin your smell
he told me.
You must be a witch. I want you so badly I will concentrate you
into my arms
willing fantasy into reality
with the repetition of prayer and
belief that our very best dreams should always come true if you only
    believe
truly enough
to warrant salvation.
He told me whatever I had done to make him like this
I must be a witch.
You are under my power I told him
hypnotizing him with my gaze
melting his man armor.
You are under my power I told him
maybe only one of us knowing the truth
he was irresistible—
he was irresistibly attractive to a certain kind of witch.
The literate type
with no talent for predicting the future or fixing the past.
At the moment I have lost most of my looks and
most of my powers yet
I'm seeing the present clearly
with a limpidlucid clarity I lacked in my younger
years. Now during this chapter of my life entitled
The Hunger Years
I understand what to say when a man
a beautiful man, a sweetkind man easy to love
when he tells you
I surrender I'm yours

I humbly confess
I know what to say now.
Yes
Yes I am a witch. But I mean you no harm.
I fling no curses. I boil no newts.
I mean you no harm.
I confess in advance. At the next interrogation
I will see clearly and speak clearly and I will say yes
I am a witch and I mean you no harm.
And when you drag me to the gallows or the drowning pool and you
    offer me
one last opportunity to repent
Before the bag goes over my head, I will say,
brothers and sisters, I mean you no harm.

—Originally published as a *Shockwire* series chapbook by
The Head & The Hand Press, Philadelphia

ACKNOWLEDGMENTS

The author is grateful to Amelia Appel and Uwe Stender of Triada US literary agency, and the entire publishing team at Diversion Books, for having the vision and passion to share this story with the world. Mark Weinstein's elegant editing, aided by Emily Hillebrand's insightful counsel, and Amy King's magical cover design, based on Jonathan Harper's photo, made a writer's dream come true. The staff of the Center for Homelessness in Hollywood, the members of the Elderberries/Have Seeds tribe, the residents of Sunset Square, the author's neighbors and friends, and his understanding wife and family—all were instrumental in welcoming Uncle Mike into our community, providing love and compassion in a time and place that often feels heartless. Thank you, everyone, for being you.

ABOUT THE AUTHOR

Formerly a professional gambler, golf columnist, improv comedian, and television commentator, MICHAEL KONIK is the best-selling author of more than a dozen books of fiction, nonfiction, poetry, essays, and memoir. He lives with his wife and dog in Los Angeles, where he grows fruits, vegetables, flowers, and fungi.